DECOLONIZING PALESTINE

DECOLONIZING PALESTINE

Hamas between the Anticolonial
and the Postcolonial

Somdeep Sen

CORNELL UNIVERSITY PRESS   ITHACA AND LONDON

First published 2020 by Cornell University Press

Library of Congress Cataloging-in-Publication Data

Names: Sen, Somdeep, author.
Title: Decolonizing Palestine : Hamas between the anticolonial and the postcolonial / Somdeep Sen.
Description: Ithaca [New York] : Cornell University Press, 2020. | Includes bibliographical references and index.
Identifiers: LCCN 2020007216 (print) | LCCN 2020007217 (ebook) | ISBN 9781501752735 (hardcover) | ISBN 9781501752742 (paperback) | ISBN 9781501752759 (ebook) | ISBN 9781501752766 (pdf)
Subjects: LCSH: Ḥarakat al-Muqāwamah al-Islāmīyah. | Palestinian Arabs—Politics and government—21st century. | Israelis—Colonization—Gaza Strip. | Gaza Strip—Politics and government—21st century.
Classification: LCC JQ1830.A98 H3775 2020 (print) | LCC JQ1830.A98 (ebook) | DDC 956.94/2055—dc23
LC record available at https://lccn.loc.gov/2020007216
LC ebook record available at https://lccn.loc.gov/2020007217

For Ma and Papa

Contents

Acknowledgments

As with most academic endeavors this book is a collective effort. First of all, this book would not have been possible without the support of my friends and interlocutors in the field. In Cairo I would especially like to thank Bassam and his family for their hospitality and my former Cairo flat mate, Jeffrey Culang, for his support, advice, and willingness to accompany me to the local café after a long day in the field. I am also grateful to Ben Silsbee, Joel Parker, Yoram Meital, Oren Barak, and Dan Miodownik for their assistance during my fieldwork in Tel Aviv, Beersheba, and Jerusalem. Conducting fieldwork in the Gaza Strip in 2013 was difficult. But it was the friendships I developed in the field that helped me weather through it. I would like to thank Ahmed, Jehad, Bahaa, Hussain, and Sayed for supporting me throughout my stay. I remain humbled by their resilience in the face of adversity, and they will forever be a constant source of inspiration for me. I am also indebted to Omar Shaban and the staff at Pal-Think for Strategic Studies for their support during my stay in Gaza.

I am immensely grateful for the support I received during my studies at the University of Copenhagen from my fellow students Salem Dandan, Lau Øfjord Blaxekjær, Ayca Uygur, Peter Marcus Kristensen, Rune Bennike, Josefine Kühnel Larsen, Kristian Knus Larsen, and Hans Dabelsteen. My supervisor Sune Haugbølle was an invaluable pillar of support. He enthusiastically took on the task of supervising a political science doctoral project that challenged some disciplinary norms and skillfully ferried me through the process of writing and defending the dissertation. Thank you also to Ben Rosamund for helpful feedback on various drafts of the manuscript that became this book. Thanks also to John Collins, Jeroen Gunning, and Noel Parker for their critical reading of earlier drafts that laid the foundations of the book in its current form. I would also like to thank the Danish Institute in Damascus and the Danish Council for Independent Research for funding part of my fieldwork in Palestine.

I thank Lene Hansen, Christian Lund and Mikkel Vedby-Rasmussen at the University of Copenhagen, Cynthia Weber at the University of Sussex, Nicola Pratt and Andre Broome at the University of Warwick as well as Carl Death at the University of Manchester, who read several versions of my book proposal and guided me through the intimidating process of steering this book to publishers. I would also like to thank Jonas, Joe, Magnus, Krista and Johan at *Roast Coffee* in Copenhagen, who kept me hydrated and caffeinated through long periods of intense writing. At Cornell University Press I am grateful to Jim Lance for taking on this book project. His keen interest in this manuscript and his enthusiasm for the final product is the kind of encouragement that fuels young scholars like me.

In the end, an acknowledgement section for this book would be incomplete without a recognition of the contributions of my family. I will remain forever grateful to my in-laws Karen Fog Olwig and Kenneth Robert Olwig for reading and rereading this manuscript. Without their extensive editorial feedback and advice this book would not have been what it is today. My partner Mette Fog Olwig was an invaluable source of support and encouragement as well. A brilliant academic, she read many drafts of this manuscript with a critical eye and her feedback has contributed importantly to the final product, even though I was not always easy to deal with throughout this process. The arrival of our son Shaan Emil and his infectious enthusiasm for life has made me realize that there is more to life than the next book, article, or grant application. Finally, I would like to dedicate this book to my parents Shelley Sen and Pradip Kumar Sen. I am immensely grateful for their enthusiasm for my academic career—this, despite the fact that I reneged on a promise to become an engineer. I see this project as a culmination of their support and the sacrifices they have made for me over the last thirty-five years.

Note on Interviews

In this book all nonpolitically affiliated interviewees have been assigned pseudonyms in the interest of their security.

DECOLONIZING PALESTINE

DECOLONIZING PALESTINE
An Introduction

> We don't know what will happen next. Life is unsure. We are not
> allowed to have a vision. People here think short-term and are
> concerned with their immediate needs because we don't know what
> destiny looms in the future. Maybe the border will be closed, maybe
> we won't get a visa. Palestinians are not allowed to dream about the
> future
>
> —Ahmed Yousef, Author Interview, Gaza City, May 2013

On May 16, 2013, after a six-hour journey from Cairo, I arrived at the Rafah border crossing between Egypt and the Gaza Strip. I was dropped off approximately a hundred meters from the border and had to walk the rest of the way through a security cordon set up by the Egyptian army. When I reached the gate of the border crossing terminal, I gave my passport and a letter to an Egyptian soldier. This letter, issued by the Egyptian Ministry of Foreign Affairs, allowed me to use the Rafah border crossing to enter Gaza within a designated time period. He examined my documents for a few seconds and then handed them to a superior officer. I waited for the next twenty minutes, still outside under the hot sun, without a passport and surrounded by the vast and desolate landscape of northern Sinai. Looking over my shoulders were Palestinian travelers, nervously waiting to be allowed to enter the border crossing terminal. There was an air of uncertainty. It was possibly a variant of the same sense of uncertainty that a prominent member of Hamas, Ahmed Yousef suggested above to me was synonymous with Palestinian life in Gaza.

Once my documents were returned and I was allowed to enter the premises of the border crossing, Ahmed Yousef's words were further validated by what I saw inside the Egyptian passport control terminal. Without an adequate system of ventilation, the sweltering summer heat inside was unbearable and some of the elderly travelers had been forced to retire to the chairs in the back of the room. Most other travelers remained gathered around the passport department, waiting patiently for the Egyptian passport control officers to bark out their names

FIGURE 1.1   Entrance to the Palestinian terminal at the Rafah border crossing. Photo by author.

on a Public Address system with only one operational speaker. The officers would then fling their passports at them. This was the stamp of approval allowing Palestinians to return home to Gaza. Those who were not "fortunate" enough to receive this stamp of approval were taken to a backroom for extra security checks.

Witnessing all this, one anxious Palestinian doctor, desperate to see his family in Gaza City, said to me, "You see here. They treat Palestinians like cattle."

Yet, despite encountering all the familiar features of a place that is besieged and colonized, at Rafah I was also confronted with another, very different image; namely, that of a place that also postures as a postcolonial state that has already risen out of the era of colonization. After spending two hours on the Egyptian side of the border crossing, I entered the Palestinian terminal. Together with a group of Palestinian travelers who had been let in at the same time as me, I was driven through a gate dominated by a sign declaring: "Welcome to Palestine" (figure 1.1). Under it were Palestinian border security personnel wearing the uniform and statelike insignia of the Palestinian Authority. All of us traveling from Egypt to Gaza had to then stand in line at an immigration terminal and, much as at any other ordinary passport control desk, I had to present the entry permit issued to me by the appropriate immigration authorities. In my case, the permission to enter Gaza had been granted by the Residence and Foreigners Affairs General Administration of the Palestinian Authority in the Gaza Strip.[1] The passport control officer asked me questions like "What are you doing here?" "Who invited you?" and "How long do you plan to stay?" Having answered them sufficiently, I was then granted a Palestinian entry stamp. Momentarily, it felt as if I had indeed arrived in the State of Palestine—one that had been liberated, was now sovereign, and encompassed a distinct territory.

Of course, the presence of these two, seemingly contradictory, images is not limited to the premises of the Rafah border crossing. In fact, the Gaza Strip as a whole became a place of contradictions when Hamas adopted a dual mode of existence following its historic victory in the 2006 Palestinian Legislative Council elections. After the unequivocal triumph of the Islamist faction, Fatah refused to be part of the Hamas government. Over the course of the 2007 Battle of Gaza, Hamas then consolidated its rule over the Gaza Strip while maintaining its commitment to the armed resistance.[2] In doing so, Hamas oscillated between the images of the postcolonial state and an anticolonial movement. As the government in the Gaza Strip, it represented a civilian authority posturing like the future Palestinian state. However, by remaining committed to the armed struggle, Hamas also recognized the fact that Palestine is far from being liberated.

The Hamas representatives I met in the Gaza Strip often embodied this dual image in their public personas. During our meeting at the Ministry of Foreign Affairs, Deputy Foreign Minister Ghazi Hamad looked like an agent of the state. Wearing a suit, with the statelike insignia of the Palestinian Authority behind him and the Palestinian flag by his side, he was more reminiscent of a bureaucrat than the keffiyeh-clad Palestinian *fedayeen* (guerrilla fighter) or the masked al-Qassam fighter I had visualized while reading about Palestinian resistance.[3] However, despite looking like the Palestinian bureaucrat, he was also quick to draw on the vocabulary of a liberation struggle. And, when I asked him to reflect on the future of Hamas as an organization, he declared, "We need to liberate the land first. Before we do anything else, we need to create a clear liberation platform and use it to acquire a Palestinian state."[4]

At the outset, it is *this* dual Hamas that I aim to explicate in this book. I ask, How should we conceptualize Hamas's politics as it wavers between the anticolonial and the postcolonial? How does its anticolonial resistance survive and find meaning for the Palestinian struggle to dismantle what I go on to conceptualize as Israel's settler colonial rule? How does the stateless Palestinian encounter Hamas's postcolonial governance, which evokes the image of an era *after* the withdrawal of the colonizer? How does the anticolonial faction rationalize the postcoloniality of its governance, while still engaged in an anticolonial armed struggle against the colonizer? And, how does this coexistence of the anticolonial and the postcolonial complicate our understanding of what it means to be liberated (and unliberated)?

In answering these questions, I draw on my fieldwork in the Gaza Strip, the West Bank, Israel, and Egypt, conducted between 2013 and 2016, to present an ethnography of anticolonial violence and postcolonial statecraft in a settler colonial condition. For instance, to capture the multiple experiences of anticolonial violence, I place a Hamas member's staunch conviction that an armed struggle is essential to the Palestinian liberation movement alongside a Palestinian restaurateur's remembrance of being tortured in an Israeli prison and a young Gazan's ambivalent stance on Palestinian armed resistance because of the scar on his body left from being shot by an Israeli soldier. Similarly, when providing an ethnography of Hamas's postcolonial statecraft, I bring together a Hamas member's insistence that governance serves a purpose for the liberation struggle, a young Palestinian's encounter with the authoritarian nature of this governance when he was publicly beaten by the police in Gaza City, and an instance that I witnessed of a violent family dispute being defused by policemen in northern Gaza. And, I place these ethnographic accounts in the context of the settler colonial narrative I encountered in Israel. These include my reflections on the absence or derogatory presence of Palestinians in exhibits at museums in Tel Aviv celebrating the Israeli "War of Independence," the Israeli appropriation of Palestinian cultural artifacts, and the almost casual way in which Palestinians carrying out stabbing attacks using knives and scissors were killed during my stay in Jerusalem in 2015 and 2016. In the end, much like the many Palestinian voices through which this text speaks, this book also oscillates between the euphoria and enigma of the anticolonial quest for change, and frequently breaks character to reveal the uncertainties surrounding this quest, especially when confronted with both the anticolonial and the postcolonial on the path toward liberation.

The Anticolonial, the Postcolonial, and the Long Moment of Liberation

Language matters.[5] And, nowhere more than in the study of Israel-Palestine. It is then of some consequence that, in the pages thus far and in those that follow, I have refrained from discussing the religiosity of Hamas's conduct. This is not to argue that religion is an unimportant facet of the organization's identity. The name *Hamas* is, after all, an acronym of Ḥarakat al-Muqāwamah al-'Islāmiyyah, or the *Islamic* Resistance Movement. Moreover, taking their point of departure in the political interest in the religiosity of the organization (especially in the post-9/11 era), several seminal works have put forth a nuanced understanding of Islamist politics in Palestine (Gunning 2007; Roy 2011; Hroub 2006; Dunning 2016). In this book, however, I aspire to globalize Hamas. In *Global Palestine* John Collins notes that, though historically characterized by a claim of exceptionalism with regard to both the character of Zionism and the suffering of Palestinians, recent scholarly works on Israel-Palestine have drawn on the "theoretical advances [made] in the study of global politics." In doing so, they have provided an understanding of politics in Israel-Palestine that resonates beyond its geographical boundaries, globalizing Palestine as a consequence (Collins 2011, 3). But this impulse has largely eluded the study of Hamas. The dearth of global theoretical discussions of Hamas is, for one thing, a consequence of the organization's relatively recent rise to political prominence. This has led to a discussion of Hamas's specificity in comparison to other Palestinian factions. But a far more important reason is its politically divisive status, which has led many to characterize Hamas as singularly contemptible in its conduct, rather than as a nonexceptional entity replicating a form of politics that already exists within and outside Palestine. Donna Nevel described this as the urge to say, "But Hamas . . ." She wrote, "In conversations about Gaza, I have heard many thoughtful people in the Jewish community lament the loss of Palestinian lives in Gaza but then say, 'But Hamas . . .' as if that were the heart of the problem" (Nevel 2014).

The tendency to perceive Hamas as singularly contemptible and thus as *the* problem hindering a solution to the Israeli-Palestinian conflict was also present in many of my encounters in the field. At a social gathering in Tel Aviv, a Swedish employee of an international NGO heard me call the siege of Gaza unlawful and responded, "But wasn't it because of Hamas? They took over Gaza in a coup, and that's why there is a siege. Hamas is the problem."[6] In December 2015, during a conversation over dinner in Jerusalem, an Israeli acquaintance who described himself as leftist readily admitted, "We are doing horrible things in Jerusalem and the West Bank." Then, referring to the ongoing stabbing attacks, he continued, "These right-wing people have gotten us here. I'm not surprised that Palestinians are responding in this way." But as soon as I attempted to conflate the Palestinian plight in Jerusalem and the West Bank with that of the Gazans, he interjected, "No. But Gaza and Hamas are a different question. We gave them freedom. Our army pulled out and we got rid of settlements.[7] And what did Hamas do? Rockets and tunnels."[8] In this book, I do recognize that Hamas is deeply shaped by the specificities of its genealogy and political history and thus my Israeli acquaintance's argument is deserving of some consideration. But my primary concern here is not the particular activities of the organization that have been characterized as being reprehensible. Instead, I bring what Collins terms the global turn, seen in the theorization of politics in Israel-Palestine in general, to this study of Hamas. I do so with regard to the anticolonial character of Hamas's armed struggle, the postcolonial nature of its governance and implications of the coexistence of the anticolonial and the postcolonial on the path to liberation. That is to say, I globalize Hamas by explicating its politics in terms of the global experience of anticolonial struggles, postcolonial states, and conceptions of being liberated (and unliberated) that go beyond the particularity of Palestine.

The Anticolonial

In this book I consider the presence of State of Israel and its endeavors in the Palestinian territories to be, in many respects, settler colonial in nature.[9] To that end, the political condition that Palestinians in general, and a faction like Hamas in particular, are meant to navigate is not unlike other colonial contexts. In general, colonialism involves the localized dominance and ascendancy of an exogenous entity that is able to perpetually "reproduce itself in a given environment" (Veracini 2010, 3–4). As Ania Loomba notes, colonialism does not just entail the expansion of "European powers into Asia, African or the Americas." The forming of colonial power also requires the "unforming or re-forming" of the communities that already exist. The practices of "unforming or re-forming" have included "trade, plunder, negotiations, warfare, genocide, enslavement and rebellions" (Loomba 1998, 2). They have equally involved institutionalized forms of cultural domination (Blusse 1995; Vishwanathan 1995). Finally, colonialism entails the creation of the (inferior) "status" of the colonized in the discourses of the colonizer. This is exemplified not least in the 1929 Rhodes Memorial Lecture delivered by South African prime minister general Jan Smuts in which he characterized "the African" as a "child type, with a child psychology and out-look" (Mamdani 1996, 4). Such institutions, practices, and discourses of domi-nation would appear to exist in Palestine, and this in turn has allowed me to draw parallels between the Palestinian condition and other colonial contexts. But, as I demonstrate further in chapter 2, the settler colonial condition is distinct in that these institutions, practices, and discourses of domination are not just meant to establish and reproduce the colonizer's localized dominance or exact the resources and labor of the colonized. The setter colonial narrative also insists that the indigenous do not exist, as a people or community with a distinct iden-tity (Wolfe 2006; Jacobs 2009; Veracini 2011). In Palestine then, the colonized are left to contend with settler colonial institutions, practices, and discourses that, in an effort to materialize this myth of indigenous nonexistence, strive to erase the signature of Palestinian presence in the "Holy Land" (Khalidi 1992; Khalidi 1997; Pappe 2006; Masalha 2012).

With this being the political "circumstance" in which Hamas operates, the anticolonial nature of its armed struggle is then "easily" established, especially when (as is the case in this book) the analysis is informed by a perspective on the anticolonial imaginary that draws on the work of Franz Fanon. I contextu-alize the anticolonial imaginary—namely the manner in which the colonized imagine their path out of the era of colonial rule and toward liberation—in relation to the stark distinction Fanon makes between the worlds of the colo-nizer and the colonized. The sector of the colonized is poor, hungry, congested, lacking permanent infrastructure and dwellings, and in want of the most basic amenities required for a dignified existence. In comparison, the colonizer's world is privileged with the permanence of stone, steel, and paved roads, and its inhabitants are satiated and rarely in want of "good things" (Fanon 1963, 4–5). In between these worlds stands the colonizer's infrastructure of oppression—barracks and police stations—that speak the language of violence, surveil the sector of the colonized, and ensure that the sectors of the colonizer and colonized remain separate and distinct (Fanon 1963, 3). This Fanonian dis-tinction would seem self-evident in Israel-Palestine. For instance, the wealth, infrastructure, and in general, material privilege I encountered in, say, Tel Aviv contrasts sharply with the poverty and congestion of the Palestinian refugee camps in the occupied West Bank and the Gaza Strip. The former symbolizes permanence and is made of stone and steel and is indeed a place that is home to the privileged. The latter is not fit for a dignified existence. Its residents are starved of the most basic of amenities like clean water and electricity, and their lives are characterized by impermanence and uncertainty. At the cusp of these two worlds are border crossings and checkpoints. Here lies the Israeli military infrastructure—armed personnel and armed vehicles—that surveils Palestinians, tempers their rebellious spirit, and ensures that the world of the colonized does not encroach on the sector of the colonizer.

The Palestinian anticolonial violence that responds to the chasm between these two worlds (and realities) mirrors the violence of armed factions in colonial (and) revolutionary contexts beyond Palestine. Fanon writes that the violence of the colonized needs to pursue an agenda of disorder and breach the material infrastructure of colonial domination (Fanon 1963, 2–3). Though Hamas's violence is materially incapable of realizing this Fanonian agenda, in chapter 4 I show that it aspires to interrupt Israel's settler colonial rule of Palestinian lands, with the hope of making it a difficult endeavor to maintain. However, the violence of decolonization has to contend with not just the materiality of a colonial project. Colonization, as Fanon demonstrates, also infiltrates the spiritual being of the colonized in a way that alienates them from their sense of self and compels them to emulate the colonizer. In Fanon's native Martinique, it was under the yoke of French colonial rule that society became alienated from its African-Caribbeanness and being white like the French in culture and language came to be seen as a vehicle of upward social mobility (Grohs 1968, 26). Fanon himself craved the colonizer's whiteness. He wrote of being unconcerned with his "negro nationality" (Fanon 1952, 157). Instead, by obtaining the love of a white woman, he hoped to access the worthiness that was associated with whiteness (Fanon 1952, 45). Tragically, though, despite craving whiteness, for the colonizer Fanon was above all a *black* man and was frequently rejected as worthy of nothing more than the jungle, as no more than a "dirty nigger" (Fanon 1952, 21).

That, in the eyes of the colonizer, the colonized is worth no more than their "jungle status" was apparent when Winston Churchill laid the blame for the Bengal famine of 1943 (Sen 1983) on Indians by saying it was the result of Indians "breeding like rabbits" (Tharoor 2017, 160). Churchill also saw the deaths of approximately three million people because of the famine as serving the purpose of "merrily culling a population" (Hari 2010; Mukerjee 2011). A similar conception of the colonized's assumed "jungle status" was also present in many of my encounters in Israel and Palestine. Whether it is a reference to Palestinians as "marauding Arab gangs" in an Israeli museum exhibit or an Israeli tour guide's insinuation that the life of a Palestinian attacker was worth no more than that of a rabid dog—these statements demonstrate that Palestinians too are assigned a "jungle status" by the colonizer. Yet, much like Fanon, the colonized in Palestine still crave the metaphorical and proverbial whiteness of the colonizer. This craving was expressed in the manner a Palestinian businessman I met in Ramallah proudly revealed that he once had Israeli friends and spoke Hebrew, in the way a young Gazan suggested to me that Palestinians should learn how to build a nation from Israelis, and as an interlocutor claimed, in the Palestinian preference for Israeli consumer products because they are considered to be "upper class." Of course, the relationship between the colonized and the colonizer described by Fanon as a racial trope was never articulated in this manner by my interlocutors during fieldwork. But as is often the case in settler colonial contexts, the whiteness of the colonizer and the blackness of the colonized are less about skin color and stand in more as a metaphor (Wolfe 2006; Jacobs 2009; Turner 1985; O'Brien 2010). So, the Fanonian analysis still finds relevance here if we treat whiteness as being synonymous with the civilized, the cultured, and the ethical, and the blackness of the sector of the colonized as representing the uncivilized, the immoral, and a realm devoid of values. Palestinians I met would never declare—as Fanon did with regard to his "negro nationality"—that they were ambivalent about their Palestinian nationality. Nonetheless, during our conversations, they occasionally glanced enviously at the proverbial whiteness and constituent goodness of the sector of the colonizer.

It is when faced with such a fractured being of the colonized that anticolonial violence, according to Fanon, needs to do much more than destroy. It also needs to be a creative force that refurbishes the colonized's fractured selves and ensures that they emerge as content in their historical indigeneity. Recognizing that anticolonial violence is indeed able to buttress the colonized's sense of self, Fanon insists that the violence of decolonization made the new decolonized person, who, having become dehumanized under colonization, becomes a human once again. In this sense, for Fanon, violent decolonization is a formative process because it purges the colonized's inferiority complex, builds their collective consciousness, and inducts them into a common national cause (Fanon 1963, 51). In this book I consider the anticolonial nature of Hamas's violence as encompassing this totalizing tactic as well. In view of, for example, the way in which a Palestinian interlocutor talked about the scars on his body from the time he was tortured in an Israeli prison, the cinematic quality of a young Gazan interviewee's memory of a Hamas rescue operation, or the ritual manner in which the Palestinian keffiyeh is wrapped around the body of a Palestinian martyr, I consider Hamas's violence to also embody the Fanonian ability to remake the colonized's humanity and create a sense of national self. That is to say, the colonized's acts of anticolonial violence or the material and human casualties that often follow rarely remain at the level of an individual experience of euphoria or tragedy. Instead, once individuals commit acts of violence or suffer the repercussions of the violent encounter with the colonizer, they transcend to the public realm and are claimed by the collective as part of the national cause. As a result, violence becomes a *Palestinian* act of violence, tragedy becomes *Palestinian* tragedy, and the armed struggle becomes a means of totalizing the national community on the path of the national cause—this, despite the settler colonial claim that Palestine and Palestinians, in effect, do not exist.

The Postcolonial

While the anticolonial finds resonance in the colonial condition, it is the appearance of the postcolonial that leads to the puzzle underlying my discussions in this book. Empirically, as I go on to argue in chapter 3, it was the Oslo Accords that introduced postcoloniality as a means of disincentivizing the often-violent anticolonial politics of Palestinian factions. However, conceptually, the postcolonial appears in two ways in this book. First, it signifies a time-bound concept, referring (chronologically) to the era *after* the withdrawal of the colonizer. Since Israel's settler colonial rule over Palestine persists, the *post*-ness specifically relates to ethnographic encounters in which the rituals and symbols one would instinctively associate with the postcolonial state were somehow performed and displayed within the colonial condition. This feeling, that the postcolonial had an anachronistic presence in what is still a colonial condition, often seemed omnipresent during my time in the field. It was present, for instance, in an entry in my fieldwork diary about my first evening in Gaza City, where I wrote,

> This place is strange. Walking through the city you forget where you are, and life seems normal. Curiously, Gaza City reminds me less of a place that is in a constant state of war and more of the urban centers of India that I have grown up loving (and hating). "Energetic" shopkeepers, honking cars, screaming children, and the smell of scrumptious street food that fills the air over Midan al-Jundi al-Majhool [Unknown Soldier's Square] put me at ease and remind me of a place that I called home for eighteen years.

In the early days of my fieldwork, I had yet to settle on the concept of "postcolonial" as a qualifier of this ostensible strangeness of Gaza. However, under the guise of terms like "strange" and "normal," I was nonetheless referring to the feeling that, despite being colonized and under siege, Gaza seemed to operate *as if* the colonizer had already withdrawn.

In the opening pages of this book, the feeling of encountering the sovereign, postcolonial state was also present at the Palestinian terminal of the Rafah border crossing, where Palestinian officials engaged in all the rituals one would expect to see at a "normal" border crossing or at the immigration desk of an airport. Similarly, the postcolonial was present in my interactions with Hamas officials like Ghazi Hamad, who, in their public persona, postured very much like the representative of an already-liberated, sovereign state. Of course, the realities of the colonial condition live firmly alongside this image of postcoloniality. Despite his outwardly postcolonial persona, Hamad ritually drew on the vocabulary of the anticolonial struggle during the course of our interview. However, the cattle-like treatment of Palestinian travelers that I experienced at the Egyptian terminal before reaching the Palestinian terminal of the Rafah border was testament to the fact that Gaza remained under siege. And, despite my initial impressions of normalcy, I went on to write the following in my fieldwork diary: "It would seem that reality is never out of reach when in the [Gaza] Strip. Pictures of the martyred, the [Hamas] police force that monitors my neighborhood with high-powered guns, or images of the Hamas official that reprimanded the owner of the café we were in for serving *shisha* to women—they all demonstrate that the uncomfortable realities of the landscape of a liberation struggle are always around the corner."

Secondly, and alongside this time-bound conception, the postcolonial in this book also refers to the specific nature of Hamas's statelike governance, as I go on to argue that the Palestinian Authority exhibits the pathologies of the postcolonial state. Joel Migdal (1988) argued that, as a new entrant into the international system, the postcolonial state is marred by "centrifugal forces." Whether a citizenry to which the state authority is invisible, alternative centers of power that challenge the political elite and the institutions in the national capital, or a territoriality that is either contested or too vast to map and control, these forces challenge the postcolonial state's ability to ensure that it is recognizable and legitimate across its demographic landscape. Christian Lund confirmed Migdal's observations in his discussion of public authority in Africa. Lund describes a disconnect between the myth of the state as a unified and coherent entity—an idea he for example often found perpetuated on the news—and the incapacity and parallel centers of authority that challenge the national capital. He further argues that many African states are characterized by much more than what lies within the walls of the official, national institutions. Instead, these states have a dispersed existence characterized by both the myths of the state as perpetuated by the national capital and the manner in which the citizen experiences this state and its myths (Lund 2006, 686–689). It is this conception of the postcolonial state that lends itself to my understanding of the postcoloniality of Hamas's role as government. For one thing, it allows me to disentangle the official institutions of the state from the practices of statecraft as experienced by the citizen. This suits a study of the Palestinian Authority well, as the existence of a colonial condition ensures that its institutions lack the resources, sovereignty, and political mandate to operate like a "real" state. Moreover, emphasizing the importance of the encounters between this state and its citizens allows me to account for both how

Hamas conceives of its postcolonial statecraft in view of its anticolonial identity, and the manner in which colonized Gazans encounter the myths of the unified and coherent state.

To be sure, the postcolonial state is frequently charged with employing the same modes of statecraft that were once used by the colonial "master." Yet, when appropriating the colonial state and its statecraft, the anticolonial faction often (cl)aims to reinterpret its institutions, taxonomies, and bureaucracies in the interest the colonized and their anticolonial struggle. Rasmus Boserup calls this a form of counter–state building.[10] For instance, when the Front de Libération Nationale, or the National Liberation Front (FLN), in Algeria adopted the form of the colonial state, it (cl)aimed to purge the colonizer's values and introduce the anticolonial ethos into its statecraft (Boserup 2009, 241–242). Similarly, echoing this form of counter–state building in Palestine, my Hamas interlocutors saw themselves as reinterpreting the Palestinian Authority and its postcoloniality, which, at its inception, was meant to disincentivize (armed) Palestinian anticolonial politics. By claiming that governing was a means of protecting the resistance movement, insinuating a synonymy between *haukama* (governance) and *muqawama* (resistance), and enforcing Hamas's authority over all aspects of politics in Gaza, the anticolonial faction in Palestine also claimed that its statelike governance was imbued with the anticolonial perspective. Thus, while once meant to serve the colonizer, this statelike governance now personifies the collective cause and being of the colonized.

While the anticolonial faction may claim to be engaged in counter–state building, its ability to propagate this myth of the state is still limited by its material inability to penetrate, regulate, and order the society it governs. Therefore, for the postcolonial state operating under colonial rule—much like its counterpart in the era *after* colonization—it is imperative that it perpetually performs its authority as a means of making itself visible to the (stateless) citizen. Indeed, the postcolonial state, whether operating before or after the withdrawal of the colonizer, stands in stark contrast to its European counterpart, which enjoys a consolidated existence, having socialized itself into the lives of its citizens and made its presence, not unlike rivers and mountains, as natural as nature itself (Migdal 1988, 15–16). Thomas Blom Hansen and Finn Stepputat, however, introduced their anthology *States of Imagination* by arguing that the postcolonial state should be treated not as an imperfect imitation of the European state but as a perspective on the manner in which the "idea of the modern state" has proliferated, especially in places where its authority is either illegitimate or illegible to the citizenry. Accordingly, the contributions in this volume focus on the postcolonial state's "language of stateness" as it engages in practical, symbolic, and performative schemes meant to naturalize its existence and legitimacy in the consciousness of the population it governs (Hansen and Stepputat 2001, 6–7). In order to bring this understanding of the postcolonial state to Palestine I have thus drawn parallels between the various schemes of the Hamas government and, for example, the mapping practices of the Ecuadorian state, which are meant to impose a uniform perspective (approved by the national capital) on its territoriality (Radcliffe 2001), the (re-)actions of the Indian state to a Hindu-Muslim riot (Hansen 2001), or the checkpoints put in place by the Sri Lankan state after a suicide bombing (Jeganathan 2004). Just as in the era of the postcolonial, these practices in the colonial condition aim to ensure that the authority of the governing anticolonial faction is naturalized among its stateless citizens.

Unsurprisingly, this postcolonial state, administered by Hamas, creates some confusion among the recipients of its governance because the instruments of postcoloniality now exist in the shadow a settler colonial endeavor (and narrative) that insists on the nonexistence of Palestine and Palestinians. For instance, speaking of the Palestinian Authority, a young Palestinian had said to me, "It is all based on an imagination, on something that is fake and the illusion of the ideal."[11] Moreover, encountering this postcoloniality, which is often marked by violence, was often a traumatic and demoralizing experience for my Palestinian interlocutors. One of them, having been a victim of the violence of both Israel and Hamas, even wondered whether there was a real difference between the governance of the colonizer and that of the anticolonial faction. Yet, while recounting their experience of Hamas's governance and criticizing it, they nonetheless referred to it as the *Palestinian* government, pursuing (and failing to fulfill) a *national* task. Certainly, this appearance of the qualifier "Palestinian" or "national" with regard to Hamas's postcolonial governance is inadvertent and does not occur in the manner intended by the anticolonial faction. Nonetheless, albeit unintended, postcolonial governance becomes socialized in the settler colonial condition, as for the colonized facing the erasure of Palestine (and their own Palestinian-ness), each bureaucratic mechanism evokes the existence of *Palestinian* government and as each act of statelike coercive violence empowers the insignia of a *Palestinian* authority.

The Long Moment

It is of course fortuitous that the colonized find a signature of their existence in their anticolonial and postcolonial acts, especially when they are compelled to contend with settler colonial institutions, practices, and discourses that insist on their nonexistence. But, then again, what other choice do the colonized have but to counter the narratives and endeavors of the colonizer? In a sense, it is this opposition—however minimal and unintended—that allows the colonized people and their cause to persist despite the material prowess of the colonizer. Yet, what the colonized aspire for is not just survival; in the end, all their efforts are meant to be in service of their liberation from colonial rule. The case of Hamas demonstrates that the anticolonial and postcolonial can indeed coexist in the era of settler colonial rule. This book then ends with a discussion of the implication of this coexistence for what it means to be liberated (and unliberated).

Ostensibly, the liberation of a people is confirmed by the momentous occasion when the colonizer renounces its rule over the lands of the colonized. It is this moment that is seen as dividing the colonized between the era of colonial rule and that of the postcolonial state. This occasion, often celebrated as Independence Day, is then meant to signify the precise moment when the colonized became truly sovereign, independent, and capable of determining their own destiny. The gravity attached to this moment was evident in Jawaharlal Nehru's speech as India's first prime minister, on the eve of the country's independence. He said,

> Long years ago, we made a tryst with destiny, and now the time comes when we shall redeem our pledge, not wholly or in full measure, but very substantially. At the stroke of the midnight hour, when the world sleeps, India will awake to life and freedom. A moment comes, which comes but rarely in history, when we step out from the old to the new, when an age ends, and when the soul of a nation, long suppressed, finds utterance. It is fitting that at this solemn moment we take the pledge of dedication to the service of India and her people and to the still larger cause of humanity.

But does the withdrawal of the colonizer pay immediate dividends in this manner? This is to ask, did the dismantling of the British Raj really result in the soul of India (and Indians) finding immediate utterance? Can the lives of the colonized be so sharply divided between the era of being unliberated and the age of liberation? Hamas and its ability to be both anticolonial and postcolonial in its conduct demonstrate that, in the era of colonial rule, a faction can indeed adopt a mode of conduct from the *other* side of this moment of liberation. To be sure, the postcolonial in Palestine is specific in its Oslo-mandate institutionalized form (i.e., the Palestinian Authority). However, it is not uncommon for the colonized still under colonial rule to posture *as if* the colonizer had long withdrawn. For instance, in *The Nation and its Fragments*, Partha Chatterjee (1993) argued that the genesis of Bengali nationalism against the Raj began in the colonized's spiritual domain wherein the precolonial cultural identity was supreme. In the material domain the West (and the colonizer) remained supreme. Yet, in the spiritual domain the colonized were able to posture *as if* in the era of the postcolonial.

Just as the postcolonial features under colonial rule, so does the struggle for liberation continue in the shadow of the postcolonial state, often being appropriated by the postcolonial elite, who use coercive modes and a language of governance that mimics the practices of the colonial state. Frantz Fanon considered this to be a pitfall of national consciousness in which the political elite of the newly liberated state was concerned with nothing more than being part of the "racket" of political leadership and, to this effect, simply paid "lip service" to the language of liberation (Fanon 1963, 100–101). In Cuba it was the victory of the July 26 Movement, marked by the overthrow of Fulgencio Batista's government, that signaled the liberation of the country from the corruption and authoritarianism of the previous regime and the imperialism of the United States. Yet the ethos of the revolution extended long after this singular moment of liberation and continued to inform life and the often-authoritarian politics of the Cuban regime. Similarly, although Robert Mugabe rose to the helm of Zimbabwean politics as a celebrated nationalist leader, the ideology of liberation persisted into the postindependence era. In the 2000s, his government viewed the forceful seizure of agricultural land from white farmers as merely the rectification of a colonial economic injustice that had persisted long after the political independence of the black Zimbabwean population.

The question then remains, what does liberation stand for if the anticolonial and the postcolonial are able to coexist on either side of the moment of liberation? Can liberation be marked by a single moment at all? At the end of this book, I conclude that the withdrawal of the colonizer as what distinguishes the era of the colonial condition from the postcolonial is an insufficient signifier of liberation. Narratives of the need to become liberated from material and spiritual colonization persist in the era of the postcolonial, and they are used in building the (formerly) colonized's peoplehood and, on occasion, misused by the postcolonial political elite. Rather than viewing the formal beginning of a postcolonial era as the mark of liberation, it is far more critical to assess the societal conditions of developing a liberated sense of the self in the era of the postcolonial. In a multiplicity of ways, the experience of colonial rule in general has left the colonized alienated from their sense of self. This alienation is even more intense under forms of *settler* colonial rule that seek to erase all evidence of the colonized's existence. Under such conditions the possibilities of leaving behind the personal ramifications of colonialism in the era of the postcolonial are even more limited. From this perspective the moment of liberation is therefore not a moment at all in the sense of an exact point in time. Instead, the moment when the colonizer withdraws is only a momentous point in a long process in which the (formerly) colonized, with little memory of their indigenous past untouched by the legacies of colonial rule, are compelled to perpetually search for a liberated identity.

Hamas's Search for Palestine

In line with this book's ambition to deliberate over the anticolonial, the postcolonial, and the long moment of liberation through the story of Hamas, chapter 2 situates the Gaza Strip within Israel's settler colonialism as a way of contextualizing the Palestinian anticolonial subjectivity. While recognizing the *Nakba*, or catastrophe, of 1948 as having begun the historical process of materializing the settler colonial "dream" of Palestinian nonexistence, in this chapter I argue that the urge to eliminate the Palestinian community remains just as important today. This is evident, for example, in the unmistakable absence of Palestinians in the exhibits at Israeli "War of Independence" museums and the swift elimination of Palestinians who carried out knife attacks. But, while this conduct is characteristic of a settler colonizer, the Gaza Strip is often perceived only as representative of an extreme case of Palestinian suffering. Moreover, with a politically divisive organization at its helm and a decade-long siege still in place, the Palestinian coastal enclave is frequently placed outside the limits of any "normal" discussion of the politics of Israel-Palestine. Yet, in this chapter I conclude that the Gaza Strip in fact personifies the norm as a spatial representative of the effort to materially realize and naturalize the settler colonial dream of Palestinian nonexistence. Specifically, as Hamas-ruled Gaza has been indomitable in its armed struggle, the treatment meted out to it by Israel, by way of a siege that has continued despite the severity of the consequent humanitarian crisis and the ruthlessness of Israeli military onslaughts, demonstrates the extent of the settler's willingness to subdue any political act or ideology that acknowledges the existence of the indigene and thus insinuates the nonindigeneity of the settler.

Chapter 3 analyzes the historical geopolitical events that led to the introduction of postcoloniality in Palestine. It argues that the Oslo Accords ensured that the postcolonial lives alongside the anticolonial in a still-persistent colonial condition in the Palestinian territories. Specifically, this is an outcome of two relevant legacies of the Accords. The first and most palpable legacy is the Accords' failure to end Israel's military rule over the Palestinian territories and establish a sovereign State of Palestine. It is this legacy that gives credence to the continued anticolonial struggle. But while many have condemned the Accords for their failures, few have discussed the manner in which these failures live alongside the agreement's generative role in changing the subjective identity of

Palestinian factions. Accordingly, the second legacy is evident in the manner in which the Oslo Accords introduced and incentivized postcoloniality, encouraging Palestinian factions to refrain from an anticolonial political conduct and instead operate in a manner *as if* the colonizer had already withdrawn. This postcoloniality is institutionally concentrated in the Palestinian Authority, which postures much like the postcolonial State of Palestine as it arbitrates the political, economic, social, and cultural lives of Palestinians—this, despite the fact that the "real" Palestinian state is far from fruition. It is thus these two legacies of the Oslo Accords which, I argue, Hamas navigates by means of its dual role. As an armed resistance movement, Hamas exemplifies a response to what the Accords failed to do, namely establish a sovereign Palestinian state and dismantle Israel's settler colonial rule. However, as the government in Gaza, it also embodies postcoloniality as instructed by the Oslo Accords, posturing as a postcolonial state and governing life and politics in the still colonized Palestinian territories.

Having thus provided a context for both the anticolonial and the postcolonial in view of the Palestinian liberation struggle, chapter 4 specifically focuses on Hamas's anticolonial resistance, not least as a means of emphasizing the colonized's existence and cultivating their liberated peoplehood. Drawing on interviews with members of the organization and Palestinians who have participated in, been witness to, or suffered the human and material consequences of Palestinian armed resistance, I argue that anticolonial violence finds relevance in light of its ability to both *unmake* and *make*. Hamas's armed resistance is assumed, by the colonized, to be capable of dismantling or *unmaking* the colonial condition. Its resistance, however, is materially deficient, and thus incapable of dismantling the occupation or defeating the Israel Defense Forces (IDF). I therefore contend that the *unmaking* potential of its violence is not expressed through its ability to destroy unequivocally the materiality of the colonial endeavor or defeat the colonizer. Rather, violence *unmakes* by nominally challenging Israel's settler colonial rule over the Palestinian territories and, in doing so, rendering it a difficult venture to maintain. The potential of violence to be a creative force, to *make*, emerges as a retort by the colonized to the colonial project's attempt to deny their inner being by imposing its own values on their identity. The colonizer, in its character and intent, may be driven by a desire to relegate Palestine to nonexistence. However, Hamas's armed resistance *makes* by allowing each act of resistance to be called an act of *Palestinian* resistance, thus enabling the subsequent suffering to be labeled instances of *Palestinian* suffering. In this way, the "new" decolonized persons emerge from instances of armed struggle, and as a consequence, Palestine and the Palestinian-ness of the colonized are rendered tangible and recognizable.

Chapter 5 demonstrates the manner in which Hamas's postcolonial governance persists in a colonial nonstate context. I argue that, despite the "real" Palestinian state being nonexistent, it is necessary to take the materiality of the imagined state seriously. However, in doing so, the aspiration is not to determine "how much" or "how little" Hamas acts like a state, but rather to illustrate the way in which its statelike conduct is socialized into a liberation context. Subsequently, I specify two perspectives on Hamas's government. The first perspective is that of Hamas. Drawing on interviews with Hamas officials, I outline the organization's perception of itself as an anticolonial faction that has now infused the postcolonial state with the ethos of the anticolonial struggle and, in doing so, reconceptualized its role as a government as a means of protecting the anticolonial armed resistance. The second perspective is that of the recipients of Hamas's governance, namely the Gazans. Based on interviews with Palestinians in Gaza, I argue that, while the colonized are socialized into the reality of their own statelessness, their encounter with Hamas's governance also emerges as a canvas on which Palestine is displayed as a state. This dynamic is reminiscent of the postcolonial state struggling to ensure that the state is indeed legible to its citizenry despite its arbitrary borders and limited coercive power. When adapted to the Palestinian liberation context, however, this dynamic becomes a means of underlining the existence of Palestine in the face of the settler colonial narrative that emphasizes the indigene's nonbeing. As Palestinians who encounter Hamas's postcolonial governance inadvertently identify it as a *Palestinian* government and chastise it for failing to fulfill the *national* task of governance successfully, this too (not unlike Hamas's anticolonial violence) becomes a way of highlighting that Palestine and Palestinians indeed do exist.

With the anticolonial and postcolonial both finding resonance in the era of colonial rule, the final two chapters discuss the implication of this for how liberation is conceived. Concerned with the Palestinian moment of liberation, chapter 6 recognizes that Hamas presents an extreme case because Palestinian postcoloniality has, to an extent, been concretized by way of the establishment of the Palestinian Authority and its accompanying institutions under the Oslo Accords. Nonetheless, the case of Hamas shows that liberation is not entirely contingent on the singular moment when the colonizer withdraws from the lands of the colonized. Instead, the colonial subject begins the process of conjuring up a liberated peoplehood while still in a colonial condition. Thus, in the case of Palestine, this means that Gaza is not just a story of siege, war, and the challenges Hamas faces while maintaining its dual role or its growing authoritarianism. If we consider the long moment of liberation to have begun already, we also notice that a Gaza Strip under the canopy of a single Palestinian leadership becomes, albeit minimally, reminiscent of the eventual liberated State of Palestine as a single territorial unit, inhabited by the Palestinian people and ruled by a Palestinian government. In chapter 7, I then take this discussion of the long moment beyond Palestine. And, using examples from India, Zimbabwe, South Africa, Tanzania, Cuba, and Turkish Kurdistan I demonstrate that, just as the postcolonial exists in the era of colonial rule, so does the struggle for liberation continue long after the withdrawal of the colonizer. This urge to keep fighting is partly driven by an effort to combat the sociopolitical, economic, and cultural remnants of colonization that often endure despite the "official" end of colonial rule. But far more critically, I argue, this urge persists because the nature (and experience) of the colonial enterprise is such that despite the (formerly) colonized's enthusiastic search for a decolonized, *post*colonial sense of self, they lack any significant memory of a past unadulterated by colonization. This dilemma is further acute for those under settler colonial rule, since the very endeavor of settler colonialism is often to erase the signature of indigenous presence. The result, I conclude, is that liberation cannot be achieved following the single moment when the colonizer withdraws. Instead, the postcolonial and the anticolonial coexist irrespective of the presence or absence of the colonizer, as the (formerly) colonized—without any way of conjuring a truly national identity sans the signature of the colonizer—are compelled to perpetually search for their decolonized sense of self, thereby generating a long and often protracted moment of liberation.

ON THE SETTLER COLONIAL ELIMINATION OF PALESTINE

On November 23, 2015, Mahane Yehuda market (or the *shuk*) in Jerusalem was the scene of a stabbing attack. The CCTV recording of the attack shows two Palestinian teenagers, Hadil Wajih Awwad, 14, and her cousin Nurhan Ibrahim Awwad, 16, swinging scissors at bystanders near a light-rail station. Soon the scene is flooded with armed men who, in their efforts to foil the attack, shoot the teenagers repeatedly until they laid lifeless on the ground.[1] Hadil was shot dead, while Nurhan was injured and afterwards charged with attempted murder. It was later reported that Hadil was the sister of Mahmoud Awwad. On March 1, 2013, Mahmoud was shot in the head by an IDF soldier with a rubber-coated steel bullet during a protest at Kalandia refugee camp. He died from his injuries later that year (Strickland 2014).

On the day of the attack involving the Awwad cousins, I was conducting interviews in east Jerusalem. When I heard about the incident, I took the light rail westward in the direction of Mahane Yehuda, expecting to see a heightened army and police presence at the scene. However, life seemed normal only an hour after the attack. The light rail was operating as usual and the hustle and bustle of the shuk had returned. The location of the attack had also been cleaned up and, with their blood washed off the sidewalk, no signs of Hadil and Nurhan remained. With nothing to see at the scene, I went inside the market and sat at a coffee shop to collect my thoughts. There I overheard a conversation between an Israeli tour guide and his client. The latter seemed shaken by the attack and said, "But they [Hadil and Nurhan] were only children." The tour guide responded, "Yes. But that's what life is here. These Arabs come here and use our schools and hospitals. Fine, you can use it. But when you come to me with a knife, I will kill you." Noticing that his client was not convinced, he added, "Look, this happens all the time. Israel attacked Hamas in Gaza, and they say a pregnant woman died. But crazy dogs get pregnant too. That doesn't mean that we don't kill them."[2] The tour guide was presumably referring to the death of Noor Hassan, who was five months pregnant when she was killed in an Israeli airstrike (Nasser 2015).

It would seem that, for the armed men and the tour guide at the shuk, there was no question that a swift death was what the young attackers deserved. This perception was also evident during an alleged stabbing attack in the West Bank, when the prominent Israeli settler and politician Gershon Mesika drove his car into sixteen-year-old Ashraqat Taha Qatnani before she was shot dead by IDF soldiers. In a nonchalant way, Mesika had said, "I didn't stop to think. I hit the gas and rammed into her; she fell down, and then the soldiers came and continued shooting and neutralized her completely" (B'Tselem 2015a). Referring to this manner of "neutralizing" Palestinian attackers, Israeli human rights organization B'Tselem wrote the following in a letter to Israeli prime minister Benjamin Netanyahu: "Even though the individuals involved had already been 'neutralized,' they were shot at again. . . . Whether or not these individuals had been attempting to perpetrate attacks is a matter that cannot obscure the harsh reality at hand: these instances constitute public, summary street executions, without law or trial. And there is reason for concern that there are other such cases as well." The letter goes on to blame the Netanyahu government for permitting the transformation of Israeli security personnel and armed civilians "into judges and executioners" (B'Tselem 2015b, 1–2).

We cannot dismiss the sense of insecurity that permeates Israeli society because of these stabbing attacks. Some would argue, this insecurity has led many Israeli civilians to act as judges and executioners. However, the urge to eliminate the indigenous swiftly is also central to a settler colonial endeavor. This impulse involves not only the physical elimination of the indigenous, but also their metaphorical erasure that occurs when Palestine and Palestinians are oddly absent in museum exhibits celebrating the Israeli "War of Independence," when Palestinian cultural artifacts are appropriated *as* Israeli, and when Gazans are reduced to a bare existence by a persistent siege. In this chapter I traverse these multifaceted ways in which the Palestinian community is erased, as I situate the Gaza Strip in the past and present of Israel's settler colonialism. I conclude that the urge to eliminate is neither exceptional nor merely an insecurity-driven act of self-defense. Rather, it is the norm that foundationally represents what settler colonialism is and does. It is this norm that then contextualizes and shapes the character of the anticolonial subjectivity and politics of an organization like Hamas.

A History of Settler Colonial Elimination

Despite their fundamentally incongruent political aspirations, the lives of settlers and natives are inseparable. During his inaugural lecture as the AC Jordan
Professor of African Studies at the University of Cape Town, Mahmood Mamdani argued that "you cannot have one without the other, for it is the relationship between them that makes one a settler and the other a native. To do away
with one, you have to do away with the other" (Mamdani 1998, 1). This relationship both builds and destroys. For one thing, it entails the dissolution of
the indigenous community. At the same time this destruction of the indigenous
community is also meant to make way for the establishment of the settler's society on the newly appropriated land, now emptied of its indigenous inhabitants.
In this sense, the settler's invasion of the indigenous community's land is not
merely an event: it is a structure (Wolfe 2006, 388). Much as in other colonial
contexts, this structure ensures the perpetual reproduction of the domination
of the colonizer (Veracini 2010, 3–4). But, to the indigenous, the *settler* colonizer does not just say "You, work for me." The settler demands, "You, go away"
(Veracini 2011, 1).

Though, in the settler's narrative the disappearance of the indigenous is not
deliberate, but simply an inevitable occurrence. The settler acknowledges (and
regrets) that there were conflicts with indigenous communities. For instance,
American folklore describing the westward expansion of settlers often includes
accounts of clashes with Native Americans. Yet, the natives' eventual demise is
deemed tragic but unavoidable in these stories because they were faced with the
settlers' far "superior technology, military prowess, and centralized state" (Jacobs
2009, 6). This belief was equally evident when an Australian administrator said
the following about the aboriginal community in 1929:

> We have the slowly advancing tide of resolute white settlers, and a receding
> tide of natives, sullen and naturally resentful. That position has been the
> same in Africa, America, Australia, and the Pacific. We have had massacres
> and ill-treatment, and there has been the same trouble, where aboriginals
> were concerned, all over the world. I say it quite frankly; these things end
> in the same way—in the domination by the whites. (Jacobs 2009, 7)

And, the Canadian-Irish painter Paul Kane also believed that the indigenous
community in Canada faced an almost inevitable extinction. So, arguing for the
need to document the ways of the fast-disappearing indigenous community, he
wrote, "The face of the red man is now no longer seen. All the traces of his foot-
steps are fast being obliterated from his once favorite haunts, and those [like
Kane himself] who would see the aborigines of this country in their original

state, or seek to study their native manners and customs, must travel far through the pathless forest to find them" (Kane 1859, xii). Despite ruing the demise of the natives, this narrative nonetheless characterizes the settler as one who heroically fled persecution and established settlements out of sheer necessity, thus deserving the credit for building a new nation (Jacobs 2009, 7).

Unsurprisingly, the indigenous do not consider the settlers' endeavors to be acts of valor. Neither do they consider their own elimination inevitable. When in the land of the indigenous, settlers intend to make this new environment their permanent home. However, in doing so they also pretend that the territory in which they are building the new nation is empty. It is then in order to ensure that this land is *indeed* empty that the settler strives not just to exploit, but to eliminate (Elkins and Pederson 2005, 2). That is, it is in order to make the "dream" of establishing the settler society on virgin territory a reality that the settler tries to displace or *re*place the indigenous from the land that the latter calls home. And while the indigenous are displaced, "[settler] colonizers come to stay" (Wolfe 1999, 1–2).

In applying this conception of settler colonialism to Israel, it would seem almost self-evident that here too the settler "destroys to replace" (Wolfe 2006, 388). European Jewish settlers considered Palestine to be "a land without a people [*terra nullis*], for a people without a land." For them, this assumption then justified the "exclusive control, ownership and domination of the land" by settlers (Masalha and Isherwood 2014, xii). Further, Nadera Shalhoub-Kevorkian adds, the phrase (a land without . . .) does not just replicate the "claim[s] of terra nullis." It "reinforces the claim that Palestinians were/are not a people." That is to say, the land was not just empty; its inhabitants were also not "a people," in the sense of a collectivity like a distinct national community (Shalhoub-Kevorkian 2015, 5). Of course, this perception of Palestinians as nonpeople was also implicit in the unequivocal manner in which Theodor Herzl, the father of political Zionism, outlined his utopian vision of a modern Jewish state. In *Altneuland*, he wrote, "If I wish to substitute a new building for an old one, I must demolish before I construct" (Herzl 1902, 38).[3]

But, the history of the material destruction of Palestinian communities, which were then replaced by (Israeli) settler communities, began with the expulsion of 750,000 Palestinians during the Nakba of 1948 surrounding the establishment of the State of Israel (Masalha 2012, 2). And Plan Dalet (or Plan D), adopted by the Jewish paramilitary organization Haganah on March 10, 1948, personified the settler colonial sentiment that "the Palestinians had to go." In his description of the plan, Ilan Pappe wrote, "The orders [for Plan D] came with a detailed description of the methods to be employed to forcibly evict the people: large-scale intimidation; laying siege to and bombarding villages and population centres; setting fire to homes, properties and goods; expulsion; demolition; and, finally, planting mines among the rubble to prevent any of the expelled inhabitants from returning" (Pappe 2006, xii). The existence of the indigenous Palestinians also seemed to have been inconsequential (and irrelevant) to Israeli military leader and politician Moshe Dayan when, in a morally indifferent tone, he said, "Jewish villages were built in the place of Arab villages. You do not even know the names of these Arab villages, and I do not blame you because geography books no longer exist—not only do the books not exist, the Arab villages are not there either" (Khalidi 1992, xxxi). Geographer David Benvenisti was similarly insistent in his erasure of Palestinians when he drew the Hebrew map of the Holy Land, while convinced of his incontrovertible "right to reclaim his ancestral patrimony" (Benvenisti 2000, 2). As his map aimed to transform the symbolic claim to the land into a material possession, it effaced all evidence of the indigenous Palestinian presence. His son Meron Benvenisti, a political scientist and former deputy mayor of Jerusalem, was too young to participate in the Israeli "War of Independence." Nonetheless, he also contributed to the settler's endeavor to replace Palestinians when he helped harvest the ripe barley left behind by expelled Palestinian farmers, assisted in the establishment of a kibbutz in an abandoned Palestinian village and uprooted Palestinian-owned olive trees in order to replace them with a banana grove for his own kibbutz, Rosh Haniqra (Ibid., 2).

This book is not an extensive study of this history of Israel's settler colonial presence. Other writers, including Ahmad Sa'di and Lila Abu-Lughod (2007), Walid Khalidi (1992), Rashid Khalidi (1997), Ilan Pappe (2006), and Nur Masalha (2012), have authoritatively demonstrated the manner in which the establishment of the State of Israel strove to make Palestine and Palestinians nonexistent. However, the Gaza Strip, as the place where I locate this book's *problematique*, bears a particularly prominent mark of this specific history. For instance, while the Palestinian "refugee problem" impacted the demographic makeup of the entire region, the impression it left on the Gaza Strip was exceptionally acute. During the Nakba the population of Gaza tripled as a result of the influx of between 220,000 and 250,000 Palestinians refugees (Roy 1995, 13; Gunning 2007, 27). This transformed the coastal enclave into not only one of the most densely populated places in the world, but also one that, demographically, was dominated by refugees (Efrat 2006, 167).

Economically, the Gaza Strip has also been far more impoverished than the West Bank. Refugees continued to live in dire conditions in overcrowded refugee camps that were first established in 1948 (Roy 1995, 19). Before 1967, Gaza's economy lacked the vibrancy, capital, or infrastructure to provide for the needs of its burgeoning refugee population. Following the Six-Day War in 1967 Israel captured the Gaza Strip and Sinai from Egypt, the West Bank and East Jerusalem from Jordan, and the Golan Heights from Syria. Under direct Israeli control, Gaza saw some economic growth, boosted primarily by the comparatively higher earnings of Palestinians living in Gaza who were now able to work in Israel. At the same time the availability of capital and Israeli business interests instigated an increase in industrial and agricultural development. This also coincided with the growing access to Arab markets. However, large-scale economic growth eluded the Gaza Strip. Despite Palestinians earning higher wages in Israel, these incomes were rarely reinvested in the Gazan economy. Additionally, Israel contributed to the enclave's stagnation by discouraging investment activities in Gaza. As a result, incomes from Israel and remittances from Palestinians abroad were largely used to buy durable Israeli consumer goods. As this did little to promote the local economy, Gaza remained disproportionately dependent on the economic tides in Israel (Roy 1987, 82–83).

As a result of the indelible impressions of the Nakba, the population of the Gaza Strip has been quite fervent in its anticolonial politics. The West Bank was "exposed to external influences" and "foreign visitors." In comparison, Gaza was largely isolated, smaller in size, had "higher fertility and lower mortality rates," and was considered to be "far more traditional" (Roy 1995, 23). Furthermore, under Jordanian rule between 1948 and 1967, Palestinians in the West Bank were socialized into state politics and were allowed to participate at the local and national level (Roy 1995, 25). Under Egyptian rule, however, Palestinians in Gaza did not have official channels to develop "their own political culture and leadership." As a consequence, violence often emerged as *the* language of political action and activism in Gaza (Roy 1995, 24). It played an important role in initiating the First Intifada, has been home to early Palestinian militant organizations in the 1950s (Roy 2011, 21), and has served as the training ground for prominent Palestinian resistance leaders and factions (Gunning 2007, 27).

So, the Gaza Strip can indeed be considered illustrative of the historical legacy of Israel's settler colonialism. Edward Said was therefore right to term both Jerusalem and Gaza as essential facets of the [liberated] Palestinian future. Jerusalem's significance, he argued, draws on the importance that "Israelis attach . . . to its enlargement and expanded colonization." Gaza, however, is the "essential core" of the Palestinian struggle. It is, for one thing, a congested, impoverished place inhabited largely by refugees that gives birth to Intifadas. It is also a place for which Israeli politicians have nothing but contempt—possibly, due to its intransigent anticolonial political spirit. Therefore, I agree with Said that to understand Gaza is to understand the Palestinian struggle (Said 1995, 47). Of course, for my purposes in this book, it is also a practical political reality that Hamas today finds its political mandate being limited to the Gaza Strip. Nonetheless, the

organization's politics inhabits a significant microcosm of the historical consequences of Israel's settler colonialism.

On the Settler Colonial Present

The settler's urge to eliminate the signature of the indigene's existence is not only
found in the past: it is a contemporary desire that makes the indigenous perpetually anxious with regard to settler colonial schemes that do not acknowledge
their presence. This anxiety was evident when the American late-night talk-show
host Conan O'Brien was confronted by (pro-)Palestinian activists in Bethlehem
while shooting for his travel special, "Conan Without Borders: Israel." The forty-
minute special released for television audiences on September 19, 2017, featured
edited footage of O'Brien's encounter with the activists, where they are seen
intently discussing the Israeli separation wall, the wider politics of the Israeli-
Palestinian conflict, and the possibilities for peace. The discussion ends with
O'Brien admitting, "There's no way my forty-minute program is going to satisfy
what it is you want me to do. What I do promise to do is to make sure the people
who watch this program will have an idea that this other reality exists."[4] However,
the most noteworthy aspect of O'Brien's encounter appears at the very outset of
the unedited version of the footage, where one of the Palestinian activists is first
seen confronting him by asking, "Did you say Shakshuka was Israeli, a couple of
days ago?"[5] O'Brien confesses that he does not know what it is but says that he
assumed it was an Israeli dish because it was served to him on an El Al flight. The
activist responds, "It's a Palestinian dish just like falafel. . . . It offends Palestinians
because they're taking the land, the food . . . there is hardly anything left."[6]

   Although O'Brien apologizes, he is visibly perplexed that calling a supposedly
Palestinian dish Israeli would matter so much. For the indigenous Palestinian
community, however, faced with the material prowess of the settler colonizer,
who insists on the indigene's nonexistence, the nonrecognition of a Palestinian dish *as* Palestinian can symbolize a step toward the materialization of the
settler colonial "dream." As Ali Abunimah of *Electronic Intifada* noted, the "cultural appropriation of indigenous Palestinian folklore and cuisine as 'Israeli'
has long angered Palestinians, especially when these same cultural products are
used in international propaganda and marketing efforts which deny Palestinians'
rights and history." In this particular case, Abunimah was responding to a video
released by an Israeli regional council in the occupied West Bank that seemed to
be appropriating as their own the allegory of olives and olive oil, which has been
regarded "the most important symbol and source of economic sustenance for
rural Palestinians" (Abunimah 2012). The Palestinian student I encountered in
2016 at a cafeteria at the Hebrew University of Jerusalem on Mount Scopus was
similarly irked. Since the names of all the dishes on offer being written in Hebrew,

I had asked an Israeli student queuing behind me to translate. While he was able to describe each dish swiftly, he hesitated when identifying what looked like *maqluba*, a quintessentially Palestinian dish. He said, "It's this Israeli rice dish. I'm blanking on the name. It has rice, chicken and vegetables. It's very good." Before I could respond, the Palestinian student standing in line in front of me interjected angrily, "It's maqluba. It's Palestinian." He then walked out of the cafeteria.

The desire to displace and *re*place the indigenous is equally present in the spatial conduct of the settler. For instance, in Jerusalem this conduct has been termed the Judaization of the city, where changing municipal regulations, the presence of a separation barrier, the plethora of IDF checkpoints, and an increasingly virulent settlement movement have helped turn the dream of Jerusalem "as the united and eternal capital of Israel and the Jewish people" into a reality (Zink 2009, 131). This materialization has come at the cost of Palestinian communities and the identity they lend to the landscape of the city (Quraishy 2009; Hodgkins 1996). Sari Hanafi further termed this spatial settler colonial tact "spacio-cide"—a juridical-political means of spatially dislocating and displacing Palestinians. He deems this process not unlike the ethnic cleansing of Palestinians in 1948, as it, by way of the systematic destruction of Palestinian living spaces, ensures that the displacement of the indigenous is all but inevitable (Hanafi 2009, 107–108). Of course, the judiciary has also been an important means through which the settler colonizer has attempted to (legally) deny the existence of Palestine and Palestinians. For example, in 2011 Amendment 40 of the Basic Principles Law, or the "Nakba Law," came into effect. It allows the Israeli Finance Ministry to revoke state funding for organizations that do not consider Israel to be a "Jewish state" or that commemorate its "Independence Day as a day of mourning" (Strickland 2015). In effect, this law criminalizes the commemoration of the Palestinian Nakba, a tragic juncture in contemporary Palestinian history that also evidences the concerted (settler colonial) attempt to materially displace and *re*place the indigenous. More recently, in July 2018, the Knesset passed the Jewish Nation-State Law that declared Israel to be the "nation-state of the Jewish people." It adds that the "right of self-determination in the State of Israel is unique to the Jewish people" (*Jerusalem Post* Staff 2018). Being a constitutional law, or an "Israeli Basic Law," it essentially strives to enshrine the Palestinians' inability (albeit, in Israeli constitutional terms) to claim liberation on, or a right to, the land that constitutes the State of Israel.

Museums celebrating the role of Jewish paramilitary organizations in securing Israel's independence erase the signature of the Palestinian presence as well. These organizations authored much of the violence that surrounded the establishment of the State of Israel. It was, after all, their sweeping military victories that led to prominent Palestinian losses of places like Jaffa, Haifa, Acre, and Tiberias. Moreover, as the historian Rashid Khalidi writes, these losses subsequently led to the expulsion of Palestinians and began the "demographic transformation" of Israel-Palestine (Khalidi 1997, 27, 178). The paramilitary organization Palmach, for instance, was established to assist British troops in case of a Nazi invasion of Palestine. Yet, in the 1940s, it not only pioneered the establishment of new Israeli settlements but was also active in "cleansing operations" in rural Palestinian communities (Pappe 2006, 45). The same tactic of cleansing Palestine and Palestinians is present today in Beit HaPalmach, or the Palmach Museum, in Tel Aviv. The exhibition at the museum is three-dimensional, and visitors walk through a film reenactment of the experience of young Palmach recruits during the Israeli "War of Independence." Each room is designed to replicate the scene(ry) in the film and thus creates an ambience conveying the impression that museum visitors are in fact accompanying the characters in the film as they fight to establish the State of Israel. While the targets of the Palmach's violence were Palestinian communities, Palestine and Palestinians are on the periphery of the exhibition's narrative. The terms *Palestine* and *Palestinians* are never used during the course of the film. Instead, Palestinians were simply referred to as "Arabs." This, in and of itself, symbolizes the nonrecognition of Palestinians as a distinct national community, not least as distinct from *other* national communities in the Arab world. But Palestinians (or "Arabs") are also relegated to the sidelines of this historical narrative in the way in which their presence is addressed. Specifically, there are only two instances when "Arabs" are mentioned in the exhibit. The first is when Palestinian troops are simply referred to as "marauding Arab gangs." The second is during a discussion between two characters in the film, where they are seen momentarily agonizing over the "problem" of Palestinian refugees. One character asks, "What should we do with the refugees?" The other, in a nonchalant tone, responds "Do what you think is best." It is as if both characters are unaware of the way in which these refugees *became* refugees and are entirely unconcerned about the consequences of the mass expulsion of Palestinians from a place they consider their national home.[7]

A similar erasure of Palestinians occurs at the Haganah Museum in Tel Aviv, especially in the exhibit on the Great Revolt of 1936–39 (figure 2.1). The historian Rosemary Sayigh describes the revolt as one of the first significant nationalist outbursts by Palestinian peasants in the long and arduous trajectory of the Palestinian revolutionary struggle for liberation (Sayigh 1979, 152). The violent response from factions like the Haganah and the consequent deaths, injuries, and incarcerations were a prelude to the "crescendo of violence" that eventually led to the Nakba of 1948 (Sayigh 1979, 4). Additionally, the uprising had regional significance as the longest lasting "militant anti-imperialist struggle in the Arab world" until the start of the Algerian War of Independence (Sayigh 1979, 43). However, the exhibit at the museum pays no heed to the historical significance of the Revolt nor does it recognize the existence of a

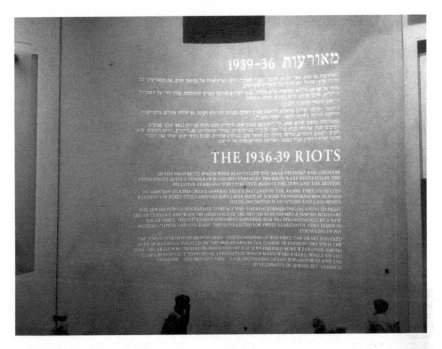

FIGURE 2.1   Exhibit on the "Great Revolt of 1936–39" at the Haganah Museum in Tel Aviv. Photo by author.

national people and their national cause in the background of the uprising. Instead, the exhibit characterizes the Great Revolt as simply "riots" and "blood disturbances" that were led by "Arabs" in Palestine and targeted Jews as well as the British. With the nationalist intentions that animated these disturbances absent from the exhibit, the museum visitor is left with the impression that the violence was conducted without cause or reason other than to harm the Jewish population. Moreover, the exhibit also communicates the futility of the Arab revolt and—much like the narrative in, say, American folklore on settlers' westward expansion—insinuates the inevitable victory of the settler following any confrontation with the indigene. It concludes,

> The Jews suffered hundreds of dead and thousands of wounded. The Arabs suffered even more losses, inflicted by the British and in the course of encounters with Jews. The Arabs who wanted to harm and hit the Jews emerged more weakened, among other reasons, due to the internal struggles in which many were killed, while on the side this brought about a strengthening of the Jewish power and the development of Jewish settlements.[8]

If Palestinians as a national people personifying (in their politics) a national cause are effaced by law, in museum exhibits, in university cafeterias, and by the spatial replanning of a divided city, where does the Gaza Strip "fit" among these multifaceted contemporary settler colonial schemes? As I have argued earlier, the Palestinian coastal enclave bears the marks of the historical legacies of the establishment of the State of Israel and the expulsion of Palestinians that consequently ensued. But does today's Gaza, besieged and with Hamas at its helm, reflect the continued settler colonial urge to ensure that the indigenous are invisible? In a sense, and unlike the contemporary settler colonial schemes I have described thus far, Gaza enjoys a hypervisibility (as opposed to being invisible), not least due to Hamas's widely held reputation as exceptionally contemptable in its political conduct. Gaza, by representing the spatial extent of Hamas's contemptable politics, is frequently treated as nothing more than a synonym for Hamas and its reputation. This synonymy is apparent in the sector of the colonizer. When I delivered a lecture on life and politics in the Gaza Strip at an Israeli university in January 2014, my focus was largely on the everyday Palestinian experiences of a siege. Yet, after my lecture, one attendee asked, "I'm wondering if we are going to see Hamas aligning with global jihad? . . . Not exactly al-Qaeda, but something like al-Qaeda, where they are not trying to build a nation state but an Islamic caliphate. A long-term 'pie in the sky' goal." His question was particularly curious since I had not mentioned "Hamas," "al-Qaeda," or "global jihad" in my presentation. However, it seemed that any mention of Gaza was perceived as an implicit reference to Hamas. Moreover, any reference to Hamas appeared to inspire parallels between this Palestinian faction and other reviled forces operating in international politics.

This synonymy was equally present in Israeli responses to the 2018 "Great March of Return." Characterized by protests on the border between Israel and Gaza, the march was meant to highlight the plight of Palestinian life under siege in Gaza, call for the end of the siege of Gaza, and underline the "right of return" of Palestinians expelled during the Nakba of 1948. Speaking to *Democracy Now*, Rashid Khalidi noted that the March of Return was a new phase in the Palestinian liberation struggle. He added, "You have literally tens of thousands of people walking to the fence, camping along the fence, carrying out protest activities, which are then met with a hail of hundreds and thousands of bullets."[9] These protesters were met with a hail of bullets precisely because, in the settler's narrative, they are not a historic or unique expression of Palestinian national aspirations, but an extension of Hamas's (contemptable) politics. For instance, responding to the widespread criticism of Israel's response to the march, the IDF uploaded a video on its Facebook page entitled "Imagine if Hamas broke through the security fence." It argued that, given the opportunity, Hamas would attack as many Israeli citizens as possible. Underlining the sacrosanct nature of the border and seemingly justifying the hail of bullets that have rained down on Palestinian protesters at the border, it concluded, "The security fence is the only thing separating Hamas from Israeli civilians."[10] The Israeli Defense Minister, Avigdor Liberman, similarly maintained that the March of Return was simply a Hamas affair when he tweeted,

> The IDF soldiers pushed back the Hamas military wing with determination and professionalism, just as we expected them to do. I fully back the [soldiers]; because of them we celebrated the Passover Seder with confidence. I do not understand the choir of hypocrites who are calling for a commission of inquiry. They got confused and thought Hamas organized a Woodstock festival and we had to give [the marchers] flowers. (*Times of Israel* Staff 2018)

In the same way, the Israel Ministry of Foreign Affairs (MFA) said the following in a press release on its Facebook page:

> The border fence between Israel and the Gaza Strip separates a sovereign state and a terrorist organization. It separates a state that protects its citizens from murderers who send their countrymen into danger. The fence separates an army that uses force in self-defense and in a focused and proportionate manner, and Hamas, an organization that sanctifies murder and death. . . . Anyone who mistakenly views in this murderous spectacle even an iota of freedom of expression is blind to the threats the State of Israel faces.[11]

Of course, it is such a conception of Hamas and, by association, Gaza(ns) in the narrative of the settler that justifies and lends impunity to this violent retaliation. In the IDF video or the statements by Liberman and the MFA, it is the contemptibility of Hamas and its politics that allows Gaza and Gazans to be painted in the same hue as the Islamic Resistance and justifies the supposedly defensive violence of the IDF that is meant to do no more than protect Israeli civilians from murderers. In fact, this perception also led the Israeli government, responding to a High Court petition filed by an Israeli human rights organization, to declare that with regard to the Gaza Strip and the conduct of the IDF during the March of Return, "The state opposes the applying of human rights law during an armed conflict" (Kubovich 2018). The perception that Gaza and Hamas are exceptional in their contemptibility has also justified the violence of each successive Israeli military campaign against the coastal enclave. This was apparent in Israeli prime minister Benjamin Netanyahu's statement on Operation Protective Edge in 2014, when he insisted, "Hamas and other terrorist groups in Gaza are firing rockets on cities throughout the State of Israel. . . . No country on earth would remain passive in the face of hundreds of rockets fired on its cities, and Israel is no exception. . . . We will continue to protect our civilians against Hamas's attacks on them."[12] This logic also extends to Israel's insistence on maintaining the siege over the Gaza Strip, which it considers purely a reflection of Israel's "legitimate security concerns" with regards to Hamas's terrorism (Israel Ministry of Foreign Affairs 2014).

As I discussed in chapter 1, the perception of a Hamas-led Gaza as exceptional was equally present in the manner in which my interlocutors in Israel often treated the organization and the plight of the besieged Palestinian coastal enclave. They were quick to utter the words, "But Hamas . . ." (Nevel 2014) to indicate that the Gaza Strip was outside the realm of any "normal" conversation on the Israeli-Palestinian conflict. However, the exceptionality accorded to Gaza is also present in narratives of its suffering. Following an Israeli decision to reduce Gaza's electricity supply, the deputy regional director for the Middle East and North Africa at Amnesty International Magdalene Mughrabi said, "For 10 years the siege has unlawfully deprived Palestinians in Gaza of their most basic rights and necessities. Under the burden of the illegal blockade and three armed conflicts, the economy has sharply declined and humanitarian conditions have deteriorated severely. The latest power cuts risk turning an already dire situation into a full-blown humanitarian catastrophe" (Amnesty International 2017). Similarly, UNICEF claimed that, as one of the most densely populated places in the world, "Gaza . . . is at risk of health and environmental catastrophe from ailing water and sanitation infrastructure" (UNICEF 2019). A 2017 UN report further declared that, as Gaza had been continuing on a path of decline since the onset of the siege in 2007, the coastal enclave would be "unlivable" by 2020 (UN 2017).

It is in no way misguided to lend hypervisibility to the Gaza Strip in this manner. There is, as Norman Finkelstein suggests, value in elaborating "what has been *done* to Gaza" especially since "what has befallen Gaza is a human-made human disaster" (Finkelstein 2018, xi–xiii). However, it *is* misguided to assume that Gaza's hypervisibility somehow contradicts the invisibility that the settler aims to impose on the indigenous. To that effect, I would argue that the perception of Hamas as exceptionally contemptible is not unlike the exhibition at the Haganah museum, as they both seem to conveniently erase the underlying agenda of a national struggle. The "Great Revolt" exhibit characterizes the Palestinian uprising no more than a riot. A similar exhibit at the Israel Defense Forces History Museum in Tel Aviv details all instances of Palestinian violence under the heading "The War Against Arab Terror" (figure 2.2). And, in this way, they erase the existence of this national struggle by portraying Palestinian violence as violence for its own sake, devoid of any politics and meant to solely inflict suffering on Israeli citizens. Deeming Hamas as exceptionally contemptable and therefore according it hypervisibility as *the* problem also overshadows

FIGURE 2.2 Exhibit on "The War Against Arab Terror" at the IDF History Museum. Photo by author.

the Palestinian national cause that has shaped all forms of Palestinian anticolonial politics, including the "brand" of politics espoused by Hamas. As a result, one needs to simply utter the words "But Hamas . . ." to detach the organization and by extension Gaza from the core of the Palestinian struggle, as it becomes an incomparable entity that is justifiably dealt with using extraordinary measures.

For those sympathetic to the plight of Gazans, the coastal enclave should enjoy hypervisibility because of the exceptional nature of its suffering. However, characterizing the socioeconomic crisis as extreme overlooks the reality that the treatment meted out to Gaza is the norm under settler colonial rule. Being a place that historically, as well as currently under Hamas rule, has displayed an indomitable anticolonial spirit, Gaza has become the target of war and siege as a means to erase this spirit and the cause that inspires it. Thus, when Yitzhak Rabin ordered Israeli soldiers to break the arms and legs of Palestinians during the First Intifada, he was not just concerned with inflicting physical violence on Palestinian bodies (Hass 2005). This physical violence, I would argue, was also meant to break the spirit of the Palestinian struggle for liberation. Similarly, when Israelis in Jerusalem aimed to bring about the Awwad cousins' biological elimination, it was not only a matter of getting rid of a group of attackers. The swift nature of the bystanders' response was also meant to instantly erase the politics (of a national cause) that the Awwad cousins embodied in their actions. Returning to Gaza, the siege and Israel's military campaigns serve a similar purpose in that they too strive to erase or, more appropriately, choke the anticolonial ethos underlying the politics emanating from there. As the siege persists, the Gaza Strip is almost ritually subjected to Israeli military campaigns because the ferocity of the anti-colonial struggle taking root in the coastal enclave persists. In this sense, I would argue, any conception of the Gaza Strip as exceptional in either its contempt-ibility or its suffering would serve only to efface the Palestinian national cause, as it would ignore the fact that the siege, perpetual violence, Palestinian deaths, material destruction, and the bare existence of life under siege in Gaza are all meant to translate into a bare existence for Palestine and Palestinians. The settler then hopes that this bare existence will eventually lead to the complete erasure of the Palestinian national struggle for liberation.

The Elimination of Palestine

On October 18, 2015, approximately a month before the Mahane Yehuda market attack, Haftom Zarhum was mistakenly identified as the accomplice of a Pales-tinian attacker at a bus station in Beersheba in southern Israel. CCTV footage shows Zarhum, an Eritrean asylum-seeker, being shot by a security officer. Over the course of the next sixteen minutes, nine people attacked Zarhum while he was lying motionless in a pool of blood. Some kicked him in the head. Others threw chairs and benches on his lifeless body. A crew member of Magen David Adom, Israel's national emergency service, can be seen being asked to attend to other injured people. Eighteen minutes after being shot, medical personnel evacuated Zarhum, who later died in the hospital.[13] Zarhum was not Palestinian. Yet, the faint possibility that he was the accomplice of a Palestinian attacker and presumably a supporter of the Palestinian national cause was enough to warrant his elimination. In this sense, and not unlike the swift elimination of the Awwad cousins, the murder of Zarhum once again personifies the settler's insistence on erasing the indigenous. Furthermore, I have demonstrated in this chapter that, while the physical elimination of Palestinians is the most brazen manifestation of the insistent eradication of Palestinians, the signature of Palestinian existence is also metaphorically erased within the walls of museums, in university cafete-rias, and in the bare existence of a besieged population. It is then not surprising that this threat of elimination fundamentally animates the colonized's political conduct, not least in its effort to embolden the signature of Palestinian existence and thus counter the settler colonial efforts to effect indigenous nonexistence.

PALESTINIAN POSTCOLONIALITY

A Legacy of the Oslo Accords

One crisp winter morning in early January in 2014, I was on my way to a taxi depot in Ramallah when I stumbled upon a scribble on a door in Arafat Square.[1] It read, "It's Nakbah, Not a Party, Idiots!" (figure 3.1). My Palestinian friends later explained to me that the writing on the door was a criticism of how the Nakba commemoration and memorial ceremonies in the West Bank had started to take the form of a *hafla*, or party. However, with my time in Gaza still in mind, it seemed instead that the words on that door were in fact emblematic of the wider political reality inhabited by Palestine. The "party" stood for an appearance of "normalcy" that one expects to see in the era of the postcolonial state (and after colonial rule), wherein the formerly colonized attempt to (re-)build their national community away from the gaze of the colonizer. The Nakba, on the other hand, signifies the persistence of Israel's settler colonialism that strives to erase the signature of Palestinian existence. In all, the slogan "It's Nakbah, not a party" symbolized a Palestine that oscillates between postcoloniality and all the familiar political and socioeconomic facets of a settler colonial situation. Of course, given the vitality of urban life in Ramallah, some may be encouraged to argue that here the party is far more boisterous than in the Gaza Strip. Nonetheless, in a Palestinian territory (i.e., the West Bank) crisscrossed by IDF checkpoints, army barracks, and settlements, here too the Nakba is never far away.

Earlier in this book I have argued that the moment of liberation from colonial rule is not a moment at all. Instead, preparations for the postcolonial era often

FIGURE 3.1   "It's Nakbah, Not a Party, Idiots!" Ramallah, West Bank. Photo by author.

begin before the withdrawal of the colonizer, while the struggle to be truly liber-ated continues long after the colonizer's departure. With Palestine still awaiting the withdrawal of *its* colonizer, in this chapter I argue that the legacies of the Oslo Accords have already triggered the Palestinian long moment of liberation in the era of settler colonial rule. By failing to secure the Palestinian state, they have, for one, spurred on the Palestinian anticolonial struggle and its violence. At the same time, the Oslo Accords were also generative as they aimed to cultivate a new Palestinian political subjectivity that veered away from an anticolonial identity and toward a more postcolonial mode of political conduct. It is therefore this ambivalent and often confusing post-Oslo political condition, oscillating between the anticolonial and the postcolonial, that Hamas was compelled to navigate following its election victory in 2006.

The Oslo Accords and the Palestinian Path "Home"

The Oslo Accords were touted as the path home for a population exiled by the Nakba of 1948. The violent establishment of the State of Israel, mired in the first Arab-Israeli war, ensured that many Palestinians lost control of all that materially entrenched them in the land they called home. What followed was the period of the "lost years," when Palestinians were not a people and their cause was invisible to the outside world (Khalidi 1997, 178). This was and continues to be the very aim of Israel's settler colonialism. But, in response, Palestinian activists and revolutionaries born and socialized in exile rejected the notion of Palestine as a memory (Turki 1972, 16). Instead, the Palestinian Revolution, strove to transform the memory of Palestine into a tangible and manifested reality (Said 1979, xli). So, while it was the Nakba that ensured that Palestinians would be dispersed across the world, it was now the task of the Palestinian liberation movement to chart "the road to the Return" out of the impoverished life of exile (Sayigh 1979, 150).

The road home, however, began long before the signing of the Oslo Accords. It saw its infancy in student organizations established across the Middle East in the 1950s by the likes of Yasser Arafat, Salah Khalaf, George Habash, and Khalil al-Wazir. Since many of these individuals went on to found prominent Palestinian factions like Fatah and the Popular Front for the Liberation of Palestine, even in their early days, these organizations together represented the Palestinian liberation struggle in exile (Khalidi 1997, 180).[2] Of course, the path home was hardly linear and was marked by, among other events, the Battle of Karameh (1968), the Black September incident (1970–71) in Jordan, the Sabra-Shatila massacres (1982) in Lebanon, and the First Intifada (1987–93), as well as countless other confrontations among the various Palestinian factions, and between them, Israel, and its Arab neighbors. These encounters with the tumultuous political landscape of the Middle East ensured that the Palestinian struggle became a formidable model for change in the region. Furthermore, as Palestinian revolutionary activism and violence won political legitimacy among the Arab masses, Palestinian-ness as an identity and Palestine as an entity once again became visible in regional politics (Kazziha 1979, 36; Sayigh 1997b, 20–23). But, despite this visibility of the Palestinian struggle, the lack of a territorial Palestinian state remained a key obstacle to the consolidation and protection of the Palestinian national identity. Therefore, for Palestinians it was this deficiency that the Oslo Accords were meant to address, as the agreement seemed to recognize the identity of an exiled population while also initiating and institutionalizing their return to a territorial home.

As a prelude to the actual signing of the Oslo Accords, letters exchanged between Palestinian Liberation Organization (PLO) chairman Yasser Arafat and Israeli prime minister Yitzhak Rabin established the norms of the agreements that would follow. In his communication to Rabin on September 9, 1993, Arafat recognized Israeli's right to a secure and peaceful existence, committed himself to the Middle East Peace Process, renounced the use of terrorism, accepted UN Security Council Resolutions 242 and 338, and assumed responsibility for all PLO personnel as a way of ensuring that they did not violate the terms of any forthcoming agreement with Israel.[3] In his response, Rabin wrote that the Government of Israel recognized the PLO as the representative of the Palestinian people and agreed to begin negotiations with the organization within the framework of the Middle East Peace Process (UNISPAL 1993). With these preconditions in place, the Declaration of Principles on Interim Self-Government Arrangements, or Oslo I, was signed on September 13, 1993.

The text of the Oslo I agreement set out the framework for the Palestinian administrative self-government (Palestinian Authority) and a legislative council (Palestinian Legislative Council) for an interim period of five years. Article V of the agreement added that permanent status negotiations on contentious issues such as the status of Jerusalem, settlements, borders, security, and refugees' right of return would "commence as soon as possible, but not later than the beginning of the third year of the interim period" (UN General Assembly/Security Council 1993, 5). The bureaucratic jurisdiction of the Palestinian self-government was limited territorially to the West Bank and the Gaza Strip during this interim period. Oslo I also stipulated that, along with its responsibilities with regard to education, social welfare, health, taxation and tourism, the Palestinian self-governing authority would also be responsible for a Palestinian police force. Article VIII nonetheless provided that Israel would continue to be responsible for the "overall security of Israelis for the purpose of safeguarding their internal security and public order" (UN General Assembly/Security Council 1993, 6).

Oslo I was followed by the Gaza-Jericho Agreement, which effectively established the Palestinian Authority as it required Israel to transfer some civilian responsibilities to Palestinians (Watson 2000, 2). Additionally, it instituted the Paris Protocol that determined the economic relationship between Israel and Palestine (NAD-PLO 1994) and established a Palestinian Civil Police Force. The Oslo II Accord was signed on September 28, 1995. Most significantly, it divided the West Bank into Areas A (under complete Palestinian Authority civil and military control), B (under Palestinian Authority civil control and Israeli military control), and C (under complete Israeli military and civil control). The majority of the territory fell under Area C. Additionally, Oslo II stipulated that neither party could initiate a change in this division of the Palestinian territories until a permanent status is agreed on (UNHCR 1995). Oslo II was followed by the Hebron Agreement (1997), the Wye River Memorandum (1998), the Sharm el Sheikh Memorandum (1999), and the Camp David Summit (2000). These negotiations worked within the limits of the Oslo parameters but failed to turn the interim agreement into a permanent settlement. Following the failure of Camp David, the Second Intifada, or Al-Aqsa Intifada (2000–2005), marked the end of the negotiations and the reemergence of Palestinian popular uprisings against the occupation.

To an extent, the Oslo Accords are just as (in)consequential and (ir)relevant as the multiplicity of other peace agreements and negotiations that have failed to liberate colonized Palestinians and establish a sovereign and viable State of Palestine. Nonetheless, it is of consequence that the Accords reaffirmed Palestinians' commitment to the anticolonial struggle while also introducing postcoloniality in a still-persistent settler colonial condition.

"Negotiations Will Never Work": Oslo and the Anticolonial Struggle

The Hamas summer camp I visited in June 2013 symbolized the emboldening effect that the Oslo Accords had on the Palestinian anticolonial struggle. At the time there was incessant international media coverage of summer camps in the Gaza Strip. News stories declaring "Gaza Children Play 'Kidnap the Soldier' at Military Summer Camp" and "Gaza Children Play War in Hamas Summer Camp" had become a summer ritual.[4] They claimed that Hamas was providing military-style training to Palestinian children at its summer camps. I was also curious about the curriculum at these summer camps. Through an acquaintance at the Hamas-run Government Media Office in Gaza, I was able to organize a tour of one such camp on the condition that I would be accompanied by a Hamas-approved interpreter.[5] The camp was held on the premises of the Asma'a

Bint Abu Bakr Low Basic Girls School for four hours every day, over a period of two weeks. It catered to Palestinian boys aged between ten and thirteen. As we entered the school, an official at the camp welcomed us. He said:

> This is a Palestinian summer camp belonging to the Hamas faction. We organize camps like this each year for Palestinian children. We named it "Generation of Return," as we believe in our right to return to our land. This camp started after the Israeli siege around the Gaza Strip. This camp is here to promote a new lifestyle for the kids and ease the pressure. Of course, some of the activities deal with the right of return.

At first glance the camp seemed to be no different than any other summer camp. It had a slip n' slide, a ping-pong table, an obstacle course, a computer gaming room, dodgeball, and soccer. As we watched the children thoroughly enjoy themselves, my interpreter said, "Our children are very simple. Anything makes them happy." Still, curious about the reputation of Hamas summer camps, I asked him about international media reports claiming that these camps train Palestinian children in the use of weapons. He responded, "They are children. Their only concern is to play. Then why should we give them weapons? We only promote entertainment, a new lifestyle, and try to remove the stress and psychological pressure of living in the Gaza Strip."

But, despite my interpreter's assurances, it was obvious to me that this camp was not *just* about summer fun. Songs celebrating the Palestinian right of return were playing in the background during our visit. Pictures of martyrs were hung around the playground. My interpreter described the obstacle course as a way of teaching the children that "*only* if we cooperate with each other can we reach our goal [of liberation]." He also described the exercise of lining up the children and marching around the school as a way of countering the Israeli claim that Palestinians were "savages or random people." Instead, the orderly march was meant to evoke the message: "We [as Palestinians] are here, we exist, and we are organized." The welcome area of the summer camp (figure 3.2) was adorned with a key symbolizing the right of return, a Quran representing the righteous path to liberation, and a wooden replica of a gun, which, according to my interpreter, symbolized "the way in which we will secure our right to return, and negotiations will never work." There was also a map of greater Palestine (figure 3.3). While pointing to it, an official from the camp said, "We [Palestinians] are a people fighting for our rights. We are under occupation, but we are committed to every inch of our land." When I joked, "Without Israeli checkpoints?" my interpreter replied, "Without Israel at all." Then there was an improvised game of snakes and ladders. The snakes were represented by caricatures of Jews, Israeli politicians, and soldiers, while al-Qassam fighters, the Palestinian fedayeen, and the

FIGURE 3.2 Entrance to the Hamas Summer Camp. Photo by author.

key symbolizing the Palestinian right of return were the ladders. The ultimate goal of the game was to reach Jerusalem (figure 3.4). So, in all, these aspects of the camp ensured that it was not just about summer fun. It was also a place where young Palestinians were familiarized with the values of the Palestinian anticolonial struggle for a national home, albeit as conceived by Hamas.[6]

FIGURE 3.3 The map of greater Palestine displayed at the Hamas Summer Camp. Photo by author.

Since the most divisive issues had been left out of the agreements, there was an expectation that the Oslo Accords would fall short of their aspirations. Tragically for Palestinians, this was indeed the case as a permanent solution to the Israeli-Palestinian conflict that was meant to follow the interim period of the

FIGURE 3.4   An improvised game of Snakes and Ladders. Photo by author.

Oslo process was never secured. Instead, during this extended interim period the Palestinian Authority has become ever less sovereign, the Israeli settlement movement has seen an exponential increase, Palestinians have been unable to access the natural resources of the Palestinian territories, and there has been a rapid economic downturn. Since sovereignty, access to land and resources, and economic viability are key to the process of state building, the Oslo Accords' most evident failure has been their inability to secure a Palestinian state. As a result, for Palestinians, the Accords often serve as a reminder of the persistence of Israel's settler colonial rule and emphasize the need to persist with the anticolonial struggle. In a sense the Hamas summer camp stood in recognition of this need (to continue fighting), not least in opposition to the norms of the Oslo Accords. For instance, when my interpreter said that the gun symbolized the futility of negotiations or that the map of Palestine in fact emphasized the nonexistence of Israel, he spoke in terms that were contrary to the mandated parameters of the Oslo process that requires Palestinians to renounce the armed struggle and recognize Israel. In the game of snakes and ladders, it is the iconic symbols of the Palestinian struggle—the fighters of the al-Qassam Brigade, the Palestinian fedayeen, and the key symbolizing the Palestinian right of return—that lead the participants closer to liberation. And, since the Oslo Accords failed to end Israel's settler colonialism that strives to render Palestinians nonexistent, the planned and ordered activities at the camp were meant as a retort to the (settler colonial) claim that Palestinians do not exist. In sum, initiatives like the summer camp demonstrate that the Oslo Accords have become a cautionary tale of the failure of negotiations, serving instead as a "point of reference" (Sen 2015b, 165) that gives legitimacy to anticolonial activism.

Of course, this legacy of the Oslo Accords also goes beyond the summer camp and provided the background to Hamas's armed struggle in the era following the signing of the agreements. While I discuss the manner in which violence finds resonance with a liberation struggle in chapter 4, at this juncture it is nonetheless important to recognize that Hamas's violence also served as a statement of opposition to the Oslo process. That is to say, as the Oslo Accords failed to secure Palestinian liberation, Hamas, by maintaining its commitment to the armed struggle against Israel, considered itself to be an embodiment of the continued relevance and prevalence of the Palestinian national struggle. This was evident when, in an interview in 1999, Hamas's cofounder Sheikh Ahmed Yassin underlined the importance armed resistance to the Palestinian liberation struggle by referencing the concessions that Palestinians were expected to make because of the Oslo Accords:

> The Palestinian people have lost all their options in fighting the enemy. Nowhere in the world do resistance movements surrender their arms until they have gained their rights, and by retaining their arms they maintain their freedom of action. But we gave up our arms at the beginning of the road and then sat waiting for handouts and rewards from the enemy. This means that we have lost the first round. (Tamimi 2007, 197)

During our conversation, Deputy Foreign Minister Ghazi Hamad similarly said: "The Oslo Accords were a mistake. In the beginning it was sold as the first step for the Palestinians to create a state. But we can see that it was false hope and painted a rosy picture. They deceived us by giving us false hope. It was a big illusion. . . . It was not there to create a state, but it is there to decrease the cost of the occupation." As a way of rectifying this mistake, Hamad then went on to conclude that the armed struggle was "a means of defending" Palestinians from the ills of the Oslo Accords.[7] And, when I asked the general manager of the Hamas-run Government Media Office Salama Maroof about the effects of the Oslo process on Hamas's politics, he said simply, "Hamas, at the very top, fights the occupation and follows the path of the liberation of Palestine. We don't care about Oslo."[8]

My (non-Hamas) interlocutors also considered Hamas's armed resistance to be a critical facet of its politics in opposition to the Oslo Accords. Gamal Abdel Gawad Soltan, a senior researcher at the Al-Ahram Center for Political and Strategic Studies in Cairo, argued that "military capabilities are closely associated with the group's identity as a resistance movement. It stands opposed to the political or diplomatic approach taken by the Oslo Accords, the Palestinian Authority and the PLO, which is seen as risking Palestinian rights."[9] Karim, a young Palestinian from Shuja'iyya, had once been a member of Palestinian factions across the ideological spectrum of the Palestinian liberation movement.[10] Today, however, he laments the human crises that often arise in the aftermath of the armed resistance. He said to me, "In some places people fight to live. Here people live to fight. What is the point of all of this? During Operation Pillar of Defense, we fought for control over three additional kilometers of sea. Three kilometers? Is that really worth all this death and destruction?" Nonetheless, Karim also acknowledged that, after the signing of the Oslo Accords, "it is not only that Hamas needed to carry out the resistance to ensure their legitimacy, but it seems that it is something that is ingrained in their struggle for existence." When I asked, "So, not unlike the Palestinian struggle in general?" he nodded in agreement.[11]

Undoubtedly, Hamas's violence found justification among Palestinians due to the failures of Oslo Accords. Nonetheless, its charity and social service operations also worked to furbish the Palestinian anticolonial subjectivity in response to the economic disadvantages of the Oslo Accords. In the post-Oslo era, the Palestinian territories saw the steepest economic downturn since 1967, triggered by the persistence of pre-Oslo structures and institutions of dependency and underdevelopment, as well as the lack of economic reform, which shrunk the already fragile Palestinian economy (Roy 2000, 16–17). Israel maintained control over all aspects of the Palestinian economy and its borders, bringing about a depreciation of Palestinian per capita income from U.S. $2,000 to U.S. $1,600 in the West Bank and from US $1,200 to US $900 in the Gaza Strip between 1993 and 2000. This led to an increase in child labor rates, with 74 percent of Palestinian children under eighteen not being enrolled in school. Without a legal and institutional counterweight to its authority, patronage politics and corruption defined the workings of the Palestinian Authority (Roy 2000, 16–23; Halevi 1998, 35–48). Additionally, the new political class within the Palestinian Authority maintained the existing economic condition of the Palestinians and ensured that wages remained low in the Palestinian territories. This then allowed "the PA [Palestinian Authority] to employ people cheaply and thereby maintain its system of patronage and dependence" (Roy 2000, 25). Consequently, this economic disenfranchisement of Palestinians led to their sociopolitical disempowerment and "a splintered [Palestinian] social being" (Turki 1996, 76). As I discuss later in this book in the context of Hamas's role as the government in the Gaza Strip, it is in the face of such immense crises that the Islamic Resistance's social service wing, which included educational institutions, medical facilities, religious institutions and organizations, and welfare activities, responded as a means of building a society capable of withstanding Israeli settler colonial rule while struggling for liberation (Pascovich 2012, 130).

To be sure, the Oslo Accords in no way inspired the Palestinian anticolonial subjectivity. The Palestinian anticolonial struggle long precedes (and exceeds) the signing of the agreements. As I have demonstrated in the previous chapter, it is shaped by Israel's settler colonial project that strives to erase Palestinian existence. That said, the Oslo Accords also provided further justification for persisting with the Palestinian anticolonial struggle, as well as for the need to continue cultivating the Palestinian anticolonial subjectivity, whether through violence, socio-civilian modes of activism, or a summer camp that declares that "negotiations will never work."

Oslo and the Postcolonial Palestinian Faction

In his poem "A Non-Linguistic Dispute with *Imru' al-Qays*," the Palestinian writer and poet Mahmoud Darwish dismissed the Oslo Accords as a mere euphemism for Israel's victory and the ever-diminishing prospect for securing the Palestinian homeland (Darwish 2000, 123). It is therefore not surprising that the agreements consequently bolstered the anticolonial fervor of Palestinian liberation factions. Yet, the legacy of the Accords is not just defined by what they failed to secure. They were also generative in that they introduced postcoloniality to the identity and conduct of the Palestinian liberation faction. Of course, this postcoloniality has less to do with the actual transition of Palestine into the era that follows colonial rule than with the recalibrating of the subjectivity of a Palestinian liberation faction so that it postures *as if* the colonizer has long relinquished its control over the colonized's land.

This recalibration of the subjectivity of the Palestinian liberation faction was exemplified by a former Palestinian fighter and Palestinian Authority policeman I met in Copenhagen in 2012. He was known to be a close associate of Yasser Arafat and a staunch member of Fatah. Since we were meeting only a few weeks after the end of Operation Pillar of Defense, I was curious about his stance on Hamas's politics and began by asking him, "You have been involved with Fatah for a long time, and you were by Arafat's side. What is your opinion of Hamas's resistance?" He responded: "Look, I was very close with Arafat. I was trained to become a fighter. I was with Arafat in Lebanon fighting the Israelis during the civil war. I saw how he was suffering. Israelis were searching for him house by house. He would sleep in one house for twenty minutes, and then we would transport him to the next house. But we fought because we were fighting for respect."

I interjected, "So then, you would agree with Hamas?"

He replied: "No. Things have changed now. With Oslo, our leader [referring to Arafat] told us that it was time that the Palestinian fighter took off the fatigues and put on a suit. I took off my military uniform and worked to build my country. I became a police officer and worked for a long time, training Palestinian Authority policemen."[12]

Owing to his allegiance to Arafat, my interviewee's Oslo-induced transition seemed almost immediate and conclusive. But while he did not necessarily rule out an armed struggle, it was not a strategy he deemed to be permanent. As a young fighter following Arafat in Lebanon, he evidently once saw value and prudence in militarily confronting Israel. But now, for him, "things had changed." In the post-Oslo era, it was time to build Palestine. He took off his military fatigues and ceased his violent struggle against Israel, looked inward, and served his country as a police officer. Even though Palestine is still under settler colonial rule he adopted the building of Palestine as his vocation, *as if* the colonized were already in the era of the postcolonial state.

In the field, the perception that "things have changed" was often evident in the way Fatah members criticized Hamas's commitment to the armed struggle. One such prominent Fatah official, sitting in the living room of his home in the midst of the iconic Jabalia refugee camp in Gaza, said, "Look at the news. These people [Hamas] can't run the government. All they do is talk about *muqawama* [resistance]. Look at the state of Gaza because of this."[13] Another Fatah-affiliated Palestinian Authority official, who refused to serve the Hamas-led government, expressed similar sentiments. When I asked him why he had not returned to his job at the Finance Ministry, he replied, "I cannot work with these people. I don't believe in violence. I don't believe in their resistance."[14] Of course, that "things have changed" is particularly evident in the comparative images and public personae of Yasser Arafat and Mahmoud Abbas. While frequently appearing next to each other on Fatah posters, Arafat is often seen covering his entire head with the Palestinian keffiyeh, a symbol of the Palestinian national struggle and the militant claim to Palestinian lands in their entirety. In comparison, Mahmoud Abbas, his successor, is mostly depicted donning a suit, while only ceremonially wearing a checkered keffiyeh around his neck. When discussing this difference in garb with Karim, he reminded me, "You know, to wear it on the head is related to Palestinian peasants, old peasants, like my grandfather used to his whole life."[15] Although this is true, it is also important to recognize that

Palestinian peasants, dependent on the land for their subsistence and livelihood, were the first to confront the occupier in the struggle to reclaim the Palestinian homeland. Rosemary Sayigh wrote, "It was the peasants who rioted in Jaffa in 1921 and in Jerusalem in 1929; it was the peasants who followed Sheikh Qassam into the hills above Haifa in 1935, and who bore the brunt of the Great Rebellion [Arab Revolt] of 1936–1939" (Sayigh 1979, 4). Thus, while Arafat led the bureaucratization of the guerrilla movement, with his keffiyeh he nevertheless symbolized the Palestinian revolutionary identity staking a claim to the entirety of greater Palestine. In comparison, Abbas, both figuratively and literally, personifies the suited bureaucrat and embodies the transformation envisioned by Oslo in its entirety. He ceremonially dons the checkered keffiyeh and speaks the language of nationalism, but he does not fight the colonizer and is simply content with the vocation of governing a sliver of what was once the Palestinian homeland.

The introduction of a formal political-administrative system also symbolizes the manner in which the Oslo Accords introduced postcoloniality into a settler colonial condition. At the very outset, it did so by creating "a realm of official Palestinian politics" encapsulated in the institutions and bureaucracies of the statelike Palestinian Authority. Only Palestinian factions that have publicly renounced the armed struggle and recognized Israel were granted access to this realm. An organization that fulfills this precondition is then deemed a legitimate representative of the Palestinian population and granted "a permanent seat in negotiations alongside Israel and Western stakeholders." Additionally, this faction would have the responsibility for governing the Palestinian territories and have access to the financial resources of the Palestinian Authority (Sen 2015b, 167). As the Palestinian Authority is responsible for key sectors such as education, culture, health, social welfare, direct taxation, and tourism, the resulting expectation was that the recognized Palestinian faction, through its entry into official politics, would be socialized into the reasoning of the state and out of the logic of the anticolonial struggle. Finally, in keeping with the statist logic of Oslo-mandated official politics (Shain and Sussman 1998, 275), and in abiding by the image of the Weberian state and its monopoly of violence, using the Palestinian Authority's internal security forces, the recognized Palestinian faction would also be responsible for ensuring the primacy of the mandate of the Palestinian Authority, especially when faced with opposition from armed Palestinian factions such as Hamas and Islamic Jihad. Thus, the Oslo norm of politics effectively criminalized the Palestinian anticolonial struggle and, through the Palestinian Authority, enforced a new political order that aimed to compel a Palestinian faction to engage in more state building and eschew fighting (Parsons 2010, 73; Sen 2015a, 212).

In this way, the Oslo Accords attempted to reconstitute the subjectivity of the Palestinian faction by incentivizing a brand of politics that entails renouncing the armed struggle and recognizing Israel's right to exist. Any Palestinian faction that adopted this brand of politics would be granted international recognition as the representative of the Palestinians and deemed a "partner for peace" (Turner 2011). Additionally, it would have the mandate to govern the Palestinian territories with statelike monetary capital and practice public violence against its detractors. The appeal of this brand of politics was personified by the former associate of Yasser Arafat who took off his fatigues, despite having spent his youth fighting Israel. It is the success of the Accords in transforming the subjective identity of a Palestinian faction that also emerged in the mocking tone of my Fatah-affiliated interlocutors when they discussed Hamas's commitment to the armed struggle. The appeal was also palpable in the dramatically transformed image and politics of the PLO. The organization was once represented by the revolutionary fighter Arafat, who, while wearing his fatigues, declared in a 1974 speech at the UN: "Today I have come bearing an olive branch and a freedom fighter's gun. Do not let the olive branch fall from my hand. I repeat: do not let the olive branch fall from my hand."[16] Implicit in this urgent appeal is the perception of the gun as central to the tactics of the revolutionary. That is to say, for Arafat, peace (symbolized by the olive branch) can be easily renounced. However, the gun will remain permanently. But, a little over a decade later, we witnessed a dramatic transformation of the PLO from being historically seeped in the revolutionary ethos into becoming a signatory to the Accords.[17] Arafat renounced the armed struggle and effectively made it an illegitimate tool for pursuing Palestinian liberation. To be sure, Arafat's concessions reflect a tired and materially challenged liberation faction (Sayigh 1997b, 638–662). Nonetheless, having been the iconic face of the Palestinian Revolution for decades, Arafat, in the public image he projected, did not entirely shed the image of the revolutionary leader. Instead, it is Abbas who personifies the completion of the transformation. As the president in a suit who only ceremonially dons a sliver of the keffiyeh—and by extension lays claim to only a sliver of greater Palestine—he is the resultant image of the renunciation of a historically foundational feature of the Palestinian liberation movement. Moreover, as he remains committed to the suit, despite the Interim Agreement failing to address inalienable aspects of the Palestinian claim to statehood, he emphasizes the pervasive appeal of the Oslo-mandated realm of official politics.

The disincentives imbued in the Oslo logic were however not just concerned with barring the entrance of noncompliant Palestinian organizations into the realm of official politics. They also ensured that activism in opposition to the Oslo Accords became a difficult endeavor. This is evident throughout most of

Hamas's development. While the Islamic Resistance was able to garner support as a movement opposed to the Oslo Accords, its operations on the sidelines of the historic yet failing Oslo process resulted in the arrests, deportations, and assassinations of its members and leadership (Kristianasen 1999, 19; Milton-Edwards and Crooke 2004, 41). Moreover, when Hamas won the Palestinian Legislative Council elections in 2006 and adopted the role of a government while still maintaining its armed resistance, it further challenged the foundational logic of the Oslo Accords and the limitations they placed on the brand of Palestinian faction that would be allowed into the realm of official politics. Hamas's victory ensured that the organization would rise to the summit of the Palestinian Authority's governance structures. Yet, by remaining committed to its role as an armed liberation faction, it also violated the preconditions that needed to be fulfilled *before* any Palestinian faction is allowed to govern Palestine. Then, following Hamas's victory in the national elections, and as a means of maintaining the limitations placed on entering Oslo-mandated official politics, what ensued was a "failed state." Sayigh described this development as intending to hinder Hamas's ability to govern, thus hampering its popularity among its own electorate and leading to the eventual restoration of the Abbas leadership (Sayigh 2007, 14).

In accordance with the strategy of creating a "failed state" and speaking on behalf of the U.S. administration after the 2006 Palestinian Legislative Council elections, Jacob Walles, then U.S. consul general in Jerusalem, communicated to the Palestinian Authority leadership that it needed to confront Hamas. If the Palestinian Authority leadership agreed, according to the "Talking Points" of the communication sent to the president of the Palestinian Authority, the United States would be willing to "support the Presidential Guard and NSF [National Security Forces]" and to provide material and political support by "lifting . . . financial restrictions . . . ensur[ing] prompt delivery of promised aid and . . . [resuming] revenue transfers" from the Israeli government (Rose 2008). Abiding by this strategy, and under the threat of U.S. sanctions, Fatah refused an offer from Hamas to form a national unity government (Sayigh 2007, 16), while government workers loyal to Fatah, including members of the security forces, refrained from assisting the newly appointed Palestinian Authority leadership in Gaza in the everyday functioning of governance institutions (Hovdenak 2009, 69). In a de facto offensive against the economy of Palestine, the European Union and the United States imposed sanctions on the Hamas-led Palestinian Authority government. Furthermore, tertiary actors were threatened with prosecution if they were found to be dealing with the Palestinian authorities, banks, and businesses (Sayigh 2007, 17–18). Subsequently, there were regular skirmishes between Hamas and Fatah cadres in the Gaza Strip and the Saudi Arabia-sponsored Mecca Agreement for power-sharing failed to diffuse the conflict (Milton-Edwards

2008, 1586). Following an open military confrontation between the two warring factions and as a way of preempting an "attempted coup by Fatah" (Rose 2008), Hamas initiated a complete takeover of the Gaza Strip in June 2007.

Many expected the organization to overcome the dictates of the Oslo Accords entirely. In a sense, Hamas did so by simultaneously adopting the postcoloniality imbued in the role of government while maintaining its commitment to anticolonial violence through successive violent confrontations with Israel, thus violating a key criterion of the Accords. Nonetheless, the infrequent and reactive nature of Hamas's violence toward Israel, the organization's the repression by Hamas of Palestinian opposition to its leadership in Gaza (see chapter 5), and its willingness to negotiate an end to the siege of Gaza[18] indicate that Hamas too has been shaped by the Oslo process.[19] When I asked Ahmed Yousef, he agreed and said: "Hamas is not the same movement it was when it first came into being. It is much more mature now. Today it pays a lot of attention to governing."[20] Ghazi Hamad similarly emphasized: "Since 2006 many things have changed. Before 2006 we have only been in the opposition and resistance. After 2006, we have been part of the PLC [Palestinian Legislative Council] and PA [Palestinian Authority]. We have agreed to the idea of a ceasefire. We have been open to the world and more realistic as a movement. Within Hamas there have been changes. We have become more democratic."[21]

Others within the organization were far more hesitant to declare unequivocally that Hamas had changed. Instead, they emphasized that the Islamic Resistance was now in a different reality and had changed its tactics accordingly. Salama Maroof noted:

> Today Hamas has had to come to terms with a new situation, circumstances, and events, and also has new responsibilities. For this reason, Hamas has confirmed that it should change. But the change is in tactics. Because from the beginning Hamas declared very clearly to all that Hamas was committed to and had a clear vision for the liberation of Palestine. So, Hamas knows that there is the continuous threat of conflict, the issue of the right of return, land grabs etc. Although the situation is very difficult, it did not change its fundamental character and survives through the occupation.[22]

In the same vein, Hamas leader Fawzi Barhoum said: "We have a new reality after the elections, and because we are now the government working within the Palestinian Authority. Also, with the Arab Spring and Israeli political weakness, the Palestinian cause is becoming more popular. Hamas has a new position in this new reality. Hamas has become a key player in Palestinian politics and the region. All this helps the Palestinian cause."[23] However, whether Hamas today is responding to a new reality with new tactics or, as Hamad and Yousef argued, is a different organization altogether, the manner in which it has been shaped by the Oslo Accords is significantly different from that of the other Palestinian signatories of the agreement. The PLO accepted the entire Oslo logic and its post-coloniality. This allowed someone like the former associate of Arafat to renounce his fatigues, condemn Hamas's violence, and unequivocally claim, "We are not like them [Hamas]!" Hamas, on the other hand, through its concurrent roles as resistance and government, personifies *all* the legacies of the Oslo Accords. Its anticolonial violence underlines what the Accords have failed to achieve. Yet, its postcolonial governance confirms the generative role of the Oslo process that aims to, through a nexus of incentives and disincentives, cultivate a new subjectivity for the Palestinian faction. Of course, this legacy of the coexistence of the anticolonial alongside the postcolonial exceeds Hamas's dual role. Seeing the persistence of Israel's settler colonial rule that remained despite the Oslo Accords, Palestine as a whole represents the need to persist with the anticolonial struggle. At the same time, the Palestinian Authority also exists as a *Palestinian* governing authority that operates *as if* it is in the era of the postcolonial state—albeit without the sovereignty, territoriality, and political mandate of the era of the postcolonial.

On Postcolonial Confusion

Postcoloniality can be a confusing affair. This confusion is often said to stem from the formerly colonized attempting to recover their indigeneity while simultaneously grasping at a form of modernity that is deeply shaped by the former colonizer (Yeoh 2001; Vale 1992; Kusno 1998; Lee and Lam 1998). The postcoloniality established by the Oslo Accords was confusing in a different way. Its specificity became very evident when I was preparing to leave the Gaza Strip in 2013. At the time I was informed by an acquaintance that I would need to register with the Internal Protection Unit (IPU). As an extension of the Palestinian Authority's security apparatus, the IPU registers non-Palestinian visitors scheduled to leave the Gaza Strip and coordinates with security personnel at the Rafah border crossing, who in turn ensure that a seat is reserved for the foreign traveler on the bus crossing into Egypt. While I was scheduled to leave a week later, rumors of a large-scale protest in Egypt, one that eventually led to the fall of the Morsi government, meant that the border crossing could be closed indefinitely. At the offices of the IPU the officials examined my passport and the itinerary of my return journey. One of them asked, "How did you enter Gaza? Tunnel or border crossing?" I answered, "border crossing." He continued examining my documents. Made uncomfortable by his silence, I impatiently explained, "I was supposed to leave next week, but there are problems in Egypt, so I'm scared the border will close." In a reassuring tone the official said, "Don't worry. It will be fine." Feeling encouraged, I responded, "Yes. I know. A friend of mine assured me that they couldn't keep the border closed for too long." Suddenly, the reassuring tone of his voice changed, and the official retorted, "Who said so? Who is your friend? We don't have any information on the border crossing. We don't know what will happen."[24]

The official's ambivalence, alternating between a tone of assuredness and one of uncertainty, exemplifies the confusion of the Oslo-induced postcoloniality in its entirety. In this chapter I have argued that the Oslo Accords required that Palestinian political factions operate *as if* the era of Israeli settler colonial rule had long passed. Therefore, by keeping up the ritual of registering me before my journey out of Gaza, the official paid "lip service" to the norms of the Interim Agreement that were embedded in the Palestinian Authority's institutions and bureaucracies that posture *as if* they were part of a postcolonial state. But the colonizer has also persisted, encouraging an organization like Hamas to maintain its anticolonial violence. Therefore, in being aware of the uncertainty and the lack of sovereignty that characterizes the life of the colonized, the official was hesitant to speculate about the future with any certainty. Instead, he admitted that "we don't know what will happen." When I asked Hussein, an instructor at a university in Gaza, about this Oslo-imposed confusion, he said, "Today we have a government without a state. We have a people without a country." He then continued, "This is incredibly disappointing to the people. We are stuck here. We are frustrated. There is no vision. We just go back and forth between fighting and governing."[25]

Nonetheless, to say that the postcoloniality established by the Oslo Accords introduced a sense of confusion is not to argue that the Palestinian liberation struggle in general and the Palestinian anticolonial subjectivity in particular have been left motionless by this confusion. The purpose of this chapter has been to simply characterize the Accords and their legacy as having triggered Palestine's long moment of liberation by introducing postcoloniality in a colonial condition that also demands an anticolonial struggle. Therefore, while the presence of the postcolonial in the era of the colonial can seem confusing, contradictory, and inauthentic, the liberation agenda persists as the colonized strive to find meaning in the cause of liberation while navigating the anticolonial and postcolonial under settler colonial rule. In the two chapters that follow, I therefore demonstrate the manner in which anticolonial violence and postcolonial governance find resonance for the liberation struggle.

ANTICOLONIAL VIOLENCE AND THE PALESTINIAN STRUGGLE TO EXIST

The manner in which Hamas's armed resistance inhabits the story of the Palestinian anticolonial struggle was first evident to me during a conversation with a young Palestinian named Bahaa.[1] I had met him in early June in 2013 at a seminar in Gaza City. After the seminar Bahaa, who had only recently returned home to Gaza after finishing a graduate program in Europe, introduced himself. We established an instant rapport, since we had both spent most of our twenties abroad. Before he left that day, we agreed to stay in touch and, some time later, Bahaa invited me to his house in Rafah for lunch. It was a hot summer's day in late June when the taxi drove me along Gaza's picturesque coast to the dusty border town. At Bahaa's home I met his mother, father, cousins, and nephews. After exchanging pleasantries, we sat down to eat lunch. As is so common in Gaza, there was a power outage midway through our meal. So, instead of sitting in the sweltering heat inside the house, Bahaa suggested that he give me a tour of his hometown after lunch. Being a Friday afternoon, the streets were largely deserted. We negotiated Rafah's trash-filled roads as he pointed out sites where Israeli settlements and army installations once stood. The dilapidated war-torn buildings were a reminder of Rafah's tumultuous past, including the dubious distinction of having been a security "buffer zone" for the IDF between 2000 and 2005. Designating certain areas in Gaza as buffer zones allowed the IDF to demolish more than twenty-five hundred Palestinian homes. Two-thirds of these homes were in Rafah (Human Rights Watch 2004, 2).

During our tour, Bahaa recounted his own life under the occupation. He reminisced about growing up in close proximity to Israeli settlements. He recalled celebrating on the streets of Rafah following the news of Israel's unilateral "disengagement" from Gaza in August 2005. But it was what Bahaa said next that stood out:

> After completing high school, I decided to come home and visit my parents in Gaza. When I reached the border by Rafah, the conflict between Hamas and Fatah was on the rise. Hamas had won the elections, and it was in the process of gaining complete control of Gaza. The Egyptians and Israelis decided to close the border. The European monitors of the Rafah border were not allowed to come across from Israel, and so the border remained closed. But when they closed the borders, all Palestinians trying to enter the Gaza Strip on that day were stuck in the passport hall of the Egyptian terminal, and we remained there for two weeks. Israel said that some could get into a bus and drive around to an Israeli checkpoint. Some decided to do this, but they would spend six hours in a bus and then wouldn't be let in. There were some Hamas activists among the travelers, and they didn't get into the bus because they knew that they would disappear forever. Within the Egyptian passport hall, times were tough. We were two thousand people waiting. Toilets were filthy. People would fight. Someone would yell at the army, and then everyone would be punished. You get one hour in a day to walk around, just like a prisoner. Food was provided by the Egyptian Red Cross. But the day that we were freed, the Egyptians didn't have guns. It was almost like they knew what was going to happen. Then, one of these masked Qassam guys came over the wall and fired two shots. Then the gate blew up and five or six black jeeps [with more masked men] pulled in. They told the Egyptians, "Sorry, but we can't keep our brothers and sisters suffering." They then asked the Egyptians to put all the passports in a box and told the Palestinians that if they wanted their passports, they should follow them.[2]

I responded, "It's like a movie, isn't it?" Bahaa laughed, "It was."

This account has always struck me as being particularly curious.[3] For one thing, the rescue operation occurred at a time when resistance had all but lost its attractions. Palestinians had turned their guns on each other during the war for Gaza and, following Hamas's takeover in 2007, the increasingly virulent rivalry between the Islamic Resistance and Fatah became further institutionalized. But, to me, it was far more noteworthy that, while the al-Qassam fighters exercised little by way of physical violence during the operation, the account somehow stood out as a tale of the poetic allure and cinematic potency of the mere exhibition of the ability to kill. Violence is often perceived as a breach of moral and ethical codes and is therefore deemed illegitimate, unacceptable, irrational, and bestial (Riches 1986, 1–2). This view accords well with the Latin etymological root of violence—namely *viol*—that relates to terms such as "defilement," "infringement," "outrage," "injury," and "violation" (Murray 1971, 3635). But imagining the balaclava-wearing al-Qassam fighters firing shots in the air, blowing up the gate that had imprisoned the Palestinian travelers, and subsequently rescuing them from a condition of utter destitution did not evoke a sense of infringement, defilement, or violation. Instead, in Bahaa's account, the gun was remembered as embodying a certain goodness. In this sense, it was truly "like a movie," not least like an old-fashioned Western where guns are fired, but no one is shot. On that fateful day at the border crossing, the gun appeared with cinematic flair at a time of crisis and suffering. Then, seemingly overshadowing the norms that encourage us to condemn it, violence, or at least ritualized theatrical violence, made a spectacularly therapeutic statement by remedying the preceding state of suffering.

In her poem "The Speed of Darkness" (1968), the American poet Muriel Rukeyser claimed that "the universe is made of stories, not of atoms." Violence and the threat of violence also encapsulates a story. In what follows, I therefore reflect on the stories Palestinians like Bahaa told of their experiences and memories of violence; stories not just of euphoria, but also of the tragedy that often follows violent encounters with the colonizer. Having already inscribed the Gaza Strip into the past and present of Israel's settler colonialism in chapter 2, the stories in this chapter thus form the basis for demonstrating the manner in which Hamas's armed resistance, or muqawama, lives and finds resonance in the Palestinian anticolonial struggle—which, at the least, strives to underline the existence of Palestine and Palestinians, despite the settlers claiming otherwise.

Thinking about Muqawama

Palestine is often considered the land of symbols. The cactus, the orange, the olive tree, the poppy—all personifying rootedness and community—are seen as symbols of Palestinian resilience to "uprooting colonial encounters" (Abufarha 2008, 365). In the previous chapter, I have briefly discussed the Palestinian keffiyeh and its symbolism as a marker of the revolutionary Palestinian claim to the national homeland. Another important example is found in the sketches of the Palestinian cartoonist Naji al-Ali, in which his character Handala's bare feet signify the plight of Palestinian refugee children, his hands folded behind his back symbolize his refusal to let the Palestinian cause be harmed, and his watchfulness represents "a radar . . . [recording] the most sensitive fluctuations of the feelings of ordinary Palestinians" (Najjar 2007, 256–257).

Muqawama similarly takes on a symbolic meaning and is often used as a term that stands for the many ways in which Palestinians resist Israel's settler colonialism. The Palestinian author Ghassan Kanafi's writings have been described as resistance literature (Harlow 1987, 2). An economy that mirrors the ethos of the Palestinian liberation movement while striving for Palestinian economic self-reliance has been called a resistance economy (Dana 2014; Tartir et al. 2012). Cultural activities meant "to revitalize and restore Jerusalem as the cultural capital of the Palestinian people" have also been described as a form of Palestinian resistance (McDonald 2006, 5). And as one would expect, Hamas officials also use the term *resistance* as representative not just of the Palestinian armed struggle but also of these various forms of social, economic, political, and cultural resilience. This became especially evident during a graduation ceremony and presentation of a master's thesis on water purification that I attended at Gaza's Al-Aqsa University. With several prominent Hamas members present, the ceremony looked very much like an Islamic Resistance affair. I sat in the audience along with students, faculty members, and parents. After the graduating student's presentation, the chief guest, the deputy speaker of the Palestinian Legislative Council Ahmad Bahar, took the podium. Bahar began by praising the master's thesis, emphasizing its importance for alleviating the water crisis in Gaza. Yet, throughout his speech, he ritually used the language of resistance and considered an effort to solve the water crisis to be synonymous with the Palestinian liberation struggle. Bahar concluded by declaring, "Studies like these will keep the resistance alive and take us to Jerusalem."[4]

For one thing, Bahar's words remind us of the historical prominence of Hamas's civilian operations, a legacy it inherited from its predecessor, the Palestinian Muslim Brotherhood (Roy 2011; Gunning 2007). But, following the 2006 elections, nonmilitary forms of resistance have largely been absorbed into Hamas's role as government, as the organization transitioned from providing socioeconomic services in the shadow of an unresponsive Palestinian Authority to becoming a statelike authority controlling all facets of life in the Gaza Strip. Hamas's civilian resistance, as pointed out by the Egyptian researcher Gamal Abdel Gawad Soltan, meant to alleviate the socioeconomic suffering of Palestinians, had now become "a matter of public policy" rather than of charity.[5] But while the armed struggle remains the primary expression of Hamas's resistance since 2006, an Israeli scholar was also correct in pointing out to me that the military muqawama is "not *just* bang, bang."[6] Armed resistance also takes on a more symbolic role whereby it is not only represented by an act of *physical* violence, but also by the narration and exhibition of the ability to conduct military operations.

In Bahaa's description of the rescue operation at the Rafah border crossing, there was the symbolic and cinematic allure of violence *without* any significant level of violence being actually practiced. On the official Arabic-language webpage of the al-Qassam Brigade, pictorial representations of Hamas's ability to engage in militant activities seem to be regarded as synonymous with the organization's ability to physically injure, maim, and kill, given that the photo gallery on the site consists largely of pictures of al-Qassam operatives posing with weapons rather than in real operations (figure 4.1).[7] This synonymy was also evident on a banner celebrating Hamas's al-Qassam Brigade, which I came across during my tour of Rafah (figure 4.2). It showed a gunman in fatigues wearing a balaclava and holding a gun. Under his left boot was the blood-stained helmet of an IDF soldier with a bullet hole. Behind him was an image of Haram al-Sharif, the holy Muslim site in Jerusalem and a symbol of Palestinian aspirations. The text in red said, "History won't say that Hamas gave up the homeland, but there will be pages of beautiful stories about the manner in which we survived treacherous ordeals."

The banner in itself is incapable of violence. Nevertheless, much like the photo gallery on the al-Qassam Brigade's webpage or the rescue operation at the Rafah crossing, it exhibits (and celebrates) the gun's supposed ability to decimate the "oppressor"—represented by the blood-stained IDF helmet—and "take back" what was once "ours," signified by Haram al-Sharif in the background. One could argue that these are *just* symbols. I will maintain, however, that the boundary

FIGURE 4.1 Image from the photo gallery of the al-Qassam Brigade's webpage. Source: www.alqassam.net/arabic.

FIGURE 4.2 Al-Qassam banner, Rafah, Gaza Strip. Photo by author.

between the act of physical violence and the symbolizing, celebration, exhibition, and recounting of violence is often blurred, and that the intermittent acts of physical violence encompassed by Hamas's muqawama are interpreted and gain meaning through symbolic acts of violence that are continually present. In the following discussion I therefore seamlessly traverse the act, symbol, celebration, exhibition, and memory of resistance as I demonstrate the manner in which Hamas's armed resistance finds relevance for the Palestinian quest for liberation as a phenomenon that both unmakes and makes.

Unmaking for Palestine

In anticolonial (and) revolutionary musings of the path to liberation, violent confrontations with the "oppressor," whether symbolic or physical, are often given sacred status because of their presumed ability to unmake the state of suffering. Driven by the "revolutionary dream" of liberation from colonial rule, Kwame Nkrumah, the first prime minister of independent Ghana, argued that an "armed struggle for freedom is neither moral nor immoral, it is a scientific historically-determined necessity" (Nkrumah 1968, 10). The influential pan-Africanist went on to claim, "The fact is that revolutionary warfare is the key to African freedom and is the only way in which the total liberation and unity of the African continent can be achieved" (Nkrumah 1968, 20–21). This story of the need to violently confront the oppressor could also be written into the struggle of the Zapatista in Mexico. The Zapatista uprising in the Chiapas was preceded by a life that, for the *campesinos* (peasants), was marred by complete socioeconomic marginalization and land grabs by "outsiders." Then, as a way of unmaking this state of suffering, a violent confrontation ensued. On January 1, 1994, the inaugural day of the North American Free Trade Agreement (NAFTA), the Zapatista Army of National Liberation (EZLN), "equipped with rubber boots, homemade army uniforms, bandanas, ski masks, and weapons ranging from handmade wooden rifles to Uzi machine guns, seized towns in eastern and central Chiapas, [and] proclaim[ed] a revolution" (Collier and Quaratiello 2005, 1). Suddenly the weak were not weak anymore, and, while confronting the Mexican state, they declared "Ya Basta!" or "enough is enough."

If an armed struggle is commonly perceived as a necessary response to oppression and as a means of possibly unmaking the condition of suffering for the marginalized in general and the colonized in particular, it is not surprising that voices from within Hamas routinely deem its armed resistance as the appropriate response to Israeli rule. This view was implicit in the aftermath of Operation Protective Edge (2014) when Khaled Meshaal, the Hamas political bureau chief at the time, unequivocally defended the organization's commitment to muqawama at a press conference. He said, "The weapons of the resistance are sacred . . . the issue is not up for negotiation. No one can disarm Hamas and its resistance." Further emphasizing that it was the armed struggle that (presumably) secured some respite for Palestinians in Gaza from years of siege, he continued, "Today we declare the victory of the resistance. Today we declare the victory of Gaza" (Bakr

2014). When the journalist Roger Gaess asked senior Hamas leader Mousa Abu Marzook if violence was indeed the appropriate tactic for dismantling Israel's military rule over the Palestinian territories, the latter began by citing instances of Israeli violence against Palestinians. Subsequently, much like Meshaal, Marzook went on to argue for the appropriateness of the Palestinian armed resistance:

> People under occupation have a right to resist that occupation. The Palestinians have had their land occupied for approximately thirty years. They have the right to fight to be free like other people so that they can determine their own future without foreign interference. You can't characterize what the Palestinians are doing against the occupation as violence. In reality, it is a form of resistance. If there was no occupation, there would be no resistance. (Gaess 1997, 117)

This perception of the Palestinian "right to fight" was also relayed to me when I first met Hamas leader Fawzi Barhoum in Gaza in early June 2013. Sitting in his office, Barhoum displayed a persona similar to that of the Hamas deputy foreign minister Ghazi Hamad (see chapter 1). In a suit and with a Palestinian flag next to him, Barhoum embodied the civilian, Oslo-mandated image of the Palestinian liberation faction. Nevertheless, as was often the case during my interviews with Hamas officials, he adamantly argued for the importance of the organization's credentials as a *resistance* organization:

> One should remember that Hamas is first a liberation organization. It's a resistance and a movement against the occupation. It is also important to remember that it's a resistance as a result of the occupation and not vice versa. . . . [We face] occupation violence, blockade, isolation and assassination. . . . Because of this we have many issues. There are infrastructural needs. Medical needs of the population. No exports. The majority of the people have problems getting by every day. We have unemployed people. Then, there is the terrorism [referring to the Israeli occupation and violence] on the people here.

By emphasizing that Hamas is an organization of resistance and liberation, Barhoum wanted to demonstrate that the Palestinian, or in this case, Hamas's armed struggle for liberation is intimately informed by Israel's denial of Palestinian rights. But, while effective in characterizing the difficulties of Palestinian life under Israeli rule, he said little about how resistance is capable of unmaking this state of affairs. So, I asked him, "But the problem of unemployment and infrastructure . . . how is the resistance helping solve these issues?" Barhoum responded, "By fighting Hamas has been successful, and the world now is with Hamas. For a long time, people have been receiving wrong information from the occupation, the West, and the U.S. But because of Hamas's resistance, we have reached a situation where Hamas doesn't need to explain itself anymore."[8] It was still unclear to me how armed resistance was able to solve the crises that order Palestinian lives in the besieged Gaza Strip. Nevertheless, what did not escape me in Barhoum's words was the almost self-evident inviolability of armed resistance in the Palestinian struggle to unmake the state of affairs that leave Palestinians weak and misunderstood.

This inviolability of the Palestinian armed struggle was once again emphasized during my interview with a Gaza-based photojournalist working for Hamas-run Al-Aqsa TV. We met at Gaza's Al-Deira Hotel, where she agreed to an interview on the condition of anonymity. As I began by explaining my research, she responded, "Resistance and government are fine. But for me the main problem is that there are so many social and moral limitations on Gaza's citizens. All I want to be is free. We don't have freedom in the Gaza Strip." At that point, it was difficult for me to gauge whether she considered the lack of freedom to be the result of Hamas's rule or the Israeli-imposed blockade. So, I asked, "Then, what is your take on Hamas's dual role as resistance and government?" She replied, "For me the muqawama is the most important. We are under occupation, and therefore we need resistance. We need a mixture [of government and resistance], but the military wing is the most important part. There is no other way ..." I interjected, "You said that 'we need a mixture.' Do you think there can be a balance between the two roles?" She replied, "If you are talking about a balance, we are forced to make one. We don't have a balance because of Israeli attacks. They have destroyed our infrastructure and prevent us from conducting proper governance. So, we are continually catching up. We are not progressing but 'breaking even.' [The] only thing people have is resistance."[9]

If there is indeed "no other way" than resistance, it would seem unproblematic to argue that it is the Palestinians' state of subalternity informed by Israel's crippling military rule and, subsequently, a denial of Palestinian aspirations of statehood that makes the armed struggle an inevitable choice of self-defense. But while Hamas's armed resistance is able to make Israeli citizens fearful and exact casualties (Gleis and Berti 2012, 162), it would be wrong to assume that its only function is to inflict suffering and anguish on the State of Israel. Instead, in view of the way Meshaal, Marzouk, Barhoum, and the photojournalist from Al-Aqsa TV saw value in resistance, I would argue that this armed struggle finds relevance (and reverence) through its presumed ability to challenge and possibly unmake the state of emergency that orders Palestinian lives. This conception of an armed struggle, appearing in the face of the "wrath" of the colonial "master" as therapeutic in its ability to rescue the colonized, is especially salient in Fanon's writings on the inalienable right to violence on the path of decolonization.

The Martinique-born "revolutionary intellectual" has often been characterized as an "apostle of violence" (Hansen 1974, 35). Surely, it is impossible to
ignore the fact that, for Fanon, violence was central to the (re-)invention of the
decolonized subject en route to liberation. However, in his works, the anticolonial imaginary often began with musings on the utter distress of the world of
the colonized. Fanon spoke of the perception that North Africans were deeply
integrated in the French nation. However, being assimilated into the colonizer's
realm did not evoke a sense of comfort. Instead, in colonial France, North Africans were insecure and unsure of their status. The North African, Fanon wrote,
"has rights, you will tell me, but he doesn't know what they are" (Fanon 1964,
12).[10] So, why was the North African insecure? The answer may lie in Fanon's
own experiences and encounters with Western civilization. Fanon was a colonial
subject assimilated into the ways of the colonizer. He was born and socialized
in the small, racially mixed bourgeoisie that emulated the white colonizer and
associated the ability to speak French impeccably with a higher social class
(Hansen 1974, 25–26). Grohs has described Martinique as the epitome of a colonized society, alienated from itself as a result of colonial rule (Grohs 1968, 544).
Fanon himself displayed a sense of self-alienation when he expressed a longing
for "lactification," as he hoped to achieve whiteness "through the love of a white
woman" (Geismar and Worsley 1969, 24). In *Black Skin, White Masks*, he further
declared, "Out of the blackest part of my soul, across the zebra striping of my
mind, surges this desire to be suddenly white." And, of the white woman who
would grant him whiteness through her love, he said, "By loving me she proves
that I am worthy of white love." In other words, in being loved by a white woman,
Fanon saw himself becoming equivalent to the white man and, much like the
white man, now capable of walking the "noble road that leads to total realization."
Moreover, with the love of a white woman ensuring that he had white culture and
beauty at his disposal, Fanon claimed that he would now be able to make white
civilization, and all its constituent goodness, his own (Fanon 1952, 45).

Race relations in Martinique, however, were considerably complex, with a
class system gradated according to a racial hierarchy that was far more varied
than a simple black–white binary (Beaudoux 2003). Fanon, being mixed race,
was relatively privileged in this hierarchy. But it was in France that he encountered the dilemma and tragedy of being a black man—a category, he soon realized, was all but singular for the colonizer (Hansen 1974, 29). Recounting his
experiences, Fanon wrote:

> While I was forgetting, forgiving, and wanting only to love, my mes-
> sage was flung back in my face like a slap. The white world, the only
> honourable one, barred me from all participation. A man was expected

to behave like a man. I was expected to behave like a black man—or at least like a nigger. I shouted a greeting to the world, and the world slashed away my joy. I was told to stay within bounds, to go back where I belonged. (Fanon 1952, 86)

It is this paradox of the colonized's subjectivity, one that oscillates between the desire for the colonizer's whiteness and simultaneous rejection as unworthy of the white world, that explains the insecurity of the colonial subject. Of course, Fanon is not the first revolutionary to strive for whiteness before being rejected. Even Mahatma Gandhi tried to emulate the English in language, education, and mannerisms, but reverted to his indigenous identity when he failed (Wolfenstein 1971, 208). But when constructing the anticolonial imaginary, Fanon conflated his own experience with that of the colonized collective and its encounter with white skin, culture, and civilization. He therefore argued that the colonizer regards the colonized as inferior and declares so in every interaction with the colonized's sector of society. Much like himself, the colonial subject is instilled with a sense of inferiority. He is constantly reminded of his "jungle status" and that it is only when he rejects his own culture and adopts the culture of the metropole that he can elevate himself. That is to say, he is human only when he renounces all that his black skin personifies—in terms of language, religion, and culture—and finally decides to put on the "white mask" of the metropolitan culture, language, and civilization (Fanon 1952, 9). Of course, whether or not he has donned the "white mask," a black man like Fanon was expected to remain within his bounds and return to where he belonged. The result is thus a colonial subject entirely unmade in his inner being. He craves whiteness and hates his blackness, but despite adopting the culture, language, and civilization of the colonizer, he is *still* rejected since, to the colonial "master," he is nothing more than a black man.

Fanon also demonstrated that this "wretchedness" of colonization, which infiltrates and (aims to) transform the subjectivity of the colonial subject, is amply supported by its material infrastructure, with important consequences for the indigenous society. The colonizer's oppression begins by compartmentalizing human society on the basis of a clear distinction between the colonized and the European colonizers. The sector of the colonized is populated by people who are submissive, inhibited, hungry, cowering, and prostrated. It is, as Fanon writes, "a sector of niggers, a sector of towelheads." As the colonized suffer, the agents of the colonizer—the military and police—keep watch as the violence of the occupier enters "the homes and minds of the colonized subject." This results in a subservient class; a realm of serfdom populated by the colonized. And, with its indigenous culture, economy, and way of life destroyed, this class is portrayed in the colonizer's bestiary as being without values, ethics, or morals, inhabiting a place that merely stinks, swarms, seethes, and gesticulates (Fanon 1963, 3–7). In comparison, and as a result of its domination and exploitation of the colonized, the sector of the colonizer is a place of privilege (Fanon 1963, 14). Its roads and dwellings are unlike the colonized's shanty towns; they are privileged with a sense of permanence. Its inhabitants are also privileged. They are satisfied, their bellies are "full of good things," and they live in a place of permanence and comfort made for white folks (Fanon 1963, 4–5).

Consequently, given the insidiousness of the colonial project, Fanon claimed that violence becomes crucial in the effort to "put an end to the history of colonization and the history of despoliation" (Fanon 1963, 15). For him, as a project of disorder, decolonization would need to "reek of red-hot cannonballs and bloody knives" because it is only through a violent confrontation that the colonized "last" can one day replace the colonizer and be the victorious and liberated "first" (Fanon 1963, 2–5). Of course, the colonized's violence is often stigmatized despite the suffering that precedes it (Fanon 1963, 34–39). Moreover, the colonized intellectual is hesitant to confront the culture of the colonizer, as it would destroy those whom he emulates. Nevertheless, Fanon insists, he (the intellectual) would need to realize that, for the colonized, violence is "the absolute praxis," and the only means by which liberation can be achieved (Fanon 1963, 44).

Frantz Fanon is unmistakably sweeping in his conception of the colonized's sector and the sufferings of its inhabitants. However, his words seem to support the need to characterize Hamas's armed resistance—reeking of cannonballs and blood-stained knives in its rhetoric and practice—as an essential destructive force, capable of eviscerating all that leaves Palestinians politically, economically, and culturally marginalized. To be sure, in the field, the relationship between the colonized and the colonizer was rarely discussed through its racial trope. But, in a settler colonial context, the colonized, their lives, and their ways are often ascribed a certain metaphorical blackness (read as, inferiority) by the settler. Such "racial regimes," Wolfe argued, are meant to "reproduce . . . [an] unequal relationship" between the colonizer and the colonized (Wolfe 2006, 387–388). This is evident, for instance, in the manner in which the 1884 Regulations of the Indian Department published by the United States Department of Interior (albeit, implicitly) considers indigenous vocations to be uncivilized. Further, it prescribes that agents of the Indian Department use all means necessary to "induce . . . Indians to labor in civilized pursuits"—namely, the cultivation of the soil (Authority of the Secretary of the Interior 1884, 84). A similar assumption of aboriginal blackness animated Australian indigenous child removal policies. Officials insisted that they only removed "neglected" aboriginal children from their parents. But their indigeneity was often seen as synonymous with neglect and both Australian officials as well as settlers assumed that aboriginal parents were unable "to take care of their children." To this end, the removal of indigenous children was considered a way for "white [settler] saviors" to rescue indigenous children from their "blackness" (Jacobs 2009, 45). Finally, the assumed blackness of the Native American population led the nonnative community in New England to also assume that the indigenous had become extinct due to their unmodern ways. Further, despite ample evidence demonstrating the existence of complex indigenous societies and institutions before the arrival of Europeans in North America (Turner 1985, 194), the settlers claimed that they (and not the indigenous community) were the first "to erect the proper institutions of a social order worthy of notice" (O'Brien 2010, xii).

In the same way, Fanon's racialized characterization of the relationship between the colonized and the colonizer can also be treated as a metaphor for the "racial regime" that orders the lives of Palestinians living under Israel's settler colonial rule. Here too, the whiteness of the colonizer does not just refer to the whiteness of the colonizer's skin color. It also represents the civilized, cultured, ethical, and moral nature of the colonizer in general. And, the blackness of the colonial subject is not only a reference to the darker skin tone of the colonized in comparison to the colonizer. It is also a representation of the colonized in general as a people who are uncivilized, immoral, and devoid of values. When abstracted in this manner, the Fanonian allegory of the "white mask" and the "back skin" became visible when one of my interviewees, a lifelong resident of the West Bank whom I met through a fortuitous encounter in a coffee shop in Ramallah, recounted his naïve attempt at friendship with Israelis. Seeing that I was alone, he asked me where I was from. This sparked what turned out to be a long conversation about my experiences in the field and his life in the occupied West Bank. As a businessman he had a particular insight into the Palestinian economy. It was within this context, while discussing economic relations with Israelis, that he proudly proclaimed, "Of course, I know that all of them [Israelis] are not bad. I had many Israeli friends. I speak Hebrew. I thought we were friends. We used to visit each other's houses. We used to have fun. We also had long political discussions." I asked, "So, do you keep in touch with them anymore?" In a dejected manner, he replied, "No. It became difficult to maintain relations with them. There is a separation. They didn't want to talk to me anymore."[11]

It would be an exaggeration to argue that his attempt at friendship with Israelis was *only* a grasp at metaphorical whiteness. In fact, no Palestinian I have met would deny their metaphorical blackness. It is often their insistent adherence to their indigeneity (i.e., their Palestinian-ness) that is seen as a means of ensuring the persistence of the Palestinian cause, especially when faced with a settler colonial narrative that insists that Palestinians do not exist. Nevertheless, the morose manner in which he claimed that Israelis did not want to talk to him anymore—as opposed to *him* not wanting to talk to them—did indicate that his grasp at friendship may have also been laced with an urge to reach out to the colonizer's whiteness. For example, that he spoke Hebrew is not uncommon for the generation Palestinians that worked in Israel. But he was proud to speak the language of the colonizer. Of course, despite trying to establish a friendship with the colonizer and attempting to "forget, forgive, and only love," he was rejected as unworthy of white (Israeli) friendship and, by extension, of symbolic "white love."

This craving for the allegorical "white love" was also visible in the way some of my Palestinian interviewees in Gaza either denigrated themselves or resigned themselves to the perceived superiority of the colonizer. During a lively discussion in a coffee shop in Gaza City on Palestinian factions' unsuccessful efforts to establish a Palestinian state, a young Gazan said, "The problem is us, not them. Look at Israel. A few decades ago there was no Israel, and suddenly there is a country that everyone recognizes. It's permanent. Palestinians would need to look to Israelis to learn how to build their country."[12] Another, insinuating an imbued morality in Israel's bombing of Gaza, said, "Israel doesn't bomb everything. They only bomb fighters. For example, one time they wanted to target an Islamic Jihad member who, at the time, was in a mosque praying with his father. Israelis waited for his father to leave. Then they bombed the mosque."[13] However, despite the seeming compulsiveness of the colonized's craving for the metaphorical whiteness of the colonizer, we also need to recognize that this craving is imposed by the colonizer. With the economy at a virtual standstill in Gaza because of an unrelenting siege and therefore unable to meet its population's requirements, supermarkets were flooded with Israeli products and foodstuffs. Emphasizing the insidiousness of the prevalence of the colonizer's goods, a Palestinian friend who accompanied me to several of Gaza's supermarkets, reminded me:

> Here you also see a class thing. A lot of Palestinians used to work in Israel, and they would bring back Israeli-made products. Slowly people here started thinking that Israeli products are better than Palestinian or Arab-made things. Yes, we often have no choice but to buy Israeli products. But it is also a class thing that we have been taught when working in Israel. Israeli things are better. So, to use Israeli products is an upper-class thing to do.[14]

This is not to say that Palestinians do not resist this infiltration of whiteness into their colonized lives. But, notwithstanding the ability and propensity to resist the "white mask," what is clear is that the colonized's sector is created in a way that also often compels the colonial subject to reject his or her "jungle status" and crave for "white culture," "white civilization," and "white love," whether through the urge to self-deprecate or the perception that Israel and Israeli goods are simply better.

What is also implicit in the above parallels between Fanon's colonized sector and its Palestinian variant is the socioeconomic degradation of the colonial subject. In Fanon's description the sector of the colonized was hungry and on its knees. And, the colonized are meant to be in a state of serfdom as a cowering subservient class with no morals, values, ethics, or "real" social fabric, watched over by the colonial military and police. In fact, this distinction is not only central to the colonizer's representation of the colonial subject, it also justifies the former's domination of the latter. Accordingly, in the West Bank, the Gaza Strip, and Israel, the disparity between the sector of the colonizer and its prosperity and the utter squalor of the realm of the colonized was unmistakable. In the previous chapter, I have already discussed the post-Oslo economic degradation of the Palestinian territories. Similarly, their ghettoization through a network of walls, checkpoints, iron gates, and roadblocks (Korn 2008, 117), as well as the siege of Gaza, remind us that the colonized's sector in Palestine can also be seen through Fanonian lenses. Much like Fanon's characterization, here too the colonized are described as prostrated and hungry, as evidenced by, for example, the shocking rates of malnutrition, especially among Gaza's young. In a report to the United Nations Relief and Works Agency (UNRWA), Dr. Mads Gilbert wrote: "Palestinian children in Gaza are suffering immensely. A large proportion are affected by the manmade malnourishment regime caused by the Israeli imposed blockage. Prevalence of anemia in children <2 yrs. in Gaza is at 72.8%, while prevalence of wasting, stunting, underweight have been documented at 34.3%, 31.4% and 31.45% respectively" (Gilbert 2014).

Similarly, the high rises on the coast of Tel Aviv, the swank boutiques that line the city's Rothschild Boulevard, and the upmarket residential towers in Ramat Aviv Gimmel, stand in stark contrast to the destruction of Shuja'iyya following Operation Protective Edge, the contaminated seawater off the Gazan coast, and the congested paths that characterize the landscapes of refugee camps like Balata and Dheisheh in the West Bank (figure 4.3). Separating these two worlds are border crossings like Rafah and Eretz (in northern Gaza) or the numerous Israeli military checkpoints one encounters in Jerusalem and the West Bank, where the colonizer's military personnel, guns, and armored vehicles—collectively, the colonizer's infrastructure of domination—watch over the sector of the colonized. We could also draw on the Fanonian imaginary in relation to the Oslo Accords and their regime of (dis)incentives (see chapter 3). The postcolonial statelike Palestinian Authority, for instance, can been seen as a euphemism for the whiteness of a colonial regime that aims to impose itself on the blackness—represented by the propensity to fight—of the colonized. Here too, the colonized is made to loathe his blackness, much like some of my Fatah interviewees who criticized Hamas's armed resistance. Moreover, the assimilated Palestinian faction (i.e., Fatah), represented by the likes of Mahmoud Abbas, serves as a testament to the manner in which the colonizer's whiteness is internalized and stands convinced of the "goodness" of "white culture" and civilization.

Viewed through the metaphors and vocabulary of Fanon's works, it is not surprising that Hamas members and affiliates accorded an inalienable right to violence as a tool for unmaking the trials of living under Israeli rule. Much as in Fanon's characterization of the anticolonial imaginary, Hamas's armed resistance, and that of other Palestinian factions, was perceived by my Palestinian interviewees as capable of removing (unmaking) the "white mask" in order to allow Palestinians to shift as a liberated people from being relegated "last" to becoming "first." But while this claim might seem self-evident, especially in light of the scenario described above, the question still remains as to what this transformation from "last" to "first," instigated by the colonized's violence, would tangibly imply for the Palestinian cause. Will it merely confirm Clausewitz's claim that war is an expression of force to impose one's own will on the enemy (Clausewitz

FIGURE 4.3A   The sector of colonizer in Tel Aviv. Photo by author.

FIGURE 4.3B The sector of the colonized in Balata Refugee Camp. Photo by author.

1976, 17)? In reality, in conflicts where the parties involved have disparate access to resources and military infrastructure, it is unlikely that the weak will be able to impose their will entirely on a stronger enemy. It is therefore highly improbable that Palestinians in general and Hamas in particular can expect to inflict a military defeat on Israel. The al-Qassam Brigade itself admits that the organization is "faced with the military and security machine of a regional superpower." For this reason, it claims a potential victory against Israel, not on the basis of its military prowess but through divine support, "belief in the justice of the Palestinian cause, and the firm belief that the will of the victims will defeat the arrogance of the aggressor" (Ezzedeen Al-Qassam Brigades—Information Office 2019). Karim, as discussed in chapter 3, also regretted the material weakness of the Palestinian resistance and wondered if it was indeed sensible to continue fighting Israel.

If such is the material ineffectualness of Hamas's resistance, then what does this process of unmaking through which the "last" becomes the "first" really look like?

As an answer, in a controversial article for *Counterpunch*, Michael Neumann noted that while Palestinians cannot expect to win militarily against Israel, violence serves as a means of "'sending a message': you really don't want to keep screwing with us. We will do anything to stop you" (Neumann 2002). A similar understanding of unmaking was also present in Jeroen Gunning's study where he argues that Hamas's credibility with the Palestinian population drew primarily on its ability to provide security and to demonstrate a willingness to fight (not win) against a militarily superior Israel, especially since Fatah is unwilling to do the same (Gunning 2007, 126–127). During my conversations with Hamas officials and affiliates, I too noticed a stark contrast between their rhetoric in public statements and their minimalist understanding of the ability of armed resistance to challenge and unmake Israel's settler colonial rule over the Palestinian territories. For instance, Fawzi Barhoum, in a public statement during Operation Protective Edge, declared, "Oh people of the West Bank. Our message to you is: Gaza is calling upon you to join the battle! Not in order to help Gaza, or for the glorified and sublime, but in order for you to become the people of purity, heroism, honor and nobility" (Al Aqsa 2014). Invoking a similar story of heroism and triumph during his victory speech following the 2014 war, Ismael Haniyeh, the Hamas prime minister at the time, asserted, "Those whose blood was spilled, and the martyrs were the fuel of this victory." Similarly, al-Qassam Brigade spokesperson Abu Ubaida had said, "Resistance unified the people. . . . The resistance forced the ceasefire out of its enemy and did not allow them any strategic or tactical achievements. . . . It crushed its pride that has been fabricated for decades through media outlets and laboratories of psychological warfare" (Ma'an 2014c). In comparison, during our conversation Barhoum rarely evoked the notion of unequivocal victory, nor did he draw on the vocabulary of "purity, heroism, honor and nobility." Instead, having already conceptualized Hamas's resistance as a consequence of Israel's violations of Palestinian rights (discussed earlier), he emphasized the utility of resistance in a minimalist fashion. While describing the manner in which Hamas balanced its dual role, he went on to list Hamas's many responsibilities, one of which he categorized as the responsibility to conduct "resistance in order to defend ourselves." After Barhoum described the challenges of maintaining this dual role as resistance and the government, I asked him, "Why does Hamas choose to do it all?" He responded, "Resistance has put pressure on the Israelis with regard to the siege, and the Israelis now have a very bad reputation."[15]

During our interview, senior Hamas member Ahmed Yousef was also unenthusiastic in his perception of armed resistance and its utility. When I specifically asked him about Hamas's armed wing he said, "We have been known because of our resistance activities. If we get rid of resistance, we will surely loose support." He continued, "[Resistance] helps with [Hamas's] credibility."[16] In a similar vein, when asked about the utility of resistance, the Palestinian Legislative Council member Atef Adwan emphasized its strategic importance. He argued, "Seven years since our elections, one can say that Hamas's resistance activities have demonstrated that it can bring Israel to make compromises. When the resistance is strong, Israel tends to retreat. The 2008–9 war on Gaza proved that we can survive. We became a model and didn't allow Israel to take over."[17] During my conversation with the photojournalist from Al-Aqsa TV, she also did not seem to view muqawama as a means of securing victory. Instead, perceiving it as a response to Israeli actions, she asserted that without resistance "Israelis are not going to listen to us."[18] Moreover, with many questioning the prudence and practicality of maintaining an armed wing while governing Gaza in the midst of a siege, Salama Maroof, general manager of the (Hamas) Government Media Office, emphasized its unmaking value when he claimed: "Within two months of being in power, it [the resistance] succeeded in capturing Gilad Shalit and forced the occupation to release more than a thousand prisoners. Hamas has therefore shown that being in power and ruling Gaza doesn't affect its abilities as a resistance organization."[19] Finally, Ghazi Hamad had begun our interview by succinctly declaring "You need to understand that we are still under occupation. So, we have to continue fighting." Subsequently, while deliberating over the utility of resistance, he explained,

> It has not been easy, but we have tried to use all resources to fight the occupation. We have kept resistance alive in our values [and] cultural outlook and made sure that resistance is mentioned in every Hamas document. Even though it is not easy, we have continually talked about resistance while being in government. In 2009 and 2012 they [Israel] reacted to Hamas being in power,[20] and yet we[21] [Palestinians] survived because of our resistance wing.[22]

This perception of Hamas's muqawama and its ability to unmake is a far cry from the revolutionary zeal that is supposed to spur an armed struggle. Moreover, even in their public speeches, Hamas officials call a ceasefire agreement (see quotes from Meshaal and Ubaida) a victory, and not the unequivocal dismantling of Israel's settler colonialism. This suggests that, for Hamas, the resistance is devoid of the revolutionary character that exuded from Bahaa's account of the rescue of the stranded Palestinians at the Rafah crossing. Nor does this story of violence seem to reek of cannonballs and bloody knives or promise a project of disorder in the manner imagined by Fanon, that would then be able to rip off the "white mask" violently imposed by the colonizers. Yet, I would argue that, despite lacking the revolutionary allure, the unmaking abilities of the armed resistance lie in its perceived ability to pressure Israel into a compromise and ensure Palestinian survival. A prominent al-Qassam Brigade operation that Hamas celebrates as symbolic of the potency of its armed struggle is a case in point.

On July 28, 2014, five al-Qassam operatives emerged out a tunnel from Gaza in Kibbutz Nahal Oz in southern Israel. A video uploaded by al-Qassam's Arabic language website shows the fighters, carrying their weapons, stealthily moving toward an IDF watchtower. The operatives sneak up to the gate of the watchtower and start shooting into the building at the IDF personnel. Then the al-Qassam men enter the building of the watchtower installation and are seen dragging out an IDF soldier screaming in agony. The al-Qassam fighters are then seen shooting the soldier at close range before escaping back through the tunnel. Five Israeli soldiers were left dead after the attack. Presumably, the attack itself is nominal, paling in comparison to the more than two thousand Palestinians who lost their lives during Operation Protective Edge. Moreover, the attack was not even able to neutralize the entire IDF infantry unit at the watchtower, as the al-Qassam fighters fled the scene when they met heavy fire. Nevertheless, its ability to unmake is evident in the emotions it evoked in Nahal Oz. One resident of the kibbutz noted, "I know that tower and am often in the vicinity—it's fucked-up—there's no other word. . . . I have no idea how families with small children will agree to return here after viewing this video—it's really frightening." Benny Sela, the security chief of Nahal Oz, said, "It's really frightening—but, then again, this whole war is frightening" (Bender 2014).

If we focus on the materiality of the attack or Hamas's armed resistance as a whole, neither has done much to unmake Israel's settler colonialism. Nevertheless, through the affect it had on the residents of Nahal Oz, one realizes that, irrespective of the material weakness of Hamas's resistance, it continues to unmake by challenging the self-conceptions of Israelis and forcing them to reevaluate them (Ayyash 2010, 16). Like other subaltern struggles, it does not destroy the "other." Yet, through the rockets it fires into Israel, the several tunnels leading from Gaza deep inside Israel that were discovered during the 2014 war (Batchelor 2014), or the operation in Nahal Oz, it unmakes the colonizer by ritually fighting and questioning the viability of maintaining the existing hindrances that prevent Palestinians from becoming the "first" as a liberated people. The fact that it "chips" away at the resolve of the colonizer is rarely evident in the grandiose manner imagined by Fanon. Nevertheless, the slow trajectory toward being the liberated "first" is evident in the fear it instills, for instance, among the residents of Nahal Oz, the 9 percent of Israeli citizens who suffer from post-traumatic stress disorder (PTSD), or for example, the "PTSD-related symptoms in several hundred [Israeli] soldiers" following the 2014 war in Gaza (Ginsburg 2014). The Hamas brand of unmaking through armed resistance is thus reminiscent of the manner in which the Zapatistas were able to travel symbolically from Chiapas to Mexico City. When Subcomandante Marcos was asked about his delusional aspirations to take over the capital city,[23] he said, "Weren't we there already by January 2nd?[24] We were everywhere, on the lips of everyone—in the subway, on the radio. And our flag was in Zócalo" (Johnston 2000, 466).[25] Similarly, through its armed resistance, Hamas also attempts to reach Jerusalem. It may not physically have the ability to march on to the compounds of Haram al-Sharif and subsequently unmake the material prowess of the IDF. Instead it unmakes by making its opponents fearful and ensuring that the Israeli rule over the Palestinian territories is too costly to maintain.

Body, Wound, and the Making of Palestine

The very nature of violence as a phenomenon that violates makes its unmaking potential self-evident. But given the "wretchedness" of the (settler) colonial endeavor that infiltrates the materiality of the colonized's sector and the inner being of the colonial subject, an armed struggle would need to do much more than merely destroy in order to serve the colonized. As they find themselves compelled to wear the "white mask" and, over time, loathe the "black skin," an armed struggle would be required to contribute to the reification of the colonized's anti-colonial subjectivity and allow them to declare, "In no way should my color be regarded as a flaw" (Fanon 1952, 59). The question then remains, how is violence able to reify the colonized's sense of self? That is, faced with the colonizer's project, which infiltrates the inner being of the colonized, can violence also (re-)make the colonial subject's inner being?

One often finds that the making ability of an armed struggle is ritually professed alongside its presumed ability to destroy. In her work on Kashmir, Gangahar recalls that, for the Kashmiri fighter, the gun was a symbol of revolt and national identity. While holding the gun, the fighter became "a hero, a martyr, a man" who remained in control against the "occupier" (Gangahar 2013, 37). The image of the fighter as a personification of the hero, the martyr, the man, and the nation also became apparent during my tour of the Palmach Museum in Tel Aviv, which ended with the statement, "their [the Palmach fighters'] bodies are the silver platters on which this country [Israel] has been gifted to us."[26] Even Fanon, often celebrated as the iconic prophet of violence and its destructive ability, recognized that it encompassed "positive [and] formative features." He argued that, as the colonized fought, they became "a violent link in the great chain" as all the (anticolonial) factions recognized each other as bounded together by a "common cause, national destiny, and collective history" and were consequently unified as a collective colonized people (Fanon 1952, 50–51).

It is in this way, as violence inducts the colonized into the collective consciousness of a population striving for liberation, that the generative qualities of violence emerge. As the choice to fight becomes inevitable in the face of the state of suffering, violence itself is evocative of who they (the colonized) are and constitutes something they have created. Being perceived as a generative force and demonstrating the ability to embody the state, nation, and those who fight for it (the revolutionary) and die for it (the martyr), violence's making potential is not lost on Palestinians either. While discussing Hamas's commitment to the armed struggle, Hamas member of the Palestinian Legislative Council, Atef Adwan noted, "They [Israel] have tried, but they cannot conquer us from inside anymore. War was able to convince people about good and bad. It provided the light at the end of the tunnel, and the young were confident. Hope went up and fear went down."[27] Instinctively, one could look at this statement as merely an exaggeration no different from the hyperbolic manner in which Meshaal declared the ceasefire agreement a victory, Ubaida claimed that Hamas's operations were able to "crush" Israel's sense of pride (quoted earlier), or an al-Qassam Brigade communiqué released on August 20, 2014, after Operation Protective Edge declared: "You ["the enemy"/Israel] have failed and so has your plan. Time after time you are proving to be a group of failures. Forty-five days since the start of the battle, despite all your intelligence-gathering activity, all you have been able to do is kill women and children" (Ezzedeen Al-Qassam Brigade 2014).

However, if we do momentarily take the assertions of Adwan and other Hamas officials seriously, it is particularly interesting that, despite its destructive abilities and, for Palestinians, its tendency to exact harsh material and human costs, armed resistance is somehow presented as a constructive process. How is it that violence is able to protect the inner self and prevent it from being conquered? What does this light at the end of the tunnel look like? Moreover, returning to Fanon, how is the collective—people, cause, destiny, and history—created through it? Detractors would ask what is the relevance (and meaning) of an unconquerable inner being if Operation Protective Edge claimed more than two thousand Palestinian lives and exacted material losses from Palestinians in the Gaza Strip amounting to approximately six billion dollars? Where is the light in this? In the face of destruction, where is the creation? To explore the possible existence of this light, which seemingly shines through armed resistance and its ability to make for the colonized, despite the destruction it inflicts on the colonized's sector, let us look at four ethnographic accounts I collected in the field.

The first was an interview I conducted in January 2013 with a young Palestinian activist in Cairo who was a close friend of a Palestinian acquaintance of mine. He had been born and brought up in the West Bank, and after finishing his education at Birzeit University, he was now working in Egypt. We first discussed the prospect of an interview over the phone, and he agreed on the condition of anonymity. Two days later we met at a café in Zamalek, an upmarket neighborhood in Cairo. He began by talking about his life in the occupied West Bank and his activism: "You notice the occupation from day one as a Palestinian. You see the destruction of Palestinian homes. My earliest memory is of a young girl being arrested for protesting the destruction of her house. So, when I conduct protests, I remember that girl, my earliest memory of the occupation." I then asked, "What are some of the challenges you faced as an activist in the West Bank?" He paused and replied, "That is an interesting question. Fighting as a Palestinian is difficult. You are young and don't have any way of protecting yourself. If you think about it, they [Israelis] own everything. They torture us and oppress us." I remember him pausing, and an awkward silence followed. I asked, "Are you okay?" He hastily replied, "Yes, Yes. It's just frustrating. Yes, we are fighting the Israelis, but the Palestinian Authority and Fatah work with them and help them. Ironically, my activism is against Israel, but I have gotten beaten up more times by the PA [Palestinian Authority]." Sensing his frustration, I interjected, "Then why do you fight? What do you get out of it?" Hearing this, the expression on his face suddenly changed. From being frustrated, it was almost as if he was surprised (and offended) that I had asked him such a question. He responded in a resolute tone, "Why do I fight? It is about power. Either they kick your ass, or you kick theirs. I know I have suffered, but I wish I suffered more, it shows that I exist, and I can survive. It is part of it all. Just like Palestine is part of me, fighting is also part me."[28]

The second account is an anecdote related to me by Bassam, a Palestinian restaurateur who was living in Cairo when I first met him. During the First Intifada, while in the West Bank, Bassam had participated in a protest. He was promptly arrested and was kept in a military prison for eighteen days. He recounted, "My hands were tied, and I was made to stand most of the time. Everyone like me who didn't confess to a crime was kept in a corridor, and soldiers would walk by and kick us and put out their cigarettes on our bodies." Bassam continued, "The only time I was allowed to sleep was between 3 am and 6 am. I lost nine kilograms in eighteen days." At this point I asked, "How did you survive?" He responded, "In jail you have to be careful what you ask for. If you ask for water, they know that you are thirsty, and they will use it against you. You also can't think good thoughts during torture." Bassam went on to explain, "It is [in] the time between torture sessions that your mind goes crazy. You need to save your good thoughts for that period. I used to think of Rana [his wife]." Then he had an encounter with an Israeli officer: "On the tenth day, one of the investigating officers put a mirror in front of me and asked if I felt pity for myself. I said, 'You feel pity for me now? Don't. I'm in prison and I'm here to be tortured. When I go home, *you* will still be weak, but I will be strong, and I will be human.'" Bassam then pointed to the scars from the cigarette burns from his time in prison and said, "For me fighting and suffering are a matter of pride, and it is what makes me Palestinian."[29]

The third encounter was an interview I conducted in the Gaza Strip with Ahmed. I was introduced to him by a Palestinian acquaintance, who told me that Ahmed has been shot by an Israeli soldier when he was young. We met at a shisha café across from Gaza City's Midan al-Jundi al-Majhool, or Unknown Soldier's Square. As we ordered our shisha, I noticed that the server's eyes were bloodshot. After he left, I asked Ahmed, "Did you notice his eyes? They were red and glazed over." He responded, "He is probably high. Tramadol or something. It is very common here. People are depressed or traumatized, and they get high." With an unemployment rate over 40 percent (GISHA 2017), war, and a persistent siege, it is not surprising that a chronic drug addiction has persisted in the Gaza Strip, despite the Hamas government's best efforts (Jalal 2013). Our discussion at the café then turned to his experience of being shot, and Ahmed relayed the following account:

> In 2000 I was eleven years old and in the sixth grade. We lived very close to a settlement. In late October, a month after the start of the Second Intifada, we were mobilized outside our school to protest against the Israeli occupation. We were young and decided to go because at that time everyone was doing it. See, people don't realize that Palestinians don't care about repercussions. We don't care because we have empty lives. We sometimes do this to feel something. Anyways, we went to the settlement. We were a group of school and college students throwing rocks at an Israeli checkpoint near the settlement, since we were not able to get into the settlement itself. These checkpoints were blocks of pure concrete with holes in them so that the soldiers could shoot at protesters through them. After one hour of throwing rocks at the checkpoint, I made the mistake of not hiding when the Israelis started shooting. I had one last rock in my hand and thought I should throw it before hiding. Then I got shot. In seconds I fell to the ground and my blood was all over the place. A young man, one of the protesters, picked me off the ground and ran with my half-dead body to the nearest ambulance. The gunshot itself was not painful . . . but it took its time and burned me up and down. Once inside the ambulance, the first aid guy assessed my injury as serious and dangerous and asked the driver to take us to al-Shifa hospital. During the drive he tried to stop the bleeding. But

the bullet had gone through my stomach and came out of my back. In fact, he needed three hands—two to stop the bleeding and the third to change the bandages. So, I just lay there bleeding and moaning until we reached the hospital. I was taken to surgery. Later I was told that my injury was severe. They had to cut some of my intestines and colon. After the surgery I was moved to a room to wake up. None of my parents or relatives were there. I was eleven, had a bullet wound and sixteen stitches in my stomach. When I came home, I was depressed. I didn't want to go to school. I had to go to therapy. I was upset that I would have this scar all my life. But what was the most tragic was that I felt that no one cared. My father has lived under occupation all his life, and my mother is a nurse. They both have seen worse times. So, for that matter, when I look at my scar, to me it is Palestine, you get hurt, you are scarred for life, but no one cares.[30]

The final encounter occurred in Beit Hanoun, a town in northern Gaza bordering the Erez crossing. It is here that I met a former al-Qassam fighter, Muhammad, the uncle of a friend who was happy to grant me an interview while taking a walk around Beit Hanoun. I was well aware that Beit Hanoun, being a border town, had a particularly tumultuous history. Nevertheless, I began by asking him to relate his experiences and confrontations with the IDF, which monitors all of Beit Hanoun with a surveillance balloon. He recounted, "Life here is tough. [Pointing to a dug-out part of the street] You see that, that's what happens. During war, they take over part of the city and barricade it and destroy the roads and streets." I then asked, "Have you personally been affected by it?" Muhammad replied, "Of course. Our house was taken over by Israelis. They put all of us in a room and took our money and gold. All the men were then taken to the Israeli side. We were let go in the middle of the night, without our clothes. We had to walk back home." Assuming then that life under occupation was the reason behind Muhammad's decision to take up arms, I asked him if these experiences encouraged him to join the al-Qassam Brigade. He answered, "No. Things like that happen all the time here. I joined because Israel murdered my friends. I joined for revenge." I would have liked to know more about his friends, but he seemed uncomfortable talking about the subject further. I therefore decided to turn to a "lighter" topic and asked, "How did you join the organization? What is the process?" He replied, "Joining Qassam is not easy. You have to show that you are a good Muslim first. You have to go to the mosque regularly. Then they take your application for approval. Once you are approved you go through basic training and you get assigned to a department. I was in the ballistics department dealing with rockets." I asked him, "What did your family think of your decision?" He replied, "My mother would cry every night, and my father would lock the doors. I would jump over the fence and go to work. I was mostly involved in nighttime patrols along the border." At this juncture I was struck by the unemotional manner in which he talked about his time in the al-Qassam Brigade. It seemed that, for this former fighter, fighting and taking up arms was *just* a job. Curious about whether it was indeed *just* as a form of employment for him, I asked, "What was your experience within the organization?" He responded, "I never got scared. There were bombings around me and shootings, but I wasn't scared. I joined for revenge, but in Qassam I felt good about being a person, being Palestinian. I felt good and moral. It made *me* feel good."[31]

Within the context of my fieldwork there are a multitude of interpretations I could write into these four, for me, poignant ethnographic encounters. Muhammad's fearlessness when faced with bombs and bullets and the Palestinian activist's commitment to continue the fight despite the tribulations of doing so are reminiscent of the manner in which many of my Palestinian interlocutors appeared able to find some semblance of normalcy, sense and meaning in utter tragedy. As a friend in Gaza once pointed out, "I'm never bothered by the sound of gunshots. You know why? Because you don't hear the sound of the gunshot that kills you."[32] Then again, does the colonial subject have any choice? The ceaseless history of wars, occupation, and siege would mean that Palestinians have no other alternative but to somehow find meaning in the suffering and trauma. One of my interlocutors, a native of Jabalia refugee camp in northern Gaza, became familiar with the essence of the tragedy of living under siege at the age of thirteen when an Israeli jet flew over his neighborhood, bombed a house and killed his friend. Because of the shock he lost his ability to speak. Nevertheless, he somehow made sense of his suffering. He explained, "I became matured. I was a man in a child's body. I recovered slowly. Recovery is important because it allows you to convert a negative into something positive. That is the strategy of the Palestinian struggle. Today I train young children who have the same problem with speaking."[33] Emad Burnat implied the same logic in the closing minutes of his 2011 documentary *5 Broken Cameras* when he claimed: "Healing is a challenge in life. It's a victim's sole obligation. By healing, you resist oppression. But when I'm hurt over and over again, I forget the wounds that rule my life. Forgotten wounds can't be healed. So, I film to heal."

Of course, the marginalized's need to make sense of the condition of subalternity that surrounds them also points to the methodological caveat of studying violence through the stories that were written into it by my Palestinian interlocutors. That is to say, invariably my interviewees, if asked, would attribute some meaning to their encounter with and experience of violence. But they recounted their experiences of violent confrontation with the enemy in very different ways, pointing to the disparate kinds of meaning that violence can acquire for individuals. During my conversation with the Palestinian activist, there was a clear sense of melancholy in the way in which he recounted his life as an activist in the West Bank. Yet, despite being beaten and tortured, he saw the fight as a means of survival and existence. For Bassam, being tortured in an Israeli military prison was an experience that instilled pride and a sense of resilience and humanity in him. In comparison, for Ahmed, being shot by an IDF soldier did not personify survival, pride, or humanity. Instead, for him, the lifelong scar that remained was a bitter reminder that resilience and sacrifice can often go uncelebrated. And for Muhammad, while the decision to join the al-Qassam Brigade was fueled by revenge, his time in Hamas's military wing instilled a certain sense of goodness and morality, which made him feel like a fearless person unmoved by the violence that is ritually inflicted on Gaza.

Ironically, however, and irrespective of the manner in which my interlocutors related their violent encounters, they all "found" Palestine in their confrontation with the Israeli authorities. The Palestinian activist in Cairo even seemed almost offended when I asked why he fought for Palestinian rights in the West Bank. This was because of the synonymy that he saw between the commitment to fight and Palestine (or being Palestinian). In other words, if he did not fight, he would not be able to identify himself as Palestinian any more. Bassam's experience confirms numerous reports by civil society organizations that claim that the torture of Palestinian prisoners is a systematic and systemic practice that begins "from the moment a prisoner is arrested" (*Middle East Monitor* 2014; also see B'Tselem 2010; B'Tselem 2017a; B'Tselem 2017b; Addameer 2012). For Bassam though, his scars were the signature of Palestine in that they were symbols of the resilience and humanity that emerge out of the continuous cycle of fighting and suffering. In stark contrast, there was no sense of euphoria in Ahmed's remembrance of being shot. For him, it was an unequivocal tragedy. Yet, he too saw Palestine as imbued in his lifelong scar. Ahmed saw the bodily blemish as a reminder of an unending national struggle where all that remains after the violent confrontation is empty and uncelebrated suffering—albeit a *Palestinian* suffering. Muhammad's decision to join the al-Qassam Brigade was an individual choice fueled by the tragedy of the death of his friends. Nevertheless, as being part of the resistance instilled a sense of morality (and seeming fearlessness) in him, it also made him feel good about being a person, a *Palestinian* person.

There is however a certain irony in the manner in which my interlocutors found Palestine in the confrontation with the "enemy." Their decision to fight—as an activist in the West Bank, by taking to the streets during the First Intifada, by throwing rocks at an IDF installation, or by taking up arms with the al-Qassam Brigade—was intimately informed by the context of the Palestinian liberation

struggle and the insufferable realities that order everyday life in the Palestinian territories. Moreover, being beaten up by the IDF and Palestinian Authority forces, being tortured in prison, being shot or having to dodge bullets and
bombs, while not unlikely occurrences, are the unintended consequences. Yet,
it is in the unintended pain, hurt, trauma, and suffering that they found some
sense of Palestine or of being Palestinian. In that way, all four of my interlocutors remind us of Loic Wacquant's boxer, who finds himself tied to the "fistic
sport" through the "double sense of *love* and *suffering*" (Wacquant 1995, 491).
Although, for a boxer, pain and suffering, while an expected outcome, may not
be the desired consequence. Nevertheless, in Wacquant's work, it was the pugilist's ability to physically withstand bodily pain that ordered his life and accorded
him honor, much like an ancient gladiator "refusing to concede and kneel down"
(Wacquant 1995, 496).

Of course, here too we could return to my earlier conversation on anticolonial
violence and the anticolonial imaginary. Fanon has already told us that torture,
trauma, pain, injury, and suffering are what inform the colonized's sector. However, he also claimed that the military infrastructure of the colonizers, their "saber
rattling exercises" and the "smell of gunpowder" have such a persistent presence
in the lives of the colonized that they do not intimidate the colonized any longer
(Wacquant 1995, 31). This may in fact explain the often mundane and sometimes
unaffected manner in which my interlocutors made sense of and dealt with their
encounter with Israeli authorities. Moreover, despite the military prowess of the
colonizer and the extent of the trauma, suffering, and pain it is able to inflict on
the colonial subject, my interlocutors were not left docile, subservient, and prostrated. Their being—with the possible exception of Ahmed—was not unmade.
Instead, what shone through the confrontation between the colonizer and the
colonized was Palestine and the latter's Palestinian-ness.

One may claim that the phenomenon of my interlocutors seeing Palestine in
their injuries, scars, trauma, and suffering is merely the case of the colonized ret-
roactively according superficial meaning to an experience that was nothing but
tragic. But, when seen through the scope of the anticolonial imaginary, we are
also reminded of the muscularity of the colonial subject's dreams. Fanon asserts
that the colonized dream of action, vitality, aggressiveness, and freedom (Fanon
1963, 15–19). That is to say, in their dreams they do not perceive themselves
as made docile by the exponentially greater military prowess of the colonizer.
This is why the Palestinian activist in Cairo refused to be characterized as someone left on his knees after being beaten and tortured and why Muhammad, the
former al-Qassam fighter, refused to become fearful. Instead they continued to
fight, as the muscular Palestinian who personifies action, vitality, and freedom.
In the same way, Bassam, having been arrested and tortured, could have been left

prostrated—that is in fact the intention of the colonizer's oppressive infrastructure. Nevertheless, he too refused to cower in fear. Instead, through the suffering he reaffirmed his own humanity and being, while finding Palestine and his Palestinian-ness etched forever on his skin. Of course, in this conversation, Ahmed is an outlier. He was not euphoric or muscular in recounting his being shot in the stomach. Nevertheless, while he himself inscribed a certain meaningless-ness to his scar, his encounter was not entirely fruitless either. Although the bullet from the IDF soldier's gun was meant to efface him—and with it his rebellious Palestinian-ness—he was also left with, albeit tragically, an emblem of Palestine.

But whether we discuss Wacquant's boxer and his attraction to the violent sport or my interviewees' recollection of their violent confrontation and their muscular dreams, I would argue that their discovery of meaning in suffering is an account of an individual experience.[34] That is, the manner in which the American, inner-city pugilist finds meaning in the "fistic sport" and my interlocutors find Palestine in their trauma, wounds and suffering may in fact be merely evocative of their individual relationships with the realities of inner-city Chicago and the Palestinian territories respectively. As Ghassan Hage noted, while the Palestinian suicide bomber is a product of the Palestinian sociopolitical experience and not an aberration (Hage 2003, 69), the suicide bombing in itself is a display of the individual Palestinian treading "a path of social meaningfulness and self-fulfillment in an otherwise meaningless life." In light of this "dire" Palestinian reality, Hage was therefore right to conceptualize suicide bombers as spectacles of individuals swapping their grim physical being for a glorious symbolic existence (Hage 2003, 80). But despite the individual being seen here as tussling with his or her *own* grim reality and, through suffering, finding meaning for him- or herself, what cannot be ignored is that the violent confrontation and the resultant pain, wounds, suffering and death are rarely limited to, or bounded by, the scope of the individual. Instead they often enter the realm of public ownership or public property in such a way that, despite being directly perpetrated (and its tragic costs suffered) by one individual, they are claimed by all.

This very character of anticolonial violence emerges in Fanon's thought. As noted earlier, he claims that violence is positive and formative and that it creates a "new man" on the path of violent decolonization (Fanon 1963, 2). This "new man," for him, is however not an isolated unit. Instead, by engaging in the violent struggle for liberation, he is inducted into the collective national cause that unites all those who are fighting the colonizer. This understanding could be attributed to the narrative style that Fanon utilized in his works, whereby he seamlessly wavered between the experiences of the colonized individual (with himself being a personification of the same) and the condition of the colonized population as a whole. Moreover, for Fanon, the synonymy between the individual and the collective was also a subjective claim about the manner in which the world needed to be remade in the interests of the colonial subject. Elaborating on this from a professional perspective as a psychoanalyst, he went on to explain, "I should help my patient to become conscious of his unconscious and abandon his attempts at a hallucinatory whitening [i.e. of the individual], but also to act in the direction of a change in the social structure [i.e. of the collective]" (Fanon 1952, 74).

As a means of exploring the infusion of the individual with the collective, let us return to the metaphor of the "fistic sport" and look at the example of the real-life Cinderella man, James L. Braddock, who fought Max Baer in a historic bout on June 13, 1935. His decision to fight may have been almost entirely informed by his individual experience (and tussle) with the realities of life during the Great Depression. But Braddock's physical confrontation with Baer somehow entered symbolically into the realm of public property and public ownership, where his every punch and eventual victory was valorized and perceived by many as the explosive arrival of the downtrodden to "center stage." Applying this discussion to my four accounts from the field, one could claim that they are but four instances. Moreover, their individual encounters are *just* their own. It is true that each rock thrown at an IDF tank and each protest bears the mark of the individual's experiences and struggles. Nevertheless, when their acts result in a scuffle with an IDF soldier, the experience of being tortured, being shot in the stomach, or simply holding a gun as a member of the al-Qassam Brigade, they become part of the collective experience of Palestinians, and the physical and emotional scars they leave come to represent Palestinian-ness.

This tendency to imbue the individual with the collective was also present in conversations with Hamas officials. As discussed earlier, Ghazi Hamad, while assessing the "value" of Hamas's armed resistance, noted that, in the face of Operation Cast Lead (2008–9) and Operation Pillar of Defense (2012), it was the organization's armed resistance that ensured the survival of the Palestinian people. In this way, as a representative of a Palestinian political organization striving for legitimacy as the rightful representative of the Palestinian population, Hamad effectively infused Hamas's *own* acts of resistance with the collective Palestinian spirit of resilience. Driven by a similar logic, a former Palestinian prisoner also insisted on prefixing his *own* experience in an Israeli prison with the collective Palestinian struggle when he noted, "First of all, you need to remember that a lot of our people spend some time in prison. There are approximately 800,000 Palestinians[35] in prison today."[36] The individual also found resonance in the collective when sixteen-year-old Mohammad Abu Khdair was kidnapped and burned alive in a "revenge attack" following the death of three Israeli teenagers in the West Bank in July 2014 (Ma'an 2014a, Ma'an 2014b). For Palestinians, the death of Mohammad became evocative of the plight of a people collectively faced with the brutality of a military occupation. In death he was a martyr for the struggle, even though he was not personally involved in the Palestinian struggle, and, with his body wrapped in the iconic Palestinian keffiyeh and the Palestinian flag, the funeral was a spectacle of mourning and protest over the suffering of a collective Palestinian people.[37] It is in this way that each individual act of resistance, whether a rock, rocket, or suicide bombing, and each occasion of suffering, whether injury, imprisonment, or death, enters into the public realm. An act of resistance fails to remain an isolated unitary instance and is inducted into the common cause, destiny, and history of the collectively colonized Palestinian population as a *Palestinian* act of resistance and an expression of *Palestinian* anticolonial fervor. Similarly, each occasion of suffering is deemed an instance of collective *Palestinian* suffering evocative of the crises faced by an entire population under Israeli rule.

In arguing for the existence of the signature of Palestine in individual acts of military resistance and the resultant suffering, this chapter walks an intellectual path already traversed by studies of nationalism in general and Palestinian nationalism in particular. These works have explicated the manner in which the soldier, the army, war, resistance, heroism, martyrdom, and tragedy are often the determining markers personifying the nation. Joseph Massad in *Colonial Effects*, for instance, emphasized the need to deliberate over the productive function of the national (postcolonial) military as an institution that "produces politics." He went on to argue that, through its coercive and disciplinary infrastructure, the army creates a specific "brand" of citizen nationals that then is disseminated through the "rest of society, through a variety of mechanisms (media, official propaganda, schools, family, military conscriptions, songs, music), new cultures and traditions that are identified as 'national'" (Massad 2001, 7). Such an understanding of the military as an institution mirrors Timothy Mitchell's perspective of the two-dimensional nature of the army in the modern state. On the one hand, he argues, it stands as a conglomeration of individual soldiers, while on the other hand, it personifies a machine capable of defining and personifying the nation and the national (Mitchell 1991, 93). A similar narrative is evident in the way violence and suffering was the vocabulary with which the story of postcolonial Namibian national identity was written. Henning Melber argued that the violence of decolonization and the consequent sufferings of the colonized are celebrated as significant facets of the Namibian national being (Melber 2003, 313). And, as was evident in the Palmach Museum, the nationalist trope of commemorating the entombed Unknown Soldier (Inglis 1993, 31) has also served as the "silver platter" on which the country has been gifted to the rest of society.

Returning to Palestine, it therefore is not surprising that the memory of battle and the remembrance or commemoration of the fighter has served as the platter for displaying Palestinian aspirations. As I have discussed in chapter 3, the keffiyeh worn by the Palestinian peasants who authored the first confrontation with the colonizer was reanimated by the Palestinian guerrilla fighter of the 1960s as a symbol of the Palestinian national collective struggle (Swedenburg 1990; 1995). Similarly, Laleh Khalili, in *Heroes and Martyrs of Palestine*, argues that tragic events such as the Nakba, the Intifadas, and the Sabra-Shatila massacres are often intertwined with a narrative of courage and heroism in the face of defeat (Khalili 2007, 153–159). Consequently, they are "wrapped in the cloak of national piety" and are turned into key markers for the creation of a narrative of Palestinian national identity and a national peoplehood (Khalili 2007, 153). Dina Matar, describing the Palestinian fighter in Lebanon, also noted that, through the launching of an armed struggle, Palestinians somehow found themselves transformed from being "passive refugees into active fighters." In light of this, the transformation is deemed virtuous and therefore demanded celebration through visual artifacts and ceremonies depicting "young and virile men, sometimes with the shoulder-length hair . . . laughingly preparing to enter conflict." Palestinian revolutionary fighters and the armed struggle they engaged in became the constituent elements of the national(ist) narrative of the Palestinian imagined community (Matar 2011, 94). So, whether an army in the postcolonial state, the liberation fighter in nationalist musings, the Palestinian peasant, or Khalili and Matar's deliberations on the Palestinian *fedayeen* as a signifier of the nation, they echo my assertion that it is in the act of violence and subsequent tragedy that one is able to find the national being. Nevertheless, the concern here is far more fundamental in that it is basically about naming. Subcomandante Marcos of the EZLN once said that "things exist only when they are named" (Johnston 2000, 466). In the same way, in using violence and its repercussions as a starting point, as recounted by my interlocutors, I suggest that it becomes possible for the Palestinians to see the "light at the end of the tunnel" in the act of simply naming confrontations as *Palestinian* acts of resistance and the suffering as *Palestinian* instances of distress.

Surely, (un-)naming is also inherent in the dynamics of life and politics in Israel-Palestine. As shown in chapter 2, the settler colonial project, by its very nature, strives to establish the settler's homeland in a territory by displacing or *re*placing the indigenous Palestinian community and, in so doing, relegating them to the realm of nonexistence. It is then not surprising that the urge to rename all that was unnamed is a vital facet of the quest for Palestinian liberation and evident in the making potential of violence. This urge to name was unmistakable in the way Bassam, with a sense of euphoria, and Ahmed, with a sense of melancholy, recounted their confrontation with Israeli authorities and found Palestine and their Palestinian-ness in their bodily blemishes. Similarly, Palestine was palpable in the manner in which the Palestinian activist saw synonymy between the commitment to fight and his Palestinian-ness and the manner in which carrying the gun as a member of the al-Qassam Brigade made Muhammad feel good as a *Palestinian* person. Of course, while inducting Hamas into this urge to name, and in arguing for the making potential as fundamental to *its* armed resistance, it may be unrealistic to expect representatives of the organization to engage philosophically with and theorize the making abilities of violence. But, in the claims of Atef Adwan mentioned earlier, or in Ghazi Hamad's assertion that the Islamic Resistance is committed to keeping the "resistance alive in our values [and] cultural outlook" and making sure that "resistance is mentioned in every document of ours," there seems to be an inherent understanding that armed resistance also makes—and not only unmakes—for the colonized. It may be for this same reason that an employee of a Hamas-affiliated media organization once quipped during our interview that "it is good that we have war every two years. In that way we remain popular."[38]

Thus, the consequence of an armed resistance that demonstrates its propensity to make is the emergence of Palestine from its midst. Whether the Palestinian armed struggle that, by means of violence, engages Israel or the pain, suffering, and death that result from it, these acts embody the "familiar properties" of Palestine that then allow Palestinians (and Israelis) to "know it . . . to recognize it [and] to give it value" (Bourdieu 1998, 47). While the denial of a Palestinian homeland, perceived as fundamental to the logic of the settler, is seen as the erasure of the signature of Palestine and Palestinian-ness, armed resistance becomes a canvass for displaying the same Palestinian-ness that in turn arrests the process of un-naming that characterizes the occupation. Here, Mbembe reminds us that "the survivor is the one who has taken on a whole pack of enemies and managed not only to escape alive, but to kill his or her attackers. This is why, to a large extent, the lowest form of survival is killing" (Mbembe 2003, 36). Consequently, a violent confrontation with Israel (aimed at killing) could also be perceived as a Palestinian attempt to survive and, in Deborah Bird Rose's terms, as a means for the colonized to interrupt the settler's project by simply staying at home (Rose 1991, 46). But the characterization of armed resistance provided in this section indicates that its practice is about much more than survival or the urge to "break even" by staying at home. Instead, violence allows Palestinians to gain some ground in the battle against the settler, as the act of naming the armed resistance and the consequent suffering as Palestinian permits the colonized to challenge the settler narrative of Palestinian nonexistence. In doing so, the armed struggle allows the proponents (Palestinians), and forces those perceived to be discontented (Israelis) with the colonized's aspirations, to "know Palestine, recognize Palestine and give Palestine value."

On Palestinian Violence

The enemy has already drawn the sword. He must, therefore, be fought with the sword.

—Subhas Chandra Bose

Is there a sword that hasn't yet been sheathed in our flesh?

—Mahmoud Darwish

In the space between the words of the Indian revolutionary leader Subhas Chandra Bose and the Palestinian poet Mahmoud Darwish lies the entirety of the story of an armed struggle for liberation. Bose, in his words and conduct, personified the violent revolutionary claim for Indian independence from British colonial rule. It is, after all, the euphoric aura around his commitment to the sword that led George E. Jones of the *New York Times* to write, "Indian nationalists are working day and night to build up Bose as the 'George Washington' of India. . . . This is particularly true of the revolutionary element in the Congress party, which spares no efforts to eulogize Bose, create a 'Bose legend' and wrap his sayings and beliefs in sanctity" (Jones 1946).[39] The aura of Darwish's words is evidently far gloomier. Hardly taken by the revolutionary aura of the sword (or the gun), he seems to recognize that, while still in the service of the liberation struggle, the sword is nonetheless sheathed in the losses of the colonized as well. It is thus in recognition of this tragic fate of the colonized and their revolutionary violence that Darwish wrote, "Here on a hill slope facing the sunset and the wide-gaping gun barrel of time near orchards of severed shadows we do as prisoners and the unemployed do: we nurse hope" (Darwish 2010, 3).

In view of my discussions in this chapter, Hamas's armed resistance also seems to be caught between these two perceptions of the colonized's violence. Its revolutionary aura as a means of unmaking the colonial condition was present during the rescue operation at the Rafah border crossing and the attack on Nahal Oz. Evidently the sword, as wielded by Hamas, is often a symbolic being and surely lacks the material capability to unmake the settler colonial condition. Nonetheless, it unmakes through its persistent attacks on the sector of the colonizer. And these attacks, while materially weak, are nonetheless capable of challenging the self-conception of the colonizer and making the settler colonial project difficult to maintain. Yet, echoing Darwish's words, Hamas's sword is also sheathed in the colonized's flesh, as violent encounters with Israel often incur greater Palestinian material and human losses. But, despite the suffering of the colonized, the violence also emerges as an embodiment of the Palestinian cause and Palestinian peoplehood. The act of resistance is called a *Palestinian* act of resistance, and the injuries and deaths that follow become instances of *Palestinian* suffering. As a result, Palestine is recognizable in a way that compels one to declare, "Palestine exists," despite the settler claiming otherwise. In the end, it is best to return to the opening pages of this chapter, where I wrote that I was interested in the stories Palestinians told of resistance. To this end, in this chapter, the discussion of Palestinian armed resistance in general and Hamas's violence in particular has been a discussion of stories. They have been stories of hope, not too different from those told by prisoners and the unemployed in Darwish's writing. Despite the material inability of Hamas's resistance to "win" when faced with Israel's military prowess and its tendency to affect greater Palestinian losses, the colonized attempt to insist on the hopeful fruitfulness of the armed struggle on the path to Palestinian liberation. In the next chapter, I will demonstrate the manner in which the story of the anticolonial struggle echoes, often inadvertently, through Hamas's state-like governance, despite its postcolonial posture and the *lack* of a "real" State of Palestine in the background.

POSTCOLONIAL GOVERNANCE
Imagining Palestine

In late May 2013 I had lunch with a young Palestinian interlocuter at his house in northern Gaza. After a delicious meal of *maqluba* and roast chicken, we moved to the living room. There he pointed to a bullet hole in the wall and remembered the time that an Israeli soldier had shot at his grandmother. The shot was meant to communicate to her that she should move away from the window. Suddenly, we heard a commotion outside. It was an argument between two brothers in the front yard of the neighbor's house. Later I was told that one owed the other four thousand dollars. As we watched, one of the brothers hurried up to the first floor of their house, picked up what looked like a bag of sand and dropped it on a car that was parked in the yard. The bag smashed through the windshield. The other brother and the father then ran up the stairs. They were accompanied by several "concerned" neighbors, looking to diffuse an argument that had clearly gotten out of hand. The women locked the brother who had broken the windshield inside the house, fearing, according to my interlocutor, that his sibling and their father would kill him. With the doors locked and not being able to enter the house, the father took off his shirt. He seemed to be getting ready for something dramatic. In the meantime, the brother outside the house found a gas cylinder, carried it up the stairs and attempted to explode it in front of the locked door. As the neighbors tried to restrain him, a police van pulled up in front of the house. Two police officers came out. Sporting closely cropped "Hamas-beards," wearing black uniforms, and carrying guns, they ran to the brother with the gas cylinder.[1] With a pat on the shoulder and a few words they were able to calm his nerves. A third police officer came out of the van and tried to disperse the crowd that had gathered. The police dragged the brother responsible for breaking the windshield out of the house and put him in their van. The women of the house screamed and cried, distraught at the possibility of a torturous night ahead for one of their sons in a Hamas police cell. As the police van left the scene, the crowd slowly dispersed.

During my time in Gaza, such incidents were not unusual. Cases of depression, domestic violence, and PTSD had increased exponentially since the start of the siege. Speaking to me over the phone in early 2015, a Hamas spokesperson had said, "Increase in unemployment rate and poverty has had a huge impact. The father cannot fulfill obligations. This has caused the mother to leave, file for divorce or has led to domestic violence."[2] He continued, "Then, you have Palestinian extended families who live in one house, say, fourteen people, and this [the siege] has increased friction. You also have hatred between brother and brother because of their different political affiliations."[3] Similarly, while speaking of the challenges faced by the youth in Gaza, a young Palestinian interviewee said: "Every day here is a struggle to stop yourself from losing your mind. You will notice that the youth in Gaza often go to university, and then on the side they do internships, volunteer, or set up organizations. All this is done to remain occupied mentally and delay the inevitable point when you lose it."[4]

Maybe what I was witnessing here was a family "losing it." In a sense, the feud confirmed that this colonized sector was indeed cast in the Fanonian image of life under colonization. The Gaza Strip I experienced was, after all, congested, starving, on its knees, and seemingly ready to tear itself apart from within. Moreover, as I have argued in the previous chapter, it is this "naked declivity" (Fanon 1952, 2) of the colonized's lives that makes armed resistance—informed by the "muscular dreams" of decolonization—an instinctive statement of rejection against the suffering that permeates Palestinian lives. But the manner in which the family dispute I witnessed ended also brought to fore another image of this colonized sector. When the armed policemen entered the scene in a situation of chaos, reined in the brother with the gas cylinder with just a pat on the shoulder, and then left with the "culprit," we were also given a glimpse of a statelike authority. The ending of the fight thus stood in stark contrast to the disarray that presumably informs life in Gaza. The armed policemen evoked the image of order as representatives of a state that wanted to ensure that its citizens respected its authority.

Naturally, the realities of life in the shadows of a persistent siege and Israel's settler colonialism, that lie in the background of this statecraft, make it problematic to apply the concept of a sovereign state to my experience in northern Gaza without further qualification. Further, given the lack of a clearly demarcated territorial mandate and the multiplicity of often competing armed factions, one may be compelled to characterize the Palestinian territories in general and the Gaza Strip in particular as less an embodiment of the ideals of the state and more a feature of the raw anarchy against which the state is meant to act as a vanguard (Hobbes 1651). That said, and as I have already argued in chapter 3, it was the Oslo Accords that established Palestinian postcoloniality by instituting the Palestinian Authority in the image of the forthcoming State of Palestine. And, while it may not "fit" the image of a "normal" state, the Palestinian Authority is not unlike the postcolonial state in that the latter is also characterized by arbitrary borders, the limited legitimacy of the sovereign authority, and a riotous citizenry. Therefore, the "problem" here is not that it displays the features of a state, albeit in the postcolonial variant. Instead, the puzzle lies in the manner in which the postcoloniality of the Palestinian Authority resides in the settler colonial condition. In other words, how does the postcolonial state persist in a political condition that, in the absence of a "real" state, has also prompted an anticolonial struggle? In what follows I therefore consider the manner in which the Hamas-led Palestinian Authority in the Gaza Strip (along with its postcoloniality) functions and finds resonance in the era of settler colonialism.

"Thinking" about the State

How are we to study a state that does not exist? When, at a conference in Vienna, I proposed "bringing back" the state into the study of Palestinian politics (Sen 2015a), one of those attending said, "We know that there is no state. That is why there is a liberation struggle. The PA [Palestinian Authority] is not a Palestinian state . . . why should we study something that doesn't exist?" She was echoing the existing disenchantment with the Palestinian Authority, a disenchantment premised on what I suggested earlier was the Oslo-mandated institution's propensity to circumscribe the liberation struggle and bureaucratize it. Given that a 2013 poll found that fewer than a third of Palestinians considered the Palestinian Authority to be an achievement and that, in a 2019 poll, 60 percent of Palestinians wanted President Mahmoud Abbas to resign, this disenchantment is largely generalizable across the Palestinian territories (Palestinian Center for Policy and Survey 2013, Palestinian Center for Policy and Survey 2019). Yet, its lack of legitimacy does not efface the materiality of the Palestinian Authority that has allowed it—albeit, to varying degrees—to arbitrate the political and economic life of Palestinians.

This materiality of the Palestinian Authority is an outcome of the post-Oslo political and financial investments made by international donors and stakeholders in the "upkeep" of its statelike institutional structures and bureaucracies (Pace and Sen 2019) and, as shown by the family dispute in northern Gaza, in its ability to exercise a modicum of the Weberian monopoly of violence. The investments began with the first donor conference in Washington, DC, held on October 1, 1993, at which forty-three donor countries raised four billion dollars to support "the historic political breakthrough in the Middle East [namely, the Oslo Accords] through a broad-based multilateral effort to mobilize resources to promote reconstruction and development in the West Bank and Gaza" (Brynen 2000, 3).

As financial contributions have grown significantly over the years, the donor commitments have been increasingly focused on building and sustaining the institutions and bureaucracies of the Palestinian Authority (Le More 2004, 210). For instance, as the single largest donor, the European Union (EU) earmarks funds for public-sector salaries, institution building, infrastructural development, and through an EU Police Mission in the Palestinian Territories, or EUPOL COPPS, the building of an efficient police force and criminal justice system. In 2008 the EU established the Mecanisme Palestino-Européen de Gestion et d'Aide Socio-Economique, or PEGASE, to provide direct financial support to the Palestinian Authority. In keeping with the Palestinian Recovery and Development Program Trust Fund's goals of institution building and reform (World Bank 2019), PEGASE's contributions aim to ensure that the Palestinian Authority is fiscally sustainable and capable of providing efficient public services (PEGASE 2017). Similarly, the mandate of EUPOL COPPS is to ensure "civilian police primacy" by training the Palestinian Civilian Police as an institution capable of "upholding law and order" (EUPOL COPPS 2014). This impetus for aid delivery is also evident in the United States' contributions to Palestine. While the humanitarian aid distributed through the initiatives of the U.S. Agency for International Development (USAID) and the need to combat Palestinian terrorism remain prominent political (and financial) priorities, the United States also provides budgetary contributions to the Palestinian Authority, as well as budgetary support for nonlethal assistance to the security sector and the criminal justice system (Zanotti 2018).

Such financial contributions have enriched the statelike qualities of the institutions of the Palestinian Authority and provided the Palestinian governing faction with the material wherewithal to pose as a state authority. As a consequence, the Palestinian Authority ostensibly encompasses all the essential facets of a functioning state. It has an executive branch headed by the president of the Palestinian Authority. The Palestinian Legislative Council fulfills legislative functions and is concerned with "administrative, regulatory, commercial and financial matters, issues pertaining to lands and services including health and education and political issues (e.g. elections, transference of powers and authorities, etc.)." The Palestinian Authority has a judicial system that includes "regular, religious and special courts" and a Supreme Court of Justice that arbitrates administrative disputes (Al-Muqtafi 2019). It also prepares its own budget for each fiscal year in accordance with Article 61 (Item 1) of the Basic Law, which functions as the temporary Palestinian constitution and requires the Palestinian government to submit a draft of the national budget to the Palestinian Legislative Council a minimum of two months before the start of the financial year (Palestinian Basic Law 2007). And, given that taxation plays an important role in fostering intrastate resource mobilization and the stimulation of state–society relations, the Palestinian Authority also enforces a tax law and collects personal income tax, corporate income tax, indirect taxes on domestic goods and services, property taxes, and taxes on international transactions (Fjeldstad and Zagha 2004, 194–199).[5]

This materiality has also translated into a situation where the Palestinian Authority has an unmistakable presence and, despite its inadequacies, one routinely encounters an institution that postures very much like a state in day-to-day matters. In the chapter 1, for instance, I described my encounter with this state at the Palestinian terminal of the Rafah border crossing, where the governing authority engages in the rituals that states often carry out at borders. As I mentioned in chapter 3, my time in Gaza also coincided with the last months of Muhammad Morsi's leadership in Egypt, which ended in the coup of 2013. Given the fact that access to the Gaza Strip through the Rafah border crossing is contingent on the ebb and flow of the political tides (and will) in Egypt and Israel, during my stay I was inundated with panicked rumors that the Egyptian army might close the border crossing. Yet, despite the evident lack of sovereignty over its borders, the governing authority in Gaza persisted with the rituals of statecraft, and much like other foreigners, I was required to register with the Internal Protection Unit (IPU) before departing from the Gaza Strip through the Rafah crossing. The presence of the state was similarly evident in my conversations in the field. During an interview with a prominent Palestinian businessman in Gaza City, I asked him to assess the economic performance of the Hamas government. Fearing retribution from Hamas, he responded, "Look, I can't be part of this officially. I don't trust these Hamas people, and what I would say may be used against me." When I agreed to conceal his identity, he said, "I have a business, so naturally the unpredictable border crossing and shortage of supplies are problems. You also have repeated Israeli attacks that make doing business very difficult." Then, specifically addressing the challenges of conducting business in the Gaza

Strip, he continued, "We have a problem with governance as well. Things are very arbitrary. We don't know how or why we are being taxed.[6] And solving problems is hampered by unnecessary bureaucracy." I asked, "Have you specifically been affected by this?" He responded, "All the time. But what we are dealing with is corruption. For example, my son owns another business, and he was robbed. He lost everything. We went to the police, but nothing happened. We are not *their* people, so we don't get any help."[7]

Interestingly, the businessman began by recognizing an overarching settler colonial condition, characterized not least by the unpredictable border crossings, the lack of supplies, and the incessant threat of Israeli military attack. Yet, he swiftly turned to judging the Hamas governing authority as a state, a "normal" state that is expected to engage in good governance, combat corruption, minimize unnecessary bureaucracy, and abide by the tax laws. In the same vein, during our interview a representative of a Palestinian professional union also began by describing the impact of the siege on economic life in Gaza. He said, "Uncertainty is the main problem here in Gaza. Tomorrow we don't know what will happen. Maybe there will be war. Of course, then you have closures and the division between Gaza and the West Bank." Yet, when I asked him how the current crisis could be alleviated, he voiced an expectation that the economic policies of the Hamas-led Palestinian Authority in the Gaza Strip should mirror those of a "normal" state: "One of the problems is banking. There are no agreements between the banks and the government, and that makes it difficult to get loans for businesses. Then, they [Hamas] say that they want to work with the private sector, but decisions are often made unilaterally, and we get the feeling that when they consult us, they have already made their decision." I interjected, "So, is there a way for Palestinian businesses to complain to the government?" He smiled, "It depends on who you are. I, for example, have met Ismael Haniyeh [the prime minister at the time] twice. That's how it works here in Gaza."[8]

Given its materiality *as* a state, it is hardly surprising that academic discussion about the Palestinian Authority also tends to judge it on the basis of its ability to mirror the normal (democratic) state. The "conversation" began with, among others, Robinson (1997), Frisch (1998) and Sayigh (1997a; 1997b) deliberating on the trajectory of the Palestinian struggle from a revolutionary claim to a homeland to state building. As the interim state persisted following the Oslo Accords, others assessed the Palestinian Authority's ability to function and fulfill its roles as a state, despite the *lack* of a "real" State of Palestine in the background. Parsons (2005) studied the institutional developments under the guise of the Palestinian Authority; Cobham and Kanafani's collection (2004) focused on the economics of Palestinian state building; and Khan, Giacaman, and Amundsen's anthology (2004) assessed the ability of the Palestinian Authority to practice good governance. Similarly, policy-oriented works have discussed the need for institutional and security sector reforms in the Palestinian territories (RAND 2005, Sayigh 2009). Criticism of Hamas's governance was also raised on the basis of its adoption of the preexisting governance apparatuses, the (re-)building of the Palestinian Authority's institutions, and the government's relationship with civil society organizations in the Gaza Strip (Knudsen 2010, Brown 2012)

To their credit, these works have provided an intricate understanding of state-craft in the post-Oslo Palestinian territories. Moreover, the materiality of this state may have compelled them to judge the Palestinian Authority, perhaps with a dose of wishful thinking, in light of what it was meant to become—namely, a sovereign, viable, and democratic State of Palestine that can be held accountable for its conduct. There is, of course, some value in judging the behavior of say the officials at the IPU or the armed policemen in northern Gaza in terms of their ability to abide by the modes of conduct expected from representatives of a democratic state. However, the foundational "problem" that this postcolonial state lives in a colonial nonstate context remains unexplored. As was evident in my conversation with the Palestinian businessman and the representative of the union, it would not be enough simply to recognize, as do the works discussed above, that state building in the Palestinian territories is hindered by a persistent settler colonial condition. Both respondents began their discussion of the economic climate in Gaza by mentioning the impact of the siege. Yet, they subsequently went on to criticize Hamas's performance as an arbitrator of economic life on the basis of the quality of its governance without making allowances for the overarching colonial condition. The fact that they emphasized the need for the government in Gaza to behave as one would expect a future State of Palestinian to conduct itself, while also recognizing the existence of an overarching colonial condition, underlines the need to analyze this state and the colonial condition in which it exists as part of the *same* conversation. Therefore, returning to my initial query: "How are we to study a state that does not exist?" I recognize that the materiality of the attendant rituals and institutions of the Palestinian Authority makes the "image of the state" (Lund 2006, 689) a qualifier for the manner in which one Palestinian faction (i.e., Hamas) conducts itself as a government. Yet, also recognizing the existence of the settler colonial condition in its background, my aim here is not to assess "how much" or "little" the Palestinian Authority acts like a state (Sen 2015a). Instead, the discussion that follows seeks rather to judge its statecraft for the manner in which it is rationalized by both the anticolonial faction that administers this state (i.e., Hamas in government) and the colonized recipients who encounter it in their everyday lives (i.e., Palestinians in Gaza). In both cases, of course, they have to do so while contending with Israel's settler colonialism.

"Together We Are Palestine": Hamas and Its Tryst with Statecraft

In chapter 3, I began my discussion of the Oslo Accords with a hasty scribble on a door in Ramallah that declared, "It's Nakbah, Not a Party, Idiots!" In Gaza, given that Hamas had indeed embraced the "party" despite the ongoing Nakba, I often began my conversations with members of the organization by asking, "Why do you govern?" I asked this very question when I sat down with senior Hamas member Ahmed Yousef for our first interview at The House of Wisdom for Conflict Resolution and Governance (HOW) in Gaza.[9] Yousef had been a senior adviser to Hamas prime minister Ismael Haniyeh and is widely considered a "moderate," albeit marginalized voice within the organization. Sitting in a large meeting room with a view of the Gaza coastline, he quietly pondered my question. I then added, "Clearly there is an occupation and siege. So, how does being a government make sense?" To this, Yousef responded,

> These operations were at the core of the beginnings of Hamas as an organization. We focused on building the Palestinian political community and winning the hearts and minds of the people. We wanted to do something for the people and care for them. Educational services were very important. It was a major field of our social services. We also provided financial support with the help of many Muslim countries that helped us in our poor situation. Our social service operations include three fields: *Da'wa* [proselytism], education and youth clubs, and charity organizations. We have had to do a lot of fund-raising work to rebuild all the houses that have been destroyed. It is because of this that Hamas has become so popular. Hamas has been the driving force for charity in Palestine working for the people. As Hamas's popularity grew through publicity and popularity, it became a significant figure in Palestine, and it could not be ignored. In student association and election meetings we started winning and won the confidence of the people through general elections.[10]

A similar argument was made by Hamas leader Atef Adwan when he explained why Hamas governs:

> Hamas's civil wing is one of the bases of this organization. Because of our social service work, our relationships became stronger and created

a brotherhood. This relationship is stronger than the bond of blood. For example, after the election victory and 2007 takeover, the [Fatah-affiliated] PA [Palestinian Authority] employees stopped working in places like schools and hospitals. It is because of this brotherhood and camaraderie that we were able to be in these areas in a week's time. If there was no faith, this would be destroyed so easily.[11]

What Adwan and Yousef were referring to is the legacy of Hamas's social service operations, which are widely recognized for their role in responding to the socioeconomic crisis in the era following the signing of the Oslo Accords (see chapter 3). The organization responded to the steady deterioration in the post-Oslo period by means of its educational, medical, and welfare institutions—a response that won it widespread Palestinian support. Although Islamic values continued to be an undertone of its operations, community development was often addressed in universal terms and geared at remedying the "fractured" being of *all* Palestinians (Roy 2011, 15). In this way, Hamas's social service operations emerged as a political response to a dismal socioeconomic situation. Its social wing acted as an intermediary between the oppressive state (i.e., the Palestinian Authority and Israel) and the citizen (Jensen 2009, 6), plugged a self-evident economic need, and in doing so, also helped build a community and rejuvenated a sense of being a strong Palestinian people able to resist oppression.

It was therefore through its activism on the margins of the Accords that Hamas secured significant victories in local elections in the 1990s (Bhasin and Hallmark 2013, 76). Professional, labor, and student union elections had become the "main site of electoral contestation," and Hamas was able to make electoral gains at the expense of Fatah. Between 1995 and 2006 it won all student elections at universities in Nablus, Hebron, and the Islamic University in Gaza and lost only three times at Birzeit University, which was considered a Fatah stronghold. Of course, Hamas's victories in local elections, while significant in reflecting the political aspirations (and needs) of the masses, were still limited in scope and unable to provide the Islamic Resistance with "real power" (Gunning 2007, 144–145). But as the municipal and legislative elections were reinstated between 2004 and 2006, Hamas secured one-third of the seats primarily in densely populated urban centers. This both indicated a significant shift in the power balance in the Palestinian political landscape and provided a foretaste of the results of the 2006 Palestinian Legislative Council elections.[12]

When it entered the echelons of the Oslo-mandated institutions of governance, Hamas was thus burdened with the public perception that it would maneuver the Palestinian political landscape out of an Oslo Accords–induced era of docility and on to the trajectory of liberation (Abunimah 2006). Not surprisingly, then,

being eager to maintain the organization's credentials as a liberation organization, representatives of the Hamas government emphasized the necessity of *their*
brand of governance as the path to Palestinian liberation. Yet, the problem of
maintaining an anticolonial armed resistance while posturing like a state that has
yet to become was not lost on Hamas members either. Recognizing this "problem" during our conversation, Atef Adwan acknowledged, "It posed a great challenge when we won the elections in 2006. We now had to go and support all the
people in Gaza and fight." I then asked him, "Since it is difficult, why doesn't
Hamas *just* fight and give up governance?" Adwan replied,

> Because of the 2006 elections, we now have an obligation to be both
> a government and resistance and therefore didn't give up. But while
> fighting is important, what does fighting mean if you can't govern
> yourself? What is the meaning of liberation? If we look at the old rulers
> [Fatah] . . . there was a huge divide between the rulers and the fight-
> ers. They were fighting amongst themselves and causing problems for
> the fighters. The people were fed up and wanted [us] to get rid of this
> system. One can say that over the last seven years, even though it is diffi-
> cult, Hamas has been a good government and resistance, and therefore
> people are on our side. . . . We are now here to help them with whatever
> they need. And we will help them as much as possible. I say to them:
> "We will protect you."[13]

In his characterization of what Hamas does as the government in Gaza, Adwan
covers a lot of ground in a manner that is all-encompassing and argues that ruling as a government, fighting as a resistance organization, and liberation are the
inescapable facets of a singular struggle. In seeing resistance in everything and
everything as resistance, he seems to echo the Hamas deputy speaker of the Palestinian Legislative Council Ahmad Bahar, who claimed that a master's thesis
on water purification held the potential to liberate Jerusalem (see chapter 4).
Yet, I see three specific modes of conceptualization in Adwan's understanding of
Hamas's governance. First, he established an unambiguous relationship between
governance and resistance by claiming that it was Hamas's responsibility as government to protect the resistance. Adwan was not the only one to view the role
of government in this manner. While listing the many responsibilities of Hamas,
Fawzi Barhoum also asserted: "We need to provide protection so that the resistance can carry out its activities without any problem."[14] Wesam Afifa, director
general of the Hamas-affiliated Al-Resalah media organization, confirmed the
same. He said, "Some in the movement justify being in government, saying that
being in power strengthens the liberation movement. The government becomes
a cover for the liberation movement. It's a sort of political protection. Earlier

the PA [Palestinian Authority] used to crack down on the movement. Now the government is there to help and support the liberation."[15]

Yaser Abu Heen, the chief editor of the pro-Hamas Palestinian Press Agency, or SAFA, also emphasized that governing was a means of protecting the resistance.[16] Before the interview, an acquaintance had already informed me that, besides working for a pro-Hamas media institution, Abu Heen was also "very connected with Hamas through his family." Then, with *misbaha* (prayer beads) in his hand and a closely cropped "Hamas beard," Abu Heen met me in his office in Gaza City. When asked to reflect on Hamas's role as the government, he said, "It was very difficult to balance government and resistance. The boycott was stupid and did not help the situation . . . but today things are better, and people can expect the same in the future. Today the government and resistance are part of each other." I then asked him, "What do you mean by 'part of each other'? Are you saying that the government and resistance are merged together?" Such a claim would be particularly provocative given that Hamas's official position is that operationally each wing of the Islamic Resistance is a self-contained unit. Further, the organization compartmentalized its operations in the 1990s in order escape complete "decapitation" by Israeli forces (Wiegand 2010, 127; Gunning 2007, 40). It is this compartmentalization that led the former deputy chairman of Hamas's Political Bureau Mousa Abu Marzook to claim in his 1997 interview with journalist Roger Gaess, "There is no contact between the political wing and the military wing, just as there is no contact between either of them and the people on Hamas's education or health staff. Each wing of Hamas is independent and works according to its own ideas" (Gaess 1997, 115). Unsurprisingly, Abu Heen swiftly rejected my suggestion, saying instead, "No, absolutely not. They are separate, but the government provides protection to the resistance. We have a formula for doing both operations." I interjected, "What is this formula? Do you prioritize one over the other?" He replied, "They are both important. The government helps create a strong society, and without a strong society, liberation cannot be achieved."[17]

Here, when contextualized in light of my earlier discussion of the Oslo Accords' attempt to bureaucratize and introduce postcoloniality into the political conduct of Palestinian armed factions, such an answer to "why we [Hamas] *need* to govern" is understandable. Nigel Parsons argued that the Palestinian Authority's policing mechanisms were another "way in which Israeli forces circumscribe Palestinian society" and its attendant struggle for liberation (Parsons 2010, 73). Before the 2006 elections these mechanisms included deportations, arrests, and targeted assassinations (Milton-Edwards and Crooke 2004). The postelection boycott, siege, and wars faced by Hamas, Sayigh (2007) explained, induced a failed state. Consequently, for my Hamas interviewees, the government and its commitment to protecting the resistance represented the continuance of the colonized's struggle to hinder the colonizer's project that aims to "socialize" the former into its schemes (Parsons 2010, 73). It was, after all, in an attempt to hinder such schemes that Hamas purged the Palestinian Authority's security sector after the 2006 Palestinian Legislative Council elections by disbanding the Presidential Guard and the Preventive Security Force. In doing so, the organization hoped to create "a new reality, new police, new security apparatus, [and] a new, legitimate judiciary" (International Crisis Report 2007, 18).

This leads to the second mode of conceptualization in the anticolonial faction's view of the role of governance in the era of colonization. Both Adwan's question, "What does fighting mean if you can't govern yourself?" and Abu Heen's claim that "the government helps create a strong society" premise Hamas's *need* to govern on governance's perceived ability to build a Palestinian society that is materially capable of withstanding the trials of a liberation struggle and is culturally attuned to the values of the resistance. Explaining this function of Hamas's governance, spokesperson Salama Maroof said,

> From the very first day in power, Hamas's slogan was, "fight occupation and serve Palestinian society." Being in government has allowed us to put this principle of resistance in every aspect of Palestinian society. For example, it builds a resistance economy. On the one hand, we see it as a way of helping the Palestinian people affected by occupation and Israel's wars on Gaza. But in doing so, we were also able to spread the values of resistance among the people here. So, Hamas has a strategy of resistance [against Israel], but as a government that is able to make sure that the same culture [of resistance] is present among the people.[18]

Maroof was unequivocal in his perception of Hamas's role as the government. For him, by serving the people and fighting for liberation, the Islamic Resistance at the helm of the Palestinian Authority was able to ensure that the culture of resistance could penetrate *all* aspects of Palestinian life. This Hamas government would foster a resistance society, a society capable of resisting the Israeli occupation. Fawzi Barhoum, in comparison to Maroof, was far more hesitant in his claims. When asked to explain why Hamas chooses to govern, he noted, "We are not happy that we are in this position. It's very difficult, and it was not easily successful. How to run the lives of the people during times of war?" But subsequently, citing Hamas's election victory as a mandate to espouse the role of government while still maintaining its posture of armed resistance, he added, "We have remained in government because the people want us to rule and fight. And we provide a service. During war we make sure that people receive salaries and that there is no crime, even though police stations were bombed. In the end we showed that there is no resistance without governance and no governance without resistance."[19]

The synonymy proposed by Hamas officials between resistance and government is not merely a rhetorical tool meant to hint at an abstract all-encompassing battle for Palestinian liberation. Historically, Hamas has maintained a dual operational profile, both socio-civilian and military, in respect of its liberation struggle (Gunning 2007; Mishal and Sela 2000). Moreover, during my fieldwork this synonymy inadvertently became apparent when Hamas's resistance activities led to Israeli military assaults on its governance institutions. While in Gaza, I frequently passed by Palestinian Authority police stations and government buildings, physical embodiments of the organization's role as a government, that were targeted and destroyed by Israeli attacks. A similar reality was evident on my way to the interview with Ghazi Hamad. The taxi picked me up from my apartment at 8:30 a.m. and when I told the driver that I needed to go to the Ministry of Foreign Affairs, he seemed to know its location. Fifteen minutes later we arrived at a building compound, but there was no sign of the ministry. The driver got out to ask for directions. When he came back, he said, "It's a different place. Every time Israel attacks the building they move to a new address." During my tour of the Hamas summer camp (see chapter 3), it was also apparent to me that Hamas's governance is never entirely isolated from the repercussions of its resistance when I walked into a room where a Palestinian Authority policeman was giving a presentation on traffic rules and regulations in Gaza. When I asked my Hamas-appointed translator if I could take a picture, he replied, "It is not a good idea. We have to be careful of his security because Israel targets our policemen."[20]

However, irrespective of whether the all-encompassing notion of governance (and resistance) is one that Hamas espouses of its own accord or one that is forced on the organization as a result of Israeli hostilities, it also suggests an organization that, as a government, is keen on asserting its own leadership over the political landscape in Gaza. Here, the third mode of conceptualization of governance emerges in the "we"—as in, "we will protect the resistance," "we have a formula for doing both [governing and protecting the resistance]," "we . . . help the Palestinian people," "we . . . spread the values of resistance." Through the "we," members of the organization I interviewed claimed a sense of leadership whereby Hamas was able and willing to protect the resistance. Yet, in doing so, the "we" signifying Hamas also became the collective "we" signifying all Palestinians, whereby all those it protected and rejuvenated were beholden to its vision and strategies.

Since Hamas's complete takeover of Gaza, it has frequently demonstrated a willingness, often publicly and forcibly, to assert its leadership. One of my

Palestinian interlocutors relayed brutal accounts of members of the organization shooting Fatah fighters in the kneecaps during the War for Gaza in 2007. Another interlocutor noted that, immediately after consolidating its control over the Strip, Hamas confiscated weapons from all non-authorized personnel, namely those not affiliated with Hamas Palestinian Authority security officials or resistance factions. Most residential buildings, cafes, offices, and hotels now carry a sign that reads "No guns allowed" (figure 5.1). Of course, with armed Hamas Palestinian Authority policemen a common sight in Gaza, it is as if the sign says, "No guns allowed, except those held by Hamas." In the same way, we could also look to Hamas's public execution of spies during Operation Protective Edge as a demonstration of its commitment to consolidating its position as the sole authority in the Gaza Strip (Akram and Rudoren 2014).

The urge to impose its authority is most obvious when one witnesses Hamas operatives' responses to acts of insubordination to its public authority in Gaza. Opposition to Hamas is often relegated to dingy cafes in decrepit buildings and the living rooms of Fatah officials, where detractors are happy to privately deride the moral bankruptcy of the resistance but dare not speak out in public. While conducting fieldwork in the Gaza Strip, there was however a rare occasion when

FIGURE 5.1   "No guns allowed." Gaza City, Gaza Strip. Photo by author.

dissent and discontent managed to ascend into the public realm. One afternoon in June 2013, as I sat on the balcony of my apartment in Gaza City trying to escape the scorching summer heat during a power outage, I heard voices chanting in unison at a distance. I looked out into the street and noticed a funeral procession for a Popular Front for the Liberation of Palestine "martyr." At the end of the street two armed Hamas Palestinian Authority police officers watched with interest but refrained from intervening. As the procession turned the corner and entered al-Shati refugee camp I heard gunshots, presumably fired in commemoration of the fallen "martyr." The policemen immediately ran to the scene with their guns pointing at the crowd and, with a few warning shots in the air, they dispersed the mourners. In doing so, they quelled any semblance of doubt in either my mind or those of the rebellious that in the Gaza Strip it is "we" as Hamas that "make the world go round."[21]

The same urge to uphold Hamas's authority and claim that "*we* make the world go round" in Gaza also appeared in my conversations with officials of the Islamic Resistance. During our interview, in between questions and while referencing a recent skirmish between the Islamic Jihad Movement in Palestine and Palestinian Authority policemen in Shuja'iyya, Adwan noted in passing, "What they [Islamic Jihad] don't understand is that you cannot work outside the control of the government. We will protect them [but] we fight together, and we declare truce together."[22] In my discussion with Ahmed Yousef, a similar, but not as paternalistic mode of argumentation was apparent when he said, "What Hamas is trying to do is work hand in hand. Instead of each faction doing something different, we have the difficult task of making sure they are working in coordination. We have to encourage them to cooperate." I then asked him, "How can Hamas do this?" Yousef replied, "We should create a cabinet that Hamas coordinates and ensure that other factions are part of it. Then we can make sure that there is a working strategy. In this forum we can discuss and solve the internal clashes."[23] Barhoum similarly concluded, "We have to make sure there is security coordination and collaboration during resistance activities with organizations such as Islamic Jihad."[24]

At least publicly, Hamas affiliates and members perceived governance as integral to the path to liberation. For them, the government is a means of protecting resistance fighters and rejuvenating a Palestinian population that finds itself materially and culturally starved under the gaze of an occupation. Yet, in doing so, much like any other political faction, it lays claim to a leading role for itself, as if to state that it is only the Islamic Resistance that possesses the appropriate vision for liberation. For the Italian journalist Paola Caridi, *this* Hamas, having come into existence following the 2006 Palestinian Legislative Council elections, is a testament to the tragically fractured nature of the Palestinian political landscape. In the "emotional epilogue" to her book, she wrote that the "war of flags" between Hamas's green and Fatah's yellow "epitomized the core issue of the post-Arafat era in Palestine: the inability to share power" (Caridi 2012, 324). Thus, for the author, the dominance of Hamas's green over the Gaza Strip today is just an illustration of the emergence of an authoritarian organization that emphasizes its control over all facets of Palestinian life in the Gaza Strip.

There is certainly no doubt that Hamas has demonstrated authoritarian tendencies since 2006. The assassination of spies, for example, reflects the brutally authoritarian means Hamas is willing to employ against traitors. Similarly, the authoritarian ways of the Islamic Resistance were confirmed by my nonpolitically affiliated Palestinian interviewees. During an interview, a Gaza-based journalist Nasser said, "You have to know that there are no rights here in Gaza. You are not allowed to have an opinion. If you are critical, you will definitely be targeted."[25] Nasser's claim seemed to be echoed by another Palestinian journalist. During our conversation, she routinely referred to the siege, war, and Israel's attacks on Palestinian journalists and the media infrastructure in Gaza as challenges she faced in her professional life. Yet, when I asked her, "Do you face any problems from people or political factions within Gaza?" I noticed an immediate sense of nervousness in her conduct. She replied, "This is a dangerous question. I'm not sure what you want me to say," thus hinting that Palestinian journalists have much to fear from within a Hamas-controlled Gaza Strip as well (Sen 2013c).[26] It was therefore not inaccurate of Nathan Brown to conclude, in his evaluation of Hamas's five years in power, that the Islamic Resistance was engaging in a "softer version of Arab authoritarianism" (Brown 2012, 3).

However, Hamas's use of censorious violence against its political detractors within the colonized's sector is hardly an anomaly in liberation contexts. During his testimony to the South African Truth and Reconciliation Commission in Johannesburg in 1996, Sergeant Olefile Samuel Mngpibisa of the South African National Defense Force (SANDF) did not talk about the atrocities of the apartheid regime. Instead, he recounted the following experience of being incarcerated at an African National Congress (ANC) prison camp in Angola:

> I love the ANC because the ANC is the people. . . . Individuals within the ANC abused their powers and they must be exposed. They hide behind the ANC and continue with their criminal activities. I once more lastly appeal to President Mandela to please take action against those who abused us in exile. This will help in healing our land. Perpetrators must be brought in front of the TRC in our presence, so that we (can) question them. (Cleveland 2005, 63)

In Algeria, the FLN (Front de Libération Nationale, or National Liberation Front) frequently engaged in disciplinary violence against Muslim Algerians who were "suspected of collaborating with the colonial state." In September 1960, in the western Algerian village of Ouled Bouchena, this violence caused the death of four men whose throats were slit with a knife. Another villager died in the hospital as result of facial amputations—having had his ears, nose, tongue and upper lip cut off (Boserup 2009, 247–248). But while for Caridi the "war of flags" was solely a testament to the inability of Palestinian factions to share power and, for Nasser, embodied the reality that it was impossible to have an opinion against the Islamic Resistance in Gaza, a far more nuanced image of the government emerges when its conduct as both government and resistance are treated as part of *same* conversation. For my Hamas-affiliated interviewees, when the organization entered the realm of official politics, it did so *as* a liberation organization. That is to say, while its governance activities alone are testament to a Palestinian faction consolidating its political authority, for the organization itself, a continued commitment to the armed struggle ensures that its anticolonial subjectivity travels with it and infiltrates the realm of official politics. Consequently, Hamas's green flags alternated with Palestinian flags along some of the major roads in the Gaza Strip, and its propensity to censor opposition became a pertinent reflection of what a government on the path to liberation is and does. Of course, this arrangement of the flags, which was presumably "approved" by the leadership in Gaza, is a bold public statement proclaiming that "Hamas is Palestine and Palestine is Hamas." Similarly, by publicly censoring critical voices, the organization seems to declare that in Gaza it is the Islamic Resistance that "makes the world go round." However, as Hamas adopts the institutions of the eventual Palestinian state as an armed liberation faction, it injects what Rasmus Boserup terms the "anticolonial perspective" into institutions and bureaucracies (namely, the Palestinian Authority) that have thus far been deemed complicit with the aspirations of the colonizer (Boserup 2009, 241).

In his study of collective violence and counter–state building in Algeria, Boserup demonstrated the manner in which the FLN, in the war against the French colonizer and the Muslim "traitor" at home, went on to consolidate its position as the embodiment of the eventual Algerian state. Moreover, in doing so, it appropriated and redefined the categories, ideologies, and taxonomies of the colonial state as a way of both countering it and engaging in its own counter–state building. Thus, the colonial state was now cast in the image and aspirations of the Algerian national community (Boserup 2009, 255–256). Similarly, when Hamas espoused the role of the government and the institutions of the Palestinian Authority that it was now mandated to administer, it also adopted the institutions, mechanism, bureaucracies, ideologies, and political norms of the colonizer and its Palestinian partner ("the traitor"). This would especially seem to be the case since the Palestinian Authority and its postcoloniality were meant to "convince" Palestinian factions of the futility of continuing the anti-colonial struggle (see chapter 3). But, while its critics would claim that, through its authoritarian tendencies, the organization has adopted the modus operandi of the colonial state, Hamas itself perceives its role as the government as one it adopted as a *liberation* faction, in a manner similar to Boserup's categorization of counter–state building. Accordingly, members of the organization view the Islamic Resistance as having appropriated that which was meant to dismantle the resistance, reconstituted it to serve as a means of facilitating the resistance, and subsequently, inducted the role of government and all that it administers into the path of the national struggle.

In this way, while the Oslo-mandated realm of official politics was meant to discourage the Palestinian liberation movement, it is now perceived by Hamas as a canvas on which to display a counternarrative. Accordingly, the unavoidable materiality and pervasive presence of statelike institutions in every aspect of Palestinian life is reimagined for the purposes of the anticolonial struggle. And, like the FLN that fought against the internal enemy as a way of embodying the singular Algerian state, Hamas's paternalistic mode of engagement with other Palestinian factions, its urge to protect (and regulate) all liberation activities, and its propensity to quell discontent also reflect a similar eagerness to embody the eventual Palestinian state. Here, we are once again reminded of Fanon's claim that the violent anticolonial struggle was capable of inducting liberation factions into a "common cause, national destiny, and collective history." Hamas, of course, sees itself as embodying a singular cause, destiny, and history. But, by unifying Palestinians as one under its governance, it also puts Palestinian factions on a "single direction," which it perceives as a way of unifying the nation and rendering the eventual Palestine indivisible even in the era of colonial rule (Fanon 1963, 50). Thus, as the organization proposes an all-encompassing notion of governance, it also presents a vision whereby the entirety of Palestine comes together under its leadership as a singular people, informed by the same history, driven by the same cause, and headed for the same destiny. For Caridi and some of my non-Hamas interlocutors, doing this may epitomize the Palestinian faction's inability to share power, but for Hamas it is a means of ensuring that it is under the auspices of its green flag that the Palestinian national community comes into being and becomes synonymous with the State of Palestine.

"Witnessing" Hamas, "Seeing" Palestine

It is not surprising that an anticolonial faction insists that it is still committed to the ethos of the liberation struggle while attempting to govern and discipline the economic and political lives of the colonial subject—especially, when many consider the institutions of governance to be an extension of the colonial state. But, despite the unequivocal manner in which the anticolonial faction makes this assertion, Fanon reminds us that the path to liberation is rarely straightforward. Instead, just as the national consciousness pioneered by the national bourgeoisie reveals "cracks in the [ideological] edifice" (Fanon 1963, 149), so too does Hamas's conception of muqawama display cracks in *its* edifice.

Ironically, though, these cracks were often revealed by those from within the cohort of Hamas affiliates and members I met in the Gaza Strip. Wesam Afifa, despite being the director general of a Hamas-affiliated media organization, admitted a certain dilemma in Hamas governing while still engaged in an anticolonial armed resistance. He said,

> The question is what comes first: building a state or liberation? Today we have a government, but it's a government without a state. And this principle is a problem of Oslo. For people in Gaza, the normal people, liberation is the most important, but what combination should we have? Not [like the] West Bank, of course. The problem now is that we don't have a term of reference. Neither are we part of the Palestinian Liberation Organization and neither are we part of the Palestinian Authority.[27]

It is particularly revealing that Afifa ended with the expression "neither are we . . . neither are we." When I think back to my interactions with Hamas officials, they often embodied this "neither . . . nor." Donning the suit, they postured like official representatives of a state that does not exist. Yet, they still celebrated the potency of army fatigues and insisted that anticolonial violence was an essential tool in their struggle for an independent state. When I specifically asked Ghazi Hamad about this dilemma, he responded by saying, "The Oslo Accords were a hypocrisy for us. It gave us a ruse of a state." I then felt compelled to ask, "Then *why* does Hamas work within this ruse?" Not as resolute in his subsequent tone, Hamad conceded, "The problem also is that everything today is on the basis of the institutions of the Palestinian Authority. Because of this, it is not easy to dismantle it and go back. The peace process has failed. So, what should we do? Should we get rid of the Palestinian Authority? We can't."[28] That Hamad seems to have become resigned to a condition of being "neither [this] . . . nor [that]" reminds us that this condition is emblematic of the postcoloniality that was imposed on the Palestinian political landscape by the Oslo Accords. I concluded chapter 3 by arguing that the state of postcoloniality introduced by the Accords was above all a state of confusion. But, how does the colonial subject make sense of this in-between, confused, and contradictory postcoloniality? For an answer, let us look at three accounts of colonized Palestinians' encounters with Hamas's practices of governance.

The first is an incident related to me by Ahmed, who I introduced in chapter 4 as a victim of a violent encounter with Israeli forces protecting a settlement in Gaza during the Second Intifada—an encounter that had left him scarred for life. But during my fieldwork in Gaza in 2013, Ahmed was also a victim of the violence of the Hamas government. At the time, given the traumatic nature of his experience, I realized that it would be unethical to ask Ahmed to recount his experience in an interview. However, a year later, I asked him to describe the events of that night. In an email, I received the following description,

> In the summer of 2013, I was relaxing on the beach with some of my friends at a small beach resort in Gaza. It was almost 2:00 a.m. when we decided to leave. While we were halfway home, our taxi was stopped at a Hamas police checkpoint. It was an irregular checkpoint. We sat in the car for approximately five minutes hoping that they would let us pass, but they did not even bother to check on us. I got stressed and started calling for the police to come and let us go. A policeman finally came to us and asked me to step off the car and then started searching me physically. I was upset and asked him to stop. He did not. I felt that it was not his right to carry out such a procedure since I'm not a suspect and wasn't caught doing anything illegal. . . . I tried to explain to him that what he was doing was not right. Then, his "boss" came along and was furious that I had challenged the authority of the police. Suddenly, the policeman hit me in the face. My glasses fell down and broke. They asked me to stand by a wall. I refused. They pulled me by my shirt and put me inside the police car. Then, a policeman came along and explained to me that the checkpoint was meant to capture drug dealers who they have been trying to capture for many years. He said it was my fault that I had acted disrespectfully towards the police while they were only doing their duty. I responded by saying that I was not informed of the procedures when I was arrested and searched. Even then, his actions were not justifiable. He then said that everything will be okay and tried to calm my nerves. He said, "I will send you home soon. Just wait for a couple of hours." The story ends with my father picking me up. Soon, I arrived home after losing all my stuff, including money, in the cab.

Then, reflecting on being scarred by both Palestinian and Israeli violence, Ahmed added, "Being subject to both Israeli and Palestinian injustices, it made me think that if the occupation treats us just as badly as the national government, what is the whole point of the struggle for freedom and independence. If independence won't give us the rights we need, maybe it is better to live oppressed under occupation."[29]

The second account was relayed to me by Nasser, the Gaza-based journalist introduced earlier in this chapter. During our second meeting we were taking a walk down the Strip's coastline. There were throngs of families around us enjoying the weekend at the beach. At regular intervals we noticed police cars parked on the side of the road. I asked Nasser, "Is it normal to have so many policemen here?" He replied, "Not sure. I think they are just here to make sure that there is no trouble because there are so many people here." Nasser then continued, "You know that I was once beaten up by the police?" Surprised, I asked, "Really? What happened?" He responded, "It was for a silly reason. I had just started working as a journalist and was writing a story on schoolchildren who had recently finished their exams. I saw a group of girls walking out of the school, and I decided to interview them. Then the police came and started asking me questions." I asked, "So they just came out of nowhere?" Nasser replied, "Yes. They were very aggressive. They started asking me if I had any permission to be out on the street questioning people. When I asked them, 'Why are you being so aggressive? You have no reason to treat me like this,' they got even more aggressive. They grabbed me by the shirt and pulled me inside the school like I was a sheep being taken to the butcher to be slaughtered." He continued, "Inside the school they asked for my ID and my ID from my job. The schoolchildren were watching me like I was a suspicious person. The policemen then said, 'Go or we will arrest you.'" Nasser stopped talking for a few seconds, so I asked, "Was that it?" He replied, "No. I said to them, 'I did nothing wrong. I hope god punishes you.' Then they started hitting me and punching me in front of all the students. They cursed me with very rude words. Afterward, I complained to every department, but there was no investigation. I even talked to a lawyer and he said that according to Palestinian law they didn't have the right to do what they did." I asked, "What reason did they give for not taking any action?" Nasser said, "They said I looked suspicious. I went to the interior ministry, and nothing. Then I talked to a senior police officer. He said he will take care of it. I thought nothing would happen, but two days later I received an official apology." I asked, "So, how long did it take for them to apologize?" He replied in a tone of astonishment, "Seven months!" I then asked him, "What impression did it leave for you about Hamas, governance, and the liberation struggle?" He paused for a moment before answering, "This is an important question. For me, Hamas is good at fighting. In government they are big losers. They cannot control Gaza because they don't have the tools or the experience. Being responsible for Gaza is a national task and the national cause. You are not above us. You need to protect and not attack us. You cannot think of yourself as god."[30]

The final account was related by Karim from Shuja'iyya, first introduced in chapter 3. A few months after I left the Gaza Strip, Karim was accepted into an MA degree program abroad. After securing a student visa, he began planning his transit journey through the Rafah border crossing before flying out of Cairo. Unfortunately, he was traveling after the fall of the Morsi government in Cairo. The Egyptian military had reversed the momentary respite provided to the Gaza Strip by the Muslim Brotherhood leadership and had begun systematically destroying the twelve hundred tunnels between Egypt and the Palestinian enclave (Saleh 2014). Moreover, as the Rafah border crossing remained largely closed under orders from Cairo, it adversely affected Palestinian students studying abroad, who, if refused transit, would lose their scholarships and student visas and be unable to enroll for the fall semester (Suliman 2013). Karim was one of these affected students, and it was the second time in his life that he could potentially be refused the opportunity to study abroad. The first time was when he was eighteen and had secured a scholarship to pursue a bachelor's degree abroad. But the siege meant that he was not allowed leave. Karim waited, cried, and slept out in the open for two days at the border before returning home. This time around Palestinian Authority President Mahmoud Abbas had called for Palestinian students to send their travel documents to the Palestinian Embassy in Cairo. It was rumored that the embassy was coordinating with the Egyptian intelligence agencies to make sure that students from Gaza were on a priority list to be granted exit out of the Palestinian coastal enclave. Karim had sent his documents a few days earlier, and on September 17, 2013, he was eagerly waiting along with other Palestinian students to be called to get on the bus to Egypt. But none of the students were on the list, presumably because Abbas's coordination with Egypt was perceived by Hamas as a Fatah-led effort to undermine its authority in Gaza. The students were angry and disappointed. They started protesting and chanting in unison "*Talaba! Talaba!* [student]." They then tried to block the loaded buses from leaving for the Egyptian side of the border. The security officials kept pushing them while one of the security personnel vehicles tried to run over the protesting students. With the media present the security officers hesitated to be more severe in their conduct, merely pushing the students and occasionally punching them. In response, the students began hitting the cars and buses. One student even broke a window on one of the buses. The officials at the crossing then tried to negotiate with the students, but Karim claimed, "They didn't seem to take us seriously." Some students yelled, "I will fail if I don't leave today." Another shouted, "My residence permit is about to finish, and I can't renew it." Someone else cried, "If we don't leave, we will not be able to register this semester, and we will lose a part of our lives." The officials instead started threatening the protesters and detained the student who broke the bus window. Then, a unit of antiriot police arrived, who then managed to end the protest. Later that day, the Egyptian authorities called on the Hamas authorities to allow the students to leave. Karim's name was the second on the list. He was finally able to leave Gaza on September 18, 2013.

After having safely arrived at his final destination in Europe, Karim and I discussed his experience at Rafah. He said, "I feel that Hamas's behavior creates a dichotomy in the Palestinian perception of the national struggle. You have a liberation struggle against Israel, and then there is a social struggle against Hamas. The outcome has confused citizens who don't know who to ask for help. Somehow both [Israel and Hamas] become enemies who conduct equal degrees of aggression against you." I then asked him, "If a liberation faction is behaving like this, how does this then affect the liberation struggle?" Karim replied, "What we are seeing here is a new generation of Palestinians who didn't grow up around Israelis. The enemy is far away and something they have never seen. The enemy flies over Gaza and bombs us during war, but at the ground level all you see is Hamas's aggression." I asked, "Surely, it is a good thing that Israel isn't present on the ground in Gaza?" He retorted, "I would in fact prefer Israel to be here on the ground. When I walk down the street, I would like to see the IDF soldier, and I want them to be aggressive towards me so that I'm reminded, and I can see the character of the occupation." I responded, "So then, do you see any sense in the *hukuma*?" Karim answered, "No. Such a form of Palestinian government doesn't make sense. It is based on aggression and fear." I followed up, "Does this affect your Palestinian identity?" He replied, "I haven't said this to anyone, but sometimes I think maybe it is good that Israel is bombing Hamas. Maybe we deserve it. I slap myself and I'm ashamed of myself. I keep saying 'Remember, Karim, Israel is the enemy. They are the ones that do all the bad things.'"[31]

Here, one could claim that the policeman at the checkpoint, the security officials at the border, and the police at the school were merely acting as representatives of a state are known to do. As these "agents" of the Palestinian Authority in Gaza emphasized their authority by hitting, punching, and arresting my interlocutors, they confirmed Charles Tilly's assertion that violence is often the tool the state uses to exact compliance from its rivals or, in the case of my interviewees, citizens who are perceived to be rebellious or insubordinate. Explicating this process of establishing its monopoly on the means of coercion, albeit in the context of European state formation, Tilly wrote that, while ordinary citizens often owned lethal weapons, rulers engaged in a systematic effort to disarm them. In doing so, as it became "criminal, unpopular and impractical" to own weapons, the state was able to ensure its primacy as the supreme coercive authority (Tilly

1992, 69–70). When faced with a rebellious citizenry unwilling to give in to its demands, the state often engaged in a process of bargaining. While the bargain sometimes took the form of negotiations and buy-offs, it often manifested itself through "exemplary punishment" meted out to the "ringleaders" of the rebellion as a means of dampening their insubordinate spirit and quelling the rest of the rebellious population (Tilly 1992, 101).

In the case of Hamas, and adding to the three accounts of its governance described above, its complete takeover in 2007 and the flight of Fatah from the Gaza Strip, its disarming of individual Palestinian citizens, and its purging of the Palestinian Authority's security forces of Fatah sympathizers signify the efforts the Islamic Resistance made to monopolize the means of coercion. Of course, much like the state in Tilly's conception of it, the Palestinian variant in Gaza also frequently encounters an insubordinate citizenry. Karim and the other protesting students at the border crossing, Ahmed at the checkpoint, and Nasser were all citizens unwilling to remain subservient to Hamas's authority. So, by beating up Ahmed; by hitting and punching Nasser in the school; and by hitting, punching, and attempting to run over the protesters at the Rafah border crossing, Hamas as the government demanded submission and compliance of the rebellious. Moreover, by inflicting "exemplary punishment" on Ahmed in front of other Palestinians waiting at the checkpoint, on Nasser while the children at the school looked on, and on the one student who was arrested while others protesting at the border watched, the government also seems to be seeking the compliance of the rest of the (potentially) rebellious population by punishing the presumed "ringleaders."

However, violence, while not an unimportant manifestation of statecraft, is but an extension of the high-modernist state's urge to order its supposedly disorderly citizenry. James Scott argued that the modern state aspires to make the society it oversees legible by sedentarizing those it governs through permanent last names, standardizations, surveys, and registers. Accordingly, while the officials governing the modern state are often far removed from the society they govern, such "simplified approximations" are an indispensable means of rendering society comprehensible and therefore easily manageable (Scott 1998, 77–78). In Palestine it is self-evident that the Hamas government in a besieged Gaza lacks the material resources to ensure that the society it governs is legible in the way prescribed by the high-modernist ideologue. Nevertheless, it too is driven by a desire to observe the (ideal) vision of what the modern state is and does. Illegible Palestinian citizens like Ahmed became legible to the Palestinian governing entity when he was forced to present his ID at the checkpoint. Nasser, the suspicious citizen, is made visible, and therefore coercible, when he is questioned by police officers outside the school and asked to present proof of his affiliation as a journalist. And, much like the lists, logs, statistics, and documents that allow the modern state to assess and intervene in the society it governs, the bureaucratic procedure of securing permission to leave the Gaza Strip, as in the case of Karim at the Rafah border crossing, also forces illegible citizens to make themselves visible to the governing authority.

To be sure, the works of Scott and Tilly are merely two among a plethora of studies on state building that could be drawn on to explicate Hamas's conduct as the government in the Gaza Strip. These works would have sufficed if my intention in this book was to judge "how much" or "how little" the Palestinian Authority and the Palestinian governing entity pose like a state. However, my goal here is to demonstrate the manner in which Hamas's governance, cast as the image of the postcolonial State of Palestine, is encountered by its colonized recipients—that is, the colonial subject's experience of governance and its postcoloniality—while simultaneously being aware of his or her statelessness. In order to do this, let us return to Ahmed, who, being a victim of the violence of the anticolonial faction *and* the colonizer, wondered whether "it is better to live oppressed under occupation." Accordingly, he presented a dilemma that often troubles the newly liberated when the euphoria of the anticolonial struggle withers away. Nevertheless, it is particularly revealing that, while reflecting on his experience, he called being hit and searched a "*Palestinian* injustice" and referred to the entity that was committing it as the "*national* government."

Karim claimed that governance, in the form practiced by Hamas, was not only futile, it "confused" the Palestinian populace. Faced with the aggression of both the Islamic Resistance and Israel, he sees Palestinians as unable to distinguish the "real enemy." Having witnessed Hamas's tyranny at the Rafah border crossing, he often finds himself being "thankful" that Hamas and Gaza were being attacked. Maybe, he thought, Palestinians deserved such a torturous fate. For this reason, in order to remember who the *real* enemy is, he preferred that Israeli authorities have a visible presence in the Gaza Strip so that, faced with the "real enemy," he would be perpetually reminded of the colonial condition in which he lives. Nevertheless, while this reflection stands as a scathing critique of the Hamas government, he chose to identify what he encountered at Rafah as representative of the *Palestinian* government, albeit a Palestinian government that for him "didn't make sense." Nasser was unequivocal in his claim that, while Hamas was successful as a resistance organization, it was a "loser" in government due to its inexperience. However, when asserting that the police officers treated him unfairly, he still used *Palestinian* law as his reference for claiming that their conduct was illegal. Additionally, while he felt that Hamas was failing as a government, governance on the path of liberation, aimed to protect the population, was still a "*national* task and the *national* cause." Thus, all three of my interlocutors, while emphasizing the futility and failures of the Hamas government in Gaza, and despite their own traumatic encounters with governance, characterized the governance as a *national* initiative, qualified the government as a *Palestinian* government, and described its failings as *Palestinian* injustice. In doing so, they remind us of the manner in which Palestine emerged out of the bodily scars, trauma, and suffering that resulted from the violent confrontation with the colonizer. Hamas's governance may be devoid of any sense of euphoria or therapeutic allure, yet my interlocutors still seem to experience Palestine in the midst of the injustices of the governance meted out to them.

Ostensibly, and with reference to my earlier discussion of Hamas's own perception of governance, my interlocutors' recognition of Palestine and the national in the Islamic Resistance's governance activities would seem to, albeit tragically, accord victory to the organization's own vision of governance in the era of colonization. Nevertheless, as the mechanisms of postcoloniality inadvertently evoke meaning for the colonized by rendering Palestine recognizable in a settler colonial context that emphasizes its nonexistence, one wonders how it is that postcolonial statecraft is able to do this in a nonstate context. Drawing parallels with its European counterpart does little to explicate the manner in which postcolonial statecraft is encountered by its recipients. But, Migdal explains the perpetual struggles of new entrants into the international system by arguing that the postcolonial state (burdened by the image of the "ideal") oscillates between attempts to successfully implement its plans and policies and the riotous realities of its arbitrary borders and often-rebellious citizenry (Migdal 1988, 4). Thus, the postcolonial state struggles, but is nevertheless driven by an effort to render the newly established state and the authority of the centralized political (and economic) elite recognizable and legitimate across its demographic landscape.

This pathology of the postcolonial state was evident in Gupta's ethnography of the Indian state. He argued that it was in the "minute texture of the everyday life"—namely the "everyday practices" of local institutions, offices, and bureaucracies—that the "translocal" state became legible to the citizen in a remote Indian village (Gupta 1995, 375). The Indian state, embodied in the national institutions in the capital New Delhi, may have otherwise been a figment of the imagination in its spatial margins. But the local bureaucracies made it a reality for the recipients of its statecraft. The Ecuadorian state was similarly unrecognizable to those in its margins. This led to a multiplicity of perspectives on its territoriality. In response, the state elite in Quito engaged in mapping practices that ensured that there was a single, state-approved conception of Ecuador's spatial composition (Radcliffe 2001, 123–126). Unsanctioned violence, bomb-ings, and riots are violations of the state's monopoly over violence. Yet, for the postcolonial elite they are also a challenge to the very ideology and being of the postcolonial state. In the face of such transgressions, the postcolonial state once again strives to emphasize its authority over the riotous citizenry. The violation in Thomas Blom Hansen's study of the myths of the postcolonial state were the Hindu-Muslim riots in Mumbai. Subsequently, in the face of the unplanned disorder that makes the citizen wonder "Where is the Indian state?" New Delhi ensured its legibility through government initiatives encouraging reconciliation and cohabitation, which were meant to underline the state's authority (Hansen 2001, 226). With regard to suicide bombings in Sri Lanka, Jeganathan similarly argues that the state placed its checkpoints in locations that were susceptible as targets. Here, through the process of checking citizens' IDs, a relationship was established "between the checker and checked." Of course, the checkpoint is a bureaucratic mechanism meant to differentiate between citizen allies and their rebellious counterparts. Nevertheless, as one is identified as allied or rebellious in relation *to something*, it is in that *something* that the state and its authority emerges—that is, the same state that was rendered illegible as a result of the sui-cide bombing (Jeganathan 2004, 79).

Faced with such persistent "centrifugal forces" (Migdal 1988) that aim to frag-ment the postcolonial state's ideology, authority, and territoriality, it would be inadequate to argue merely that this state is solely driven to enforce centralized authority. It is also burdened with the task of making the state itself recognizable, legible, and meaningful for its own citizens. It is this mechanism that then helps us better understand the image (and meaning) that postcolonial statecraft evokes from its stateless Palestinian recipients. Except, when adapted to the context of the Palestinian liberation struggle, and with Palestinians facing a settler colonial project claiming that the colonized do not exist, the mechanisms of postcolonial-ity emerge as a means of emphasizing that Palestine indeed exists. Returning to my ethnographic accounts, it thus becomes possible to treat Ahmed's experience at the checkpoint, Karim's encounter at the Rafah border crossing, and Nasser's encounter with the police outside the school as representative of the instances of statecraft cited throughout the course of this book. That is to say, these three accounts bear synonymy with the "Welcome to Palestine" sign at the Rafah bor-der crossing, the Internal Protection Unit, the Palestinian travelers waiting to be granted a permit to leave Gaza, the police officers who diffused the fight in north-ern Gaza, or for that matter, the expansive materiality of the Palestinian Authority described earlier in this chapter. They can, of course, be considered bureaucratic practices and institutions that are drowned out and rendered mundane in the face of the bombastic statements of liberation and resistance. But, as my interlocutors encountered Palestine and the national in these instances of the mundane every day, their experiences indicate that in the context of a liberation struggle the mundane also enjoys some meaningfulness.

The domestic fight in northern Gaza, the prevalence of drug dealers, Ahmed challenging the policemen's right to search him, Karim protesting at the border crossing, and Nasser "looking suspicious" were instances where Hamas's authority as the government was (perceived to be) challenged. In response, as the policemen arrested the enraged brother, set up checkpoints, hit Ahmed, assaulted Nasser, and attempted to run over the protesting students, they subsequently forced the recognition of a *Palestinian* governing entity on the recipients of their governance. Similarly, the siege of Gaza and the inability of the Hamas government to control the movement of people in and out of the territory represent transgressions of the statelike authority's control of a specific territorial mandate. However, by ensuring the existence of the "Welcome to Palestine" sign at the Rafah border crossing—and not unlike the creation of the Ecuadorian state through mapping practices—Palestine also emerges in the effort to specify the territoriality and physical geography that the Hamas government aspires to control. Finally, the blockade may ensure that the governance structures in Gaza are materially starved and lacking in sovereignty. But, the bureaucracy of having to apply for a permit and then wait for it to be granted makes the *Palestinian* authority legible, much like the translocal state becomes legible in the spatial margins of the Indian state through its minute bureaucratic practices that rural citizens are made to encounter.

It is thus in this way that, for the colonized Palestinian, postcolonial statecraft inadvertently becomes a means of emphasizing the existence of Palestine despite settler colonial claims to the contrary. As noted earlier, the Palestinian Authority's materiality has ensured that it arbitrates life in the Palestinian territories. Consequently, in doing so, it personifies all the symbols of state authority. When Nasser refers to Palestinian law in his criticism of the policemen's conduct, he reminds us that there is a semblance of legal premises and of the discourse of a state(-like) authority. The existence of the IPU, the bureaucratic procedure of requiring a permit to leave Gaza, and the existence of checkpoints demonstrate that symbols and rituals exist in the form of physical government structures. And, while the Hamas government may lack the material ability to map the Palestinian territories, by maintaining a sign that proclaims "Welcome to Palestine" and by regulating the movement of people in and out of the territory (say at the Rafah border crossing), it demonstrates a desire to map the territory of the national home that would presumably be informed by the common Palestinian national identity and culture. Consequently, as this state authority, its materiality, and its symbols are encountered by my interlocutors, they became symbols of a *Palestinian* state authority, while the role of government becomes part of the colonized's struggle as it ensures that the Palestine that was once unnamed in the physical landscape of Israel-Palestine reemerges as recognizable. Naturally, the Palestine that becomes visible in this manner cannot lay claim to the Weberian territorial state. Nevertheless, it becomes naturalized in the consciousness of the ordinary Palestinian, as it speaks like Palestine and, through its bureaucracies and statelike institutions, ensures that the idea of Palestine is continuously reproduced and inducted into permanence (Hansen and Stepputat 2001, 5–8). Here it would be presumptuous to claim that the Hamas government or, for that matter, its counterpart in the West Bank has intended Palestine to become recognizable in this manner. Nevertheless, taking the perspective of the recipient of Hamas's role as government, I would posit that, like resistance, governance also is a means for the colonized to render Palestine legible, albeit an inadvertent one.

On Palestinian Governance

In his essay "The Morning After," Edward Said scathingly criticized the Oslo Accords and all that resulted from it. Ostensibly, as I have argued in chapter 3, the Accords promised a secure path home after decades of exile, established a precursor to the State of Palestine by way of the Palestinian Authority, and promised to grant Palestinians sovereignty after an interim period. Yet, Said had realized early in the aftermath of the agreement that it was deeply flawed. He wrote of the vulgarity of the ceremonial manner in which the Accords were signed at the White House and the degrading manner in which Yasser Arafat thanked everyone—all of which, for Said, failed to obscure the fact that the Oslo Accords symbolized the "astonishing proportions of the Palestinian capitulation" (Said 1993, 3). With this assessment in mind, it may not be surprising that the primary manifestation of the Accords—namely, a Palestinian Authority that poses like the postcolonial state—is frequently dismissed as a corrupt form of statecraft that is useless to the purposes of the liberation struggle. Yet, the Palestinian Authority and its attendant postcoloniality has persisted for more than two decades, leading to the postcolonial persisting in a settler colonial condition. The question thus addressed in this chapter is what happens to this postcoloniality in a settler colonial (nonstate) context?

The anticolonial faction insists that, by adopting the role of government, it ensures that the anticolonial ethos enters the Palestinian Authority—an institution that many argue is but an extension of the colonial state. Accordingly, Hamas maintains that it protects the anticolonial struggle, rejuvenates the values of resistance among a population under siege, and by claiming that "we will protect the resistance," demonstrates an eagerness to emphasize its sole leadership over the Palestinian political landscape. Some have argued that Hamas and its conduct as a government is merely a reflection of an organization striving to institute its own authoritarian dominance over everything and everyone. However, placed within the context of a liberation struggle, I see a far more nuanced reality in which, by suggesting a path to liberation under the auspices of its *own* leadership, Hamas also perceives its mandate as a government to be to collect the multitude of actors and political allegiances under the canopy of a single Palestinian struggle on a singular path to liberation. In this vein, as the "leader" it hopes that the Palestinian national community will come into being under the auspices of its green flag.

For colonized Palestinians in Gaza, at the outset, the experience of Hamas's governance convinces them of the futility of governance. Yet, when my interviewees described their encounters with Hamas's postcolonial governance, they nonetheless identified the government in Gaza as the *Palestine* government and its failings as *national* failings. This, I have argued, is an effect of what the postcolonial state is and does. Faced with arbitrary borders and a rebellious citizenry, the postcolonial state struggles to ensure that its authority is recognizable to its citizens. When this quality of the postcolonial state is adapted to the colonial condition, it seems to serve a similar purpose; except, for the colonized, the postcoloniality becomes a means of emphasizing the existence of Palestine. In this way, as Hamas's governance encompasses a statelike legal premise, symbols, bureaucracies, and institutions, it speaks like Palestine and ensures that the idea of Palestine is constantly reproduced and naturalized in the consciousness of the colonized recipients of its governance. Consequently, Hamas's governance inadvertently seems to compel the colonized who encounter it to recognize the signature of Palestine in its midst.

Taking together the perspectives of the anticolonial faction that governs and the colonized who are governed, this chapter concludes that Hamas's governance finds relevance for the Palestinian liberation struggle in a manner not unlike its armed resistance. That is to say, much like its anticolonial violence, Hamas's postcolonial governance also displays the signature of Palestine in the face of a settler colonial endeavor that works to efface Palestine and Palestinians from the landscape of the "Holy Land." This signature is evident under the canopy of Hamas's leadership, in its urge to induct *all* Palestinians on a single path to liberation, and in the manner in which the colonized accord a certain Palestinian-ness to the brand of governance they encounter. In the next chapter I will then consider the implications of both anticolonial armed resistance—reminiscent of the period of colonial rule—and postcolonial statecraft—associated with the era *after* the withdrawal of the colonizer—finding resonance in and relevance for the liberation struggle in the era of settler colonial rule.

THE PALESTINIAN MOMENT OF LIBERATION

Nasser and I took a stroll along Gaza's picturesque coastline in late June 2013.[1] He insisted that we walk, despite the searing summer heat. "I walk everywhere," he said. When I asked him why, he replied, "I think walking is the best strategy here. It makes Gaza feel bigger than it is."[2] Halfway through our stroll we decided to sit down for a cup of tea. As we drank it facing the vast Mediterranean Sea and watched the sun set in the horizon, there was a gradual lull in our conversation. Suddenly, in a tone of abrupt realization and in seeming conclusion to all that we had discussed thus far, Nasser said, "You know . . . one day I will be back in Jaffa. That is where I'm from, and that is my destiny. Life here in Gaza is meaningless." Neither Nasser nor his parents had ever been to Jaffa. It was his grandparents who had last set foot in their ancestral home before Jaffa was overrun by Jewish paramilitary forces (Pappe 2006, 102). Nonetheless, hearing the resolve in his voice, I momentarily forgot how unlikely it was that he would ever return to his ancestral home. It was almost as if he had said, "Come what may, I will return home to Jaffa one day." Six months after this encounter, I was in Jaffa and naively wondered if I could find the plot of land where Nasser's ancestral home once stood. With directions from Nasser I wandered the streets late one night. Unsurprisingly, there was no remnant of Nasser's home or his past, nor, therefore, of what he imagines his future to be.

By placing his past in Jaffa, rejecting his present existence under siege and exiled in Gaza, and pining for a future that sees him return to his ancestral home, Nasser is testimony to the fact that liberation is rarely *just* about the expulsion of the colonizer. At the outset this book was concerned with the manner in which Hamas's anticolonial violence and postcolonial governance "live" and coexist in the context of a liberation struggle. But in relaying the story of Hamas and thus tacking back and forth between the postcolonial and anticolonial, I have also presented an account of a similarly wavering assemblage of the past, present, and future. The past first appeared in chapter 2, where I discussed the settler colonial "dream" of Palestinian nonexistence. Historically, the Nakba of 1948 personifies the settler colonial urge to materially "cleanse" Palestine and Palestinians from the landscape of the "Holy Land." Yet, I argued, this erasure has continued and persists today in the indifferent way a young Palestinian scissors-wielding attacker was shot dead in 2015 near the shuk in Jerusalem, in the derogatory narrative told at Israeli museums like Beit HaPalmach in Tel Aviv, and in the way the siege of the Gaza Strip has relegated life and politics in the coastal enclave to a bare (in)humanity. It is this effort to dematerialize the colonized's existence that, I concluded, drives them to retort: "We are here, we exist, and we are organized."

This retort is boldly written into Hamas's anticolonial violence. In chapter 4 I argued that Hamas's armed resistance finds value for the Palestinian struggle for liberation in its ability to unmake and make. Anticolonial violence unmakes by dismantling the settler colonial condition that starves the colonized subject and subjectivity, both materially and culturally. Certainly, Hamas's violence is materially incapable of challenging the IDF, let alone unraveling the entirety of Israel's settler colonial presence in the Palestinian territories. However, its violence unmakes not by defeating or ousting the colonizers but by minimally (yet, persistently) challenging their presence in the colonized's lands, with the hope of rendering the colonial endeavor a difficult venture to maintain. Alongside its ability to minimally unmake, Hamas's violence can also function as a creative force. Seeing that this violence often incurs greater material and human costs for its author (the colonized) than its primary victim (the colonizer), it would seem difficult to argue that it can embody an ability to make. Yet, I demonstrated that Palestine and my interlocutors' Palestinian-ness were inscribed in the tragic repercussions that often follow anticolonial violence. That is to say, the suffering and deaths that result from acts of anticolonial violence are not merely tragic and undesirable outcomes of confrontations with a materially superior colonizer. They also allow for such clashes to be called *Palestinian* acts of resistance, and the subsequent suffering to be identified as instances of *Palestinian* sacrifice and tragedy. As a result, anticolonial violence and its repercussions become a canvas for the display of Palestine and Palestinian-ness and allow the colonized to recover their indigeneity, which faces erasure from a settler colonial enterprise. In this way, through violence, the colonized are able to build their sense of self and, while striving for a liberated future, declare their existence.

It is not surprising that the violence of the anticolonial faction serves to counter the settler's narrative of Palestinian nonexistence. Further, Hamas's violence mirrors the important status often accorded to violence in the context of revolutionary (and) anticolonial struggles in general. From the Kashmiri liberation movement and Basque struggle for independence to Kwame Nkrumah's writings on revolutionary warfare, violence is often deemed to be a sacred expression of anticolonial (and) revolutionary subjectivity and will. But the far more puzzling reality is that Hamas does not just pose as an anticolonial faction. It also displays postcoloniality in its statelike governance of the Gaza Strip. How is it that the postcolonial exists in a settler colonial condition that also inspires an anticolonial struggle? In chapter 3, I argued that this puzzling condition is a legacy of the Oslo Accords. Touted as the first *real* agreement between the State of Israel and Palestinians, the Accords were meant both to recognize the existence of the Palestinian population exiled after the Nakba and to institutionalize their return home, not least by way of the establishment of a sovereign Palestinian state. The Oslo process, however, did not result in the establishment of the State of Palestine and did little to stem the expansion of Israel's presence in the Palestinian territories. As a result, while Israel's settler colonialism continues to shape the Palestinian anticolonial struggle, the Accords further spurred the anticolonial politics (and not least the violence) of an organization like Hamas that, seeing the failures of the Accords, was convinced of the futility of negotiations with Israel. However, aside from what the Oslo Accords did *not* secure (i.e., the Palestinian state), the agreement was generative in that it introduced postcoloniality into Palestinian politics as it attempted to incentivize a brand of political conduct among Palestinian liberation factions that involved *more* state building and *less* fighting. In doing so, the Oslo Accords effectively criminalized the Palestinian anticolonial struggle in return for granting political capital, economic incentives, and tools of coercion—all institutionally brought together in the Palestinian Authority—that encouraged Palestinian factions to operate within the realm of official statelike politics and behave *as if* the colonizer had long since withdrawn. What resulted from this is a confusing political condition in which an organization like Hamas confirms the existence of the colonial condition by persisting with its anticolonial violence while, as a government at the helm of the Palestinian Authority, also posturing *as if* it were in the era of the postcolonial.

The question remains, How does the postcoloniality of Hamas's statelike governance operate in a settler colonial condition? In answering this question in chapter 5, I was largely unconcerned with the extent to which the bureaucracies and institutions of the Palestinian Authority in the Gaza Strip postured as a "real," democratic, and sovereign state. With Israel's settler colonialism and a siege as its background, the Hamas-ruled, statelike Palestinian Authority in the Gaza Strip would undoubtedly pale in comparison to a "real" state. Its postcolonial existence therefore needed to be examined within a political context characterized by the nonexistence of a state. Accordingly, I discussed Hamas's governance through the perspectives of both its provider (i.e., Hamas itself) and its recipients (i.e., colonized Palestinians in Gaza). As Hamas entered the Palestinian Authority with its "celebrated" status as a resistance organization, which, unlike Fatah, was still committed to fighting Israel, its members and affiliates perceived resistance to be inalienable on the path to liberation. For them, the role of government, under the auspices of a Hamas leadership, was thus inducted into the path of liberation, imbued with the ethos of the liberation struggle and embodying the anticolonial perspective. Consequently, according to my Hamas interviewees, what was once meant to operate *as if* in the era of the postcolonial came to embody the values of the anticolonial struggle. Moreover, with Hamas as a government alluding to its own leadership over all aspects of political life, my interlocutors also demonstrated a tendency to perceive the organization as an embodiment of the eventual Palestinian state, as if to say, "Hamas is Palestine and Palestine is Hamas." Hamas's governance of Gaza was nevertheless often experienced by Gazans as that of an increasingly authoritarian Palestinian faction. Indeed, in many ways the Hamas-ruled Palestinian Authority replicated the postcolonial state in having to struggle continually to emphasize its own existence to a citizenry for whom the state is either illegitimate or illegible.

When the pathology of the postcolonial state is introduced into the settler colonial condition, the institutions of governance are not satisfied by the mere emboldening of the signature and legibility of the centralized authority. Instead, much as is the case with resistance, governance becomes a means of rendering the signature of Palestine and Palestinian-ness legible and recognizable. Insofar as my interlocutors identified the Hamas government as a *Palestinian* government and saw its shortcomings as symbolizing Hamas's failure to fulfill the *national* task of governing Palestine, the government also became a canvas displaying the continued existence of the colonized. I thus concluded that the postcoloniality of Hamas's governance, when viewed within the context of the Palestinian liberation struggle, also becomes a means of emphasizing the existence and persistence of the colonized, despite the narrative of the settler claiming otherwise. In this way, the anticolonial retort that "we exist" resonates through both Hamas's anticolonial violence, despite its material weakness, and its mode of governance, despite its postcoloniality. In what follows I consider the two implications of this: the arrival of the Palestinian "moment of the liberation," and "the bad state."

The Palestinian "Moment of Liberation"

It is difficult to predict the future of the Gaza Strip. As has been evident in the words of several of my interlocutors, uncertainty is what marks life and politics in the besieged Palestinian enclave. It is therefore often most appropriate just to resign to this reality and admit, "We don't know what will happen." This uncertainty applies equally to the future of Hamas and its search for Palestine as both a resistance movement and a government. Officially, abiding by the terms of the latest reconciliation agreement signed with Fatah on October 12, 2017, Hamas claims to have renounced its role as a government and, with it, its administrative control of the Gaza Strip. In return, as the West Bank–based Palestinian Authority assumed complete control of the Palestinian coastal enclave, the latest deal between the two warring factions was meant to ease the siege of the Gaza Strip (Beaumont 2017). However, ten weeks after the agreement was signed, the current Hamas chief in Gaza Yahya Sinwar declared, "The reconciliation project is falling apart. Only a blind man can't see that." Accusing Fatah and international stakeholders of trying to force Hamas to disarm, Sinwar further noted, "Reconciliation is collapsing because some people want to get from it the relinquishing of arms and the closing of tunnels." Fatah officials have claimed, however, that Hamas has yet to hand over administrative control of the Gaza Strip (Reuters 2017). Many of my interlocutors in Gaza have confirmed that Hamas's rule over the enclave has remained largely intact. One of them, now living in Europe, added,

> They are in full control of the internal economy and security. This is because they still run the whole bureaucracy. They have consolidated this [control over the bureaucracy] for years, and it will take years to reverse this. The only thing Hamas did is allowing Abbas's security people to control the border crossings and letting them collect taxes on goods entering Gaza. Because there is [a] problem with cash-flow in Gaza, this allows the PA [Palestinian Authority] from the West Bank to take responsibility for paying the salaries of government employees in Gaza.[3]

Despite a sense of opacity around what is really happening, Hamas seems to have somewhat maintained its *official* commitment to the armed struggle while continuing *unofficially* to govern most aspects of life and politics in Gaza. For one thing, this demonstrates the persistence of the "idea of liberation" even when *actual* liberation is unlikely. That is to say, irrespective of whether a political act is considered materially capable of securing the liberation of a colonized people, it can nevertheless be draped in the language and symbols of the national struggle. For instance, Hamas's armed struggle is materially incapable of dismantling Israel's rule over the Palestinian territories. Nonetheless, the organization's violence also finds value when it makes it difficult for Israel to maintain control over the area and when the tragic repercussions of muqawama become a means for displaying Palestinian existence. Similarly, the pretended postcoloniality of Hamas's governance, that mainly evokes the image of a state that is yet to arrive, has little apparent value for the liberation struggle. However, it too becomes socialized into the Palestinian liberation struggle both as a means of expressing the anticolonial perspective and, with Gazans viewing the Hamas government as a *Palestinian* government, as a way of performing a *national* undertaking that displays Palestinian existence. In this sense, liberation is not a political expression meant solely to impose the colonized's will on the colonizer. It also finds fruition in the very practice of performing political acts that can be perceived as important facets of the struggle for liberation.

It may be questioned whether Hamas's minimalist understanding of what counts as an act in the service of liberation bodes well for the colonized. Given the military prowess of the colonizer and the consequent implausibility that an act for liberation will lead to the actual unraveling of the colonial endeavor, it would be futile for the colonized to judge the value of every political act in terms of its ability to physically oust the colonizer. Therefore, a far more significant outcome of this minimalist conception of liberation is the limited importance attached to the physical withdrawal of the colonizer. To be sure, the ultimate aspiration of the Palestinian liberation movement, like that of any other anticolonial struggle, remains the total dismantling of the colonial enterprise. Yet, the political conduct of the colonized is not shaped solely by this momentous occasion, which bifurcates the lives of the colonized into the eras of colonial rule versus the postcolonial state. Instead, concerned primarily with ensuring that the liberation struggle persists through minute, minimal, mundane, and materially weak political acts, the colonized blur the boundary between the colonial and postcolonial. In doing so, they are able adopt postcoloniality alongside the anticolonial struggle *before* the withdrawal of the colonizer. And, as I go on to argue in the final chapter, the struggle for liberation also continues in the era of the postcolonial state, long *after* the withdrawal of the colonizer. The case of Hamas thus demonstrates that the moment of liberation is not a single moment at all but a long moment that begins in the era of colonial rule, as the colonized adopt both anticolonial *and* postcolonial modes of conduct.

Of course, this limited importance given to the presence or absence of the colonizer has its specificity in the case of Palestine. The postcoloniality adopted by the anticolonial faction here is not one it assumes or conjures up on its own. It was introduced, and also imposed, by the Oslo Accords and hyperinstitutionalized by means of a Palestinian Authority that postures as a postcolonial state. Moreover, as noted earlier, by preempting Palestinian postcoloniality, the Accords were meant to restrain Palestinian anticolonial politics. Yet, Hamas's persistence with the simultaneous roles of resistance and assumption of governmental authority confirmed that the anticolonial and postcolonial can indeed coexist in the era of colonial rule in service of the liberation struggle. The case of Hamas thus suggests that the Palestinian long moment of liberation might have already begun, despite the postcolonial being externally imposed. Certainly, the coexistence of the postcolonial and the anticolonial is not unique to the Gaza Strip. Yet, in comparison to the West Bank, where Palestinian factions have chosen in the main to be either anticolonial or postcolonial in their conduct, both facets of the long moment of liberation are (albeit, for now) consolidated under Hamas's leadership, isolated and besieged within the spatial limits of the Gaza Strip, and uninhibited by IDF checkpoints or a pervasive settlement movement. In chapter 2, I argued that the besieged Gaza Strip was an extension of a settler colonial urge to dematerialize the colonized's existence. At the same time, the Gaza Strip under Hamas's leadership as both anticolonial resistance *and* postcolonial government is also a microcosm of the entirety of the Palestinian long moment of liberation. Facets of this long moment may exist dispersed in the Palestinian territories outside the Gaza Strip, but it is the Palestinian coastal enclave that exemplifies the long moment before the withdrawal of the colonizer in its entirety, consolidated under a single leadership, with the colonizer visible only at a distance.

The Bad State

My stay in Gaza coincided with the finale of Season 2 of the television music competition *Arab Idol*. It was a special occasion for Gazans because one of their own, Mohammad Assaf, had reached the finale and was widely considered to be the favorite to win. At the time, Assaf had also become the face of the struggles of life under siege in Gaza. The story of his trials traveling from Gaza through the Rafah border crossing and Egypt had become well known across the Arab world and beyond. In the hours before the final episode there was a palpable mood of anticipation in Gaza, as if Assaf had already won and the Palestinians were merely waiting for the official announcement from the judges in Beirut. When the announcement was made of his victory a celebratory roar reverberated across the Gaza Strip in unison, and immediately afterward the celebrations spilled onto the streets. Many had wondered if they would be an opportunity for the otherwise censored and muted opposition groups to demonstrate against Hamas's rule over Gaza. There were some Fatah flags, and some young Palestinian men seemed to be keen on testing the patience of the Palestinian Authority policemen patrolling the streets. But the number of opposition flags was negligible compared to the flood of Palestinian flags on the streets that evening. The policemen also seemed to have been instructed not to react to provocations, as they turned their backs on the boisterous crowds and had their guns pointed toward the ground.

The evening and night went without incident. Yet, I was struck by the intensity of the festivities. Convoys of cars and motorcycles donned with flags and posters of Assaf formed a celebratory procession that filled the streets of Gaza City and slowly made its way to Midan al-Jundi al-Majhool, or Unknown Soldier's Square. The crowd at the square danced, sang, screamed, and cried, and it felt as if this moment of joy and revelry was long overdue (Sen 2013b). But why did this victory matter? Was it not just a television program, which, after all, could do very little to alleviate Gaza's and Palestine's troubles under settler colonial rule? To an extent this was indeed the case, but the young Gazan's victory in a television show filmed in Beirut mattered because it could not be disputed. In a place where victory is frequently preceded by a lengthy series of armed hostilities with the IDF that leaves thousands of people dead and millions in material losses, triumph is often denoted by mere survival, permitting Palestinians to fight another day. In comparison, Assaf's victory did not have any human costs, did not inflict suffering, and did not require Palestinians to mourn. In a way, it represented a true "break" from the perpetual suffering that defines life in Gaza. As it represented a true victory, the celebrations at the Unknown Soldier's Square were marked by pure joy and bliss. Surely, those celebrating on the streets the night of Assaf's victory knew well that this momentary "break" would soon pass, and that the settler colonial condition would once again take center stage the very next day.

Much like Assaf's victory, my findings in this book also might seem to propose a "break" from the usual conversations about Gaza. No doubt, as Norman Finkelstein rightly argues, the story of Gaza's past and present is the story of utter loss and multiple atrocities (Finkelstein 2018, 4). Yet, despite these atrocities, as I have argued, Hamas's politics and the manner of its struggle for Palestine somehow make sense. Despite their faults and inadequacies, both resistance and governance somehow evoked the colonized's retort, "We are here, we exist, we are organized." And, even though *actual* liberation is far from being realized, the Palestinian *long* moment of liberation has already begun under the auspices of Hamas's rule over Gaza.

But just as Assaf's victory could not erase the reality that Palestinian victories are otherwise lined with tragedies, "finding" Palestine in this manner in the politics of Hamas cannot ignore the realities of life in the Gaza Strip. Nonetheless, this book's attempt to break with the usual narrative on Gaza as a place of suffering might be incorrectly perceived to be an attempt to efface the cost of Hamas's persistence with its dual role. As a proponent of a "barefoot" approach to anthropology, Nancy Scheper-Hughes, for example, would most likely argue that my theoretical abstractions and rhetorical figures of speech have served to aestheticize the suffering of the colonized; and further that, by focusing on the creativity of governance and resistance on the path to liberation, this book has ignored the "muddied" reality that the path to dismantling a settler colonial condition is lined with oddities and discrepancies, often lacking the allure of the therapeutic or euphoric (Scheper-Hughes 1995, 416). This, of course, was not my intention. However, nearing the end of this book, it would be prudent to address the location and character of the tragedy that lies in the background of my discussions.

Certainly, there is much in the current condition of the Palestinian territories in general and of the Gaza Strip in particular that warrants "shock and awe" and requires alarmist descriptions and analyses that would both outrage the reader and be morally demanding in form and intent (Scheper-Hughes 1995, 417). However, in keeping with the focus of this book, the most shocking and awe-inducing facet of my discussion of Hamas's politics has been the seeming inalienability of violence as the currency of politics. Specifically, the violence perpetrated in the search for a Palestinian state, discussed in chapter 4, and the violence conducted *as* the Palestinian statelike authority, addressed in chapter 5, were canvases on which Palestine and Palestinian-ness were displayed. My interlocutors were adamant in emphasizing that this violence had tragic consequences. Karim, while remembering his tussle with Hamas's border security personnel in Rafah, claimed that the coercive practices of the Islamic Resistance were creating confused citizens, who, faced with Israeli attacks, sometimes wondered (as he did), "Maybe we deserve it." Ahmed, as a victim of the violence of both the colonized and the colonizer, further emphasized the tragedy of life under the gaze of colonization when he asked, "If the occupation treats us just as badly as the national government, what is the whole point of the struggle for freedom and independence?" In essence, they wondered, if the colonized population perpetually finds itself at the wrong end of the barrel of a gun, whether facing the colonial state or its indigenous variant, is there any wisdom in the struggle for liberation and the aspiration to achieve sovereign statehood?

The scope of this book limits the extent to which I can deliberate further on how or why violence is synonymous with the state. Nevertheless, because of the scars and bruises incurred by my interlocutors during their struggles with the statelike authority in Gaza, we are reminded of the need to criticize the way violence is or has become an exemplification of both the way a state impresses itself on people and the currency through which it deals with them.[4] Charles Tilly (1992) tells us that wars make states. This claim, having reached a level of theoretical truism, has been the subject of intense academic deliberation as many have wondered if war-making is *indeed* necessary for state building (Malesevic 2012; Herbst 1996–97; Leander 2004). But, regardless of whether it is necessary, violence is clearly endemic to the very being of the state. And, it is therefore not surprising that those preparing for independence, for example, in the Palestinian territories find themselves described through the vocabulary of the violent speech that permits the centralized political elite to emphasize the primacy of its logic and ideology. However, an intellectual stance in countering the internalization and acceptance of the state's violence should not be based on whether or not violence makes states, especially since answering such a question would not change the practical functioning of the state. Instead, we would need to discuss the violence conducted under the auspices of the state's insignia in light of the shock, panic, suffering, pain, and death to which it usually leads. This ensures that the state is represented by its tendency to demand compliance from the cowering citizen under the threat of the clenched fist.

The "Good," "Bad," and the "Moment of Liberation"

The case of Hamas tells us that liberation is not *just* about liberation. It is as much about the colonized's perceptions of who they were, who they are, and who they ought to be in their liberated future. Nor is liberation solely a story of the triumph of "the good" (i.e., the colonized) over "the bad" (i.e., the colonizer). To an extent, it is indeed about the discovery of something "good," like the Palestinian "moment of liberation" in the utter tragedy of life under colonial rule. However, this encouraging "moment" for the Palestinian struggle also lives alongside something "bad," that is, the brand of Palestinian statehood that seems to be in the offing if the future State of Palestine simply mirrors the violent characteristics of the Israeli state. In this way, the story of Hamas's search for Palestine as resistance and government shows us that a struggle for liberation is rarely as linear or euphoric as is often told in the nationalist narrative of the anticolonial struggle. Due to the vastness of the material infrastructure that constitutes the colonial endeavor, liberation is instead a protracted affair that has ebbs and flows and is often much more about the colonized's struggle to sustain the cause of liberation than about the achievement of *actual* liberation. This means that, for one, the successes and failures of political acts conducted in the service of liberation during the course of this protracted struggle are rarely contingent on their ability to instigate the withdrawal of the colonizer. Moreover, as I have concluded in this chapter, the limited significance of the presence or absence of the colonizer also means that liberation is not about the singular moment of *actual* liberation from colonial rule. Instead, it is a long moment that begins before the colonizer withdraws, as the colonized adopt both anticolonial and postcolonial modes of conduct as means of underlining the existence and persistence of the colonized as a people and a cause, while a settler colonial narrative insists otherwise. Of course, aside from the specificity of the Palestinian condition, where postcoloniality was externally induced, it is the limited importance placed on the moment of liberation that *allows* the liberation faction to blur the colonial–postcolonial divide in order to adapt the postcolonial to the era of settler colonial rule and the anticolonial struggle. Yet, as I discuss further in the final, concluding chapter, the same limited significance accorded to the moment when the colonizer withdraws also means that the struggle for liberation continues in the era of the postcolonial state; that is to say, the struggle to be liberated does not cease in the absence of the colonizer.

ON LIBERATION

When I hear the term *liberation*, I am reminded of two events in my life. The first occurred when I was ten years old, while spending time with my grandfather. In our family, he was always described as a gentleman. In the middle-class Bengali circles of Kolkata where I grew up, being a gentleman meant being dignified, well-mannered, and educated. My grandfather's status as a gentleman was also due to his English sensibilities. He spoke English, read books on Indian revolutionary thinkers and freedom fighters in English, named my mother Shelley after the English poet Percy Bysshe Shelley, and wore tailored suits imported from London. He was a high-ranking manager at a bank, and his reputation as an incorruptible employee was well known. Dadu, as I used to call him affectionately, was also the only member of our family who had traveled abroad. I cherished my time with him. Dadu was worldly and a vivid storyteller. When he read to me, I simply marveled at his command of the English language. I too aspired one day to be as English as he was. In due time, with a few years of private English-medium education under my belt from a school where we began the day saying the Lord's Prayer and were reprimanded if we spoke Hindi or Bengali, I had become quite confident of my ability to speak English. So, one day, as my grandfather attempted to explain a verse of an English poem, I said to him proudly, "Dadu, I can speak English too." He replied in a dismissive tone, "You can say you speak English only if you dream in English. Do you dream in English?" I did not, and mumbled under my breath, "No." He responded with a grin, "Then you don't really speak English."

The second event occurred fourteen years later in 2008 at Central European University in Budapest, Hungary. I was among a group of students who were about to begin a graduate program in International Relations and European Studies. It was our department's orientation meeting, and we went around the room stating our names, countries of origin, and areas of research interest. When it was my turn I said, "I'm from India." However, having lived abroad since 2003, I somehow felt compelled to let the other students know that I was not *just* Indian—I was more than that. I quickly added, "But I have lived abroad for some time now." Then it was the turn of the Kosovar student. He ended his introduction by proudly declaring, "I'm from Kosovo. The newest independent country in the world." While most of those in the room clapped and cheered him on, the Serbian student was unmoved and remained with his arms folded. A few days later, I ran into him on the way to a lecture. I asked him what he thought about the Kosovar student's declaration. He shrugged and replied, "If they are so proud to be liberated from Serbia, why do they still get free electricity."

So, what does it mean to be liberated? The *Oxford Dictionary* defines "liberation" as "the action of setting someone free from imprisonment, slavery, or oppression," a "release" and as "freedom from limits on thought or behavior" (Oxford Dictionary 2010, 1018). It would seem, then, that if liberation, at its core, signifies "freedom from" something, none of the individuals mentioned above were truly liberated. Surely, if asked, they would say that they had certainly secured their freedom from the oppressor. My grandfather would have said that he distinctly remembered listening to Jawaharlal Nehru's speech declaring India's independence. For him, Nehru's speech would have marked the withdrawal of colonial rule from India. The Kosovar student would similarly say that his country had secured its liberation when, on February 17, 2008, the Assembly of Kosovo declared its independence from Serbia. But did the withdrawal of the oppressor really mean the liberation of the oppressed? Undoubtedly, Dadu had witnessed the material dismantling of the British Raj in India. Yet, possibly out of habit, he kept up with the colonizer's ways in his mannerisms and language. He advised me that to claim that I spoke English, I needed to dream in English as well. Today I dream only in English, I am unable to conduct a conversation solely in Bengali (my native tongue), and at the orientation meeting in Budapest, felt that it was not enough to be *just* Indian. The colonizer withdrew thirty-seven years before I was born. But am I a liberated individual if I struggle to embrace my indigeneity in this manner? Can my grandfather be deemed liberated when being English remained such an integral facet of his identity? And, while I was unable to judge the Serbian student's assertion, can a national people claim to be liberated if they remain economically dependent, despite having secured political independence?

The Palestinian long moment suggests that the presence/absence of the colonizer is an insufficient marker of liberation. In this chapter I then venture beyond Palestine, as I further explore both the concern with the postcolonial in the era of colonial rule as well as the continued struggle for liberation after the withdrawal of the colonizer. The question remains, however, what are the possibilities of securing *actual* liberation if the presence or absence of the colonizer is an insufficient signifier of "freedom from" colonialism? In a sense, the case of Hamas represents the very vocation of the colonized. By this I mean that, faced with the continued vast and tenacious material infrastructure of the colonizer's rule, it is expected that the colonized are content to find only the signature of their cause everywhere and in everything—no matter how minimal or tragedy-ridden this may be. Moreover, as I have argued in the previous chapter, this "tactic" may in fact help sustain the cause of the liberation. But, in end, I suggest that the nature of the (settler) colonial endeavor, and its ability to alienate the colonized from their sense self, is such that the struggle for liberation from the legacies of colonial rule may persist perpetually—even when there is no memory of the colonial presence.

Postcolonial, Anticolonial, and Colonial Presence/Absence

Beyond Palestine, the colonized have routinely shown concern for the postcolonial, and not least the character of the postcolonial national community, *before* the withdrawal of the colonizer. In 1916, thirty-one years before Indian independence, this concern was visible when the Bengali polymath and Nobel Laureate Rabindranath Tagore wrote *Ghare Baire* (The Home and the World). Earlier, in his poem "The Sunset of the Century" (1899), Tagore had already expressed his misgivings about revolutionary anticolonial nationalism. He wrote,

> The last sun of the century sets amidst the blood-red clouds of the West and the whirlwind of hatred.
> The naked passion of self-love of Nations, in its drunken delirium of greed, is dancing to the clash of steel and the howling verses of vengeance.
> The hungry self of the Nation shall burst in a violence of fury from its own shameless feeding.

In *Ghare Baire* the character of Sandip symbolizes the uncompromising and "self-loving" nature of revolutionary nationalism that is solely concerned with the hunger for the nation. In his vengeance against the colonizer, Sandip is largely unconcerned with the cost of his revolutionary ways. The character of Nikhil, a wealthy landowner, is far more discerning. He *is* concerned with the cost of the all-encompassing, uncompromising greed of nations. He is also a progressive figure who sees value in the adoption (and not just rejection) of aspects of the West, especially for the emancipation of his wife Bimala from the strict boundaries of a traditional Bengali household and marriage. Bimala, the object of both Nikhil and Sandip's affection, represents the innocence of Bengal, caught between the two ways forward on the path of decolonization. She is initially devoted to her husband but is eventually taken in by the radicalism of Sandip's politics.

The characters in his novel, one imagines, symbolize Tagore's own struggle to determine the ideal path to liberation. Through the voice of Bimala, Tagore expresses his discomfort with the sudden and all-encompassing way in which the *Swadeshi* movement in Bengal demanded the complete rejection of foreign goods. Bimala ponders, "One day there came the new era of Swadeshi in Bengal. . . . There was no gradual slope connecting the past with the present. For that reason, I imagine, the new epoch came in like a flood, breaking down the dykes and sweeping all our prudence and fear before it. We had no time even to think about, or understand, what had happened, or what was about to happen" (Tagore 1919, 344). However, for Tagore the concern is not just the path of liberation but also the manner in which a particular chosen path of decolonization shapes the eventual postcolonial national community. Specifically, Tagore fears that the same nationalist ideology and political project that intends to corrode the colonizer's influence on the colonized community will prove indiscriminate in its corrosive effects, eventually affecting the postcolonial nation that will emerge out of the national struggle. Nikhil therefore does not attribute a sacrosanctity to the nation. He says, "To worship my country as a god is to bring a curse upon it" (Tagore 1919, 73). Further cautioning against the radicalism of the Swadeshi nationalist, Nikhil warns, "To tyrannize for the country is to tyrannize over the country" (Tagore 1919, 514). In this sense, Tagore anticipates the disadvantages of the sense of pride that informs the radical nationalist ideology and argues that, in the era of the postcolonial state, this pride will turn into arrogance and lead to "the repression of others." In the end, the novel is an expression of Tagore's call for a new world order. The world that results from the schemes of the nationalist, according to him, will lead to the destruction of "freedom and individuality." Instead, Tagore desires a world where individuality, diversity, and the "mutual interaction of all people" can thrive (Atkinson 1993, 98).

While directed toward the newly liberated and the many yet to be independent national communities in the African continent, Frantz Fanon's writings offer a similar reflection on what the postcolonial nation ought to look like. Concerned with the "trials and tribulations of national consciousness," Fanon is deeply critical of the new and forthcoming postcolonial political elite, deeming them both ill-prepared for national leadership and unconcerned with the welfare of the national community (Fanon 1963, 97–144). In his essay "On National Culture," Fanon also criticizes colonized African intellectuals for their attempts to revive the national community by uncovering what they consider to be the authentic precolonial culture. For Fanon, however, any such effort to recover a cultural identity that is untarnished by the colonizer is doomed to fail because it aims to demonstrate the existence of a "Negro" or "Negro-African" culture—a culture that is entirely a construction of the colonizer. It is the colonizer who does not care to differentiate among the various national communities living on the continent and instead categorizes the entirety of the inhabitants of Africa as a single "Negro" population, albeit, one that lacks a discernable cultural heritage. To speak of a precolonial "Negro" culture will therefore be to speak in categories that are essentially colonial and not national. Instead, Fanon imagines the national community and culture coming to fruition from the midst of the national struggle. Culture, for him, is an outcome of the nation, not vice versa. Therefore, emphasizing that the national struggle in and of itself is an expression of national culture, Fanon argues, "The conscious, organized struggle undertaken by a colonized people in order to restore national sovereignty constitutes the greatest [national] cultural manifestation that exists" (Fanon 1963, 178).

Of course, the concern for the postcolonial in the era of colonial rule is not just a matter of intellectual musings. While lacking the hyperinstitutionalized form in which it is performed in post-Oslo Palestine, postcoloniality has nonetheless been practiced by national communities still awaiting the withdrawal of the colonial occupier. For instance, in the eyes of the Turkish nationalist the Kurdish national community does not exist. It is this forceful denial of the existence of Kurdishness that led the Turkish state and its armed forces to etch Turkish nationalist iconography on the built and natural landscapes of Turkish Kurdistan. However, while the hills overlooking Kurdish-majority cities like Diyarbakir and Van may display the famed words of Mustafa Kemal Ataturk: "Ne mutlu Türküm diyene [How happy is the one who says I am Turkish]," the Kurdish residents living in their shadow are largely unconcerned with this message.[1] Instead, during my field research in 2015 on the Turkification of urban landscapes in Turkish Kurdistan, it was evident to me that they look to the era *after* the withdrawal of the occupier and are concerned with building the national community that will constitute the eventual, liberated Kurdistan. Thus, referring to the Turkish nationalist symbols in Diyarbakir's Dağkapı square, an interlocutor said, "It is nothing to deal with. It is there, but it doesn't change me or my life. Today it may not seem that we are struggling against Turkey, and Dağkapı is still there. But I still hold on to my Kurdish language and Kurdish heritage. That is how I fight . . . this is what is important for Kurdistan."[2]

In *The Nation and its Fragments*, Partha Chatterjee cites the writings of the Swadeshi movement leader Bipinchandra Pal, who described the way in which student messes in Calcutta had already begun to function like a democratic republic long before Indian independence from the British Raj. With this "republic," in its form and conduct, presumably mirroring what the future nation aspired to be in the postcolonial era, Pal wrote:

> Everything was decided by the voice of the majority of the members of the mess. At the end of every month a manager was elected by the whole "House," so to say, and he was charged with the collection of the dues of the members, and the general supervision of the food and establishment of the mess. . . . Disputes between one member and another were settled by a "Court" of the whole "House." (Pal 1973, 157–160, cited in Chatterjee 1993, 11)

Chatterjee also writes of the way a realm of national sovereignty was constructed in the middle-class Bengali household. During colonization, *bahir* (the material world outside) was a place dominated by the colonizer's rule of law, economy, and technologies (Chatterjee 1993, 26). It was also a place where trenchant material interests and the practical considerations for the Bengalis' material survival were of the utmost concern. In comparison, *ghar* (the home) was where the spiritual self was cultivated and protected (Chatterjee 1993, 120). Whether through language, religion, or the particular "elements of personal and family life," these features of the home were not just the bases for establishing cultural differences between the colonizer and the colonized, they were also a microcosm of the practice and performance of national sovereignty (before the acquisition of *actual* sovereignty), a realm distinct and free from the gaze of the colonizer (Chatterjee 1993, 26).

To be sure, the colonized are compelled to somehow concern themselves with the postcolonial while still living under colonial rule, and the ability to practice or perform *as if* one is in the era after the withdrawal of the colonizer therefore becomes a central facet of the liberation struggle. This is an outcome of the colonizer's claim, especially in settler colonial contexts, that the colonized do not exist as a distinct national community. The Israeli settlers premise their colonization schemes on the claim that Palestinians do not exist as a distinct national community. It was thus as a retort to such a claim that the Hamas summer camp I discussed in chapter 3 was meant to display and demonstrate the fact that Palestine and Palestinians exist and are organized. Fanon, as noted, was critical of the colonized African intellectuals for attempting to demonstrate the existence of a

"Negro" culture. But I would claim that, despite its faults, here too the colonized intellectuals feel compelled to display the existence of a national community and culture that constitute the postcolonial state because the colonizer insists on their nonexistence. In the same way, as the dominance of the colonizer in the material world outside leaves little room for the national community to emerge, it is in the Bengali home that the national culture takes form. The home provides a realm of sovereignty independent of the colonizer where the national identity can be nurtured and primed for the eventual confrontation between the colonizer and colonized. Of course, the colonized also need to perform or practice postcoloniality because they themselves must be convinced of the existence of their distinct national peoplehood, one that demands national liberation. As I have discussed in this book in the context of Fanon's works, the colonial endeavor is not just material in its nature. It also emaciates the colonized's spiritual being, alienating them from their sense of self as they strive after the metaphorical whiteness of the colonizer. My Palestinian interlocutors, for instance, reached out for this whiteness when they looked to Israel to learn how to build a (permanent) Palestinian state, through their past friendships with Israelis, and in their preference for Israeli consumer products because they were considered "upper class" (see chapter 4). But, being able to practice postcoloniality *as if* the colonizer has long withdrawn is self-referential as it becomes a way for the colonized to demonstrate to themselves that they *indeed* exist, are organized, and are deserving of national liberation.

Yet, just as the concern for the postcolonial persists alongside the struggle for liberation before the withdrawal of the colonizer, the struggle for liberation also continues in the era of the postcolonial state. Language, or what is considered to be the distinction between the vernacular languages and the language of the colonizer, is often the pretext for demanding liberation even in the absence of the colonizer. For my late grandfather and the Bengali middle-class circles of my upbringing, the ability to converse in English is undoubtedly a necessity for upward socioeconomic mobility. Of course, as Aijaz Ahmad rightly points out in *In Theory: Nations, Classes, Literatures*, the English language cannot simply be expunged or dismissed for its colonial heritage. "History," Ahmad cautions, "is not really open to correction through a return passage to an imaginary point, centuries ago, before the colonial deformation set in" (Ahmad 1992, 77). However, when the colonizer's language is accorded such prominence, language does become an important platform for nationalist contention for liberation, both before and after the flight of the colonizer.

The empowerment of Swahili vis-à-vis English, for example, was a significant facet of the Tanzanian independence struggle and in the activism of Julius Kambarage Nyerere. In his speeches Nyerere used Swahili vocabulary. As president of the Tanganyika African National Union (TANU) he introduced Swahili as the second language of legislative council meetings, and as part of the general liberation struggle, he emphasized the use of Swahili as a language that would standardize national(ist) communications (Legere 2006, 374–379). However, the cultivation of a national language as a platform for the cultivation of a national community did not cease with Tanzanian independence because Swahili became the language of the struggle to rebuild the nation from the shambles of colonial rule. Swahili was the language through which Nyerere's *Ujamaa* policy of "villagization" (i.e., the conglomeration of "smaller villages into larger communes") was discussed and explained within the country. The national language was also promoted as an essential facet of Nyerere's Education for Self-Reliance initiative, aimed at ensuring that primary education was sufficient "for the needs of the majority of the school-going population." The ability to read and write Swahili was then deemed integral to an education that promoted national self-reliance. In this sense, language became the tool of national emancipation. And, as was the case under colonial rule, Swahili remained a "vanguard of nation building" in the absence of the colonizer, as it idealized Tanzanian (and African) values, fostered national unity, provided for an egalitarian tool of communication available to everyone, and served as an expression of "racial pride, freedom, *Ujamaa* and anticolonialism" (Topan 2008, 258–259).

The struggle to liberate the once-colonized was also apparently the aim of a radical land acquisition program in Zimbabwe. In February 2000, the Robert Mugabe-led Zimbabwean African National Union-Patriotic Front (ZANU-PF) government failed to secure a majority "yes" vote in a referendum on constitutional reforms that would have both strengthened the executive branch and extended its ability to seize land without compensation. With the newly established Movement for Democratic Change (MDC) having campaigned for a "no" vote, Mugabe responded to the growing political opposition by calling for radical land redistribution as promised at independence. In doing so, he gave his "official blessing" to land occupations led by the War Veterans Association and amply supported by the army (Human Rights Watch 2002, 9–10). Dubbed the Fast-Track Land Reform Program (FTLRP), the government specified the types of land that were to be occupied. Land determined to be unused, underutilized, absentee owned, owned by someone with multiple farms, above a certain size and adjoining communal areas were slated for reclamation. White landowners were given ninety days to vacate their commercial farms. The government directive that designated twenty-nine hundred commercial farms for redistribution specified that the owners would be "compensated for improvements made on the land, but not for the land itself, as this land was stolen from the original owners in the colonial era." Although the FTLRP was to end in August 2002, in fact it continued until 2004. There were extensive reports of the violation of the "one person, one farm" policy by the (pro) ZANU-PF black political and economic elite. In 2005 the Mugabe government passed a constitutional amendment that established state ownership of all agricultural land. This led to the seizure of agricultural land from four thousand white farmers, as "72,000 large farmers received 2.19 million hectares and 127,000 smallholders received 4.23 million hectares" (Mamdani 2008, 17–21).

The controversial and radical nature of the FTLRP has spurred a vibrant and politically divisive discussion of the politics of the program and its wisdom. For some, FTLRP was indicative of the overt undermining of the judiciary by the executive branch (Masiiwa and Chipungu 2004). Others have described the corruption and political mismanagement of the land acquisitions, as well as the detrimental economic effects of a fast-track land reform initiative (Krinninger 2015; *The Economist* 2017; Alexander 2006; Meredith 2002). More recently, some have questioned the conventional wisdom concerning the FTLRP and argued that there has been a growth in production, investments, and in general, economic activities in the Zimbabwean agricultural sector despite the dismantling of large white-owned commercial farms (Matondi 2012; Scoones et al. 2010). However, here I am interested in the way the metaphor and imagery of the liberation of *black* Zimbabweans from the *white* (colonial) settlers defined the politics of the proponents of the FTLRP—this, despite two decades having passed since the official end of colonial rule. Land reform was a key aspiration of the Zimbabwean liberation struggle, and the white ownership of the large majority of the agricultural landscape was an unmistakable marker of the existence of settler colonial rule. For this reason, in the Lancaster House Agreement that led to the establishment of the Zimbabwean republic out of the Republic of Rhodesia, the acquisition and use of land and racial discrimination with regard to land tenure were extensively addressed (Lancaster House Agreement 1979; Dekker and Kinsey 2011; Cliffe et al. 2011). In 2000, with the remaining land ownership still being racially skewed to the advantage of white settlers, Mugabe readily embraced the concept of the FTLRP as part of a continued liberation struggle in the era of the postcolonial state. In his speech at Mount Olivet Baptist Church in Harlem on September 8, 2000, Mugabe declared,

> Although independence had come, it had come to us only in political terms. Some other people continued and still continue to deprive us of our economic independence. The land we had hoped would come to us easily after the understanding we had reached in 1979, as we negotiated for independence with the British at Lancaster House and they had agreed to fund the process of land acquisition and settlement, . . . the land we thought would come still hasn't come.[3]

Of course, the metaphor of a continued liberation struggle was embodied in Mugabe himself, as he posed as an iconic revolutionary figure who had once spearheaded Zimbabwean independence and who continued to do so in the era of the postcolonial state, albeit now under the pretext of a fast-track land reform.

Finally, the perception of the FTLRP as the continuation of a historical anti-colonial struggle is also apparent in the way it is occasionally called the Third Chimurenga.[4] The First Chimurenga was an uprising of the Ndebele and Shona tribes in Matabeleland and Mashonaland between 1896 and 1897. They revolted against white settlers, who, following their arrival, stole Ndebele and Shona land and cattle and imposed taxes to force tribal members "to sell labour" (Dawson 2011, 145). While Dawson considers the uprising to be much more complex than a national struggle, the First Chimurenga is nonetheless often described as an early expression of African anticolonial nationalism (ibid). The Zimbabwean independence struggle, or the Rhodesian Bush War, is then called the Second Chimurenga, thus drawing on the legacy of the Ndebele and Shona uprising (Martin and Johnson 1981; Kriger 1991). Then, by calling land reclamation in the 2000s the Third Chimurenga, the FTLRP also embeds itself in the long, historical legacy of an anticolonial struggle against the schemes of the white settlers.

This way of struggling for liberation long after a population has secured political independence is equally present in many other postcolonial and postrevolutionary political contexts. For example, the settler colonialism of the apartheid regime in South Africa also led to the minority white settler population owning a majority of the agricultural land (Cliffe 2000; Cousins 2009). But while the apartheid regime was officially dismantled in 1991, the struggle for the economic liberation of South Africa's black population is seen as still relevant almost two decades later. Accordingly, the aptly named Economic Freedom Fighters (EFF) party proposed an amendment to Section 25 of the South African constitution that "would allow expropriation of land without any financial recompense." When the proposal was approved by a parliamentary vote on March 1, 2018, Julius Malema, the leader of the EFF, declared to Parliament, "We must ensure that we restore the dignity of our people without compensating the criminals who stole our land" (Osborne 2018).

The Cuban Revolution is also said to have liberated the country from the authoritarian, corrupt, and imperialist-backed regime of Fulgencio Batista, who came to power following a military coup in 1952. However, while the guerrilla uprising led by Fidel Castro eventually ousted the Batista regime and established a revolutionary state in 1959 (Perez-Stable 2012, Paterson 1994), this did not necessarily mark the end of the cultivation of the revolutionary ethos in the postrevolution era. Julie Bunck, for instance, writes that, while Castro's leadership failed to build a revolutionary gender consciousness, work ethic, or youth consciousness, it nonetheless succeeded in cultivating a revolutionary sports culture. For the revolutionary regime at home, sport became a platform to mobilize citizens, build a healthier population to improve labor and military performances, and educate Cuba's citizens politically. In essence, through sport, "the government effectively controlled much of the leisure time of children, students and workers" (Bunck 1994, 186). Of course, the cultivation of a revolutionary culture in the era following the revolution was not just a means of control. Writing about cultural politics in the Cuban public sphere, Sugatha Fernandes argues that this sphere is also a platform in which revolutionary ideology is adopted and challenged, as well as one where the Cuban government tolerates counternarratives so that they can be eventually "reincorporated in official institutions, traditions and discourses in ways that bolster the state's popularity" (Fernandes 2006, 12).

In this section I have attempted to impart the limited significance of the presence or absence of the colonizer in determining what it means to be liberated or unliberated. Not unlike the manner in which the postcolonial was socialized into the liberation context in post-Oslo Palestine, a concern with the era of the postcolonial is often present among those striving for liberation *before* the actual dismantling of colonial rule. In the same vein, the struggle to liberate the colonized does not end with the official declaration of independence. Whether through the promotion of a national language under the pretext of national self-reliance, in the quest to liberate the formerly colonized who are yet to be freed from the colonial economic injustices that persist in the postcolonial state, or in the attempts to inculcate the ethos of revolution in all aspects of postrevolution life—liberation continues to be a concern long after formal political liberation. In the context of the Palestinian moment of liberation (see chapter 6), I argued that national liberation is a protracted affair that constitutes many ebbs and flows because of the vastness of the colonial endeavor that perforates almost every aspect of the colonized's lives. Often, it is this vastness that leads the colonized to be less concerned with the presence or absence of the colonizer than with maintaining the cause of liberation. This involves, for one thing, the colonized displaying to the colonizer that the national community indeed exists. Further, as I have argued earlier in this chapter, the colonized are compelled to perform *as if* the colonizer has withdrawn in order to convince, or remind, themselves that, despite the trials of life under colonial rule, liberation is a deserved and worthwhile aspiration.

The materiality of the colonial endeavor is also the pretext for the use and misuse of the narrative of liberation in the postcolonial and postrevolutionary era. It is the minimal rectification in the postindependence era of the uneven, racialized distribution of land ownership established under colonial rule that has allowed the minority white settlers in Zimbabwe and South Africa to remain proprietors of the majority of the agricultural land in the postcolonial state. Land, in this sense, was a key avenue of economic oppression for the colonized population living under settler colonial rule and continued to be perceived as such after independence. Then, under the premise of securing the colonized's economic independence, the apparently corrupt and economically unviable modes of redistribution were justified by the revolutionaries. Similarly, the prominence of the colonizer's language, often accorded during colonial rule, frequently "spills over" into the postcolonial era in which the ability to speak like the colonizer is still perceived as the sole means of socioeconomic advancement. As a result, the cultivation of a national language is pursued before and, more importantly, *after* the colonizer's withdrawal under the auspices of a continuing anticolonial struggle in order to rectify the prominence often accorded to aspects of the colonizer's cultural identity.

It is therefore in view of the regularity with which the postcolonial appears in the colonial condition and the frequency with which the anticolonial struggle continues after the withdrawal of the colonizer that we should be wary of exaggerating the importance of the colonizer's presence or absence. This is not to say that the withdrawal of the colonizers is not a momentous occasion: on the contrary, it is a significant point in the historical narrative of the liberation struggle when the colonizers officially announce their inability to persist with their colonial project. Yet, the colonized and the once-colonized do not make their aspirations and destiny contingent on this single moment. When it is deemed appropriate, they routinely draw from the other side of this moment in their quest to cultivate the postcolonial in the era of colonial rule. And, when it is both politically relevant and advantageous to do so, they persist with the liberation struggle even when the colonial state has officially been dismantled. It is this mode of rendering porous, if not entirely irrelevant, the colonial–postcolonial division in the lives of those who are striving for liberation that ensures that the moment of liberation is not a moment at all in the sense of a single occasion. Instead, liberation stretches out on both sides of this unique occasion as a complex psychological and cultural mix of the postcolonial and the colonial.

"But We Were Colonized, Just Like You"

Having reached the closing pages of this book, I do wonder whether struggles for liberation (long and protracted, as I have claimed thus far) ever end or find a conclusion. That is to ask, is there an end to this search for liberation? While visiting Dar es Salaam in early 2018, the struggle indeed seemed never-ending. My partner warned me that, although I had been able to build a relationship with many of my Palestinian interlocutors during my travels in Palestine because

I "looked Palestinian" and was, occasionally, just as much an object of suspicion to Israeli authorities as Palestinians were, things would be different in East Africa. Here, as an Indian, I would look like a member of the economic elite that had rapidly risen up the socioeconomic ladder as a beneficiary of the colonial administration. Today, while Tanzanians of Asian origin lack any significant political power, their economic power allows them to "lord" over black Tanzanians. In his book on Asian business elites in East Africa, Gijsbert Oonk describes South Asians as "settled strangers" who, after "three or four generations . . . find that it is never enough to be accepted as locally loyal" (Oonk 2013, 7). In his lecture at the University of Cape Town, Mahmood Mamdani asked, "When does a settler become a native?" Himself a Ugandan of Indian descent, Mamdani then went on to distinguish between civic and ethnic citizenship. The settler in East Africa, whether White, Asian, or Arab, may well secure civic citizenship in due course, yet, he argues, when it comes to ethnic citizenship the settler can never become a native (Mamdani 1998, 3). Of course, from the lofty views of my comfortable, sea-facing hotel in Dar es Salaam, it seemed that the settlers had no interest in descending from their socioeconomic heights to become natives anyway. While the South Asian-owned supermarket frequented by expats employed Africans, the managerial staff and, in particular, those who processed credit card payments were Asian. At the hotel restaurant, I too was both literally and figuratively at the same table as the whites, served by the all-black waiting staff. Ironically, I would have cherished a place at that table in my place of domicile in Denmark, where refugees, asylum-seekers, and immigrants alike struggle to cope with the draconian and ever more stringent immigration regulations. Yet, in Dar es Salaam, I wanted to be off that table, I wanted equality in subalternity. "I'm just like you," I wanted to say, "we were also colonized."

In my naïve and self-indulgent quest for *this* equality, I ventured toward downtown Dar es Salaam, to Kisutu, a neighborhood that is home to the city's South Asian residents. I was searching for KT shop—a hole-in-the-wall tea, samosa and kebab shop that sold South Asian delicacies to a racially mixed customer demographic. A *Vice* magazine story called it "a hot bed of diversity . . . bridging cultural divides in Tanzania" (Dehnert 2017). Surely, I hoped, a place like the KT shop would erase my privileged status. The very nature of the chaotic environment and service at the shop was an instant "equalizer" that ensured that its black and brown clientele rubbed shoulders, sat at the same tables and conversed with each other on equal terms. Yet, the KT shop represented the limits of this equality. Outside, I watched black Tanzanian workers labor in the hot sun while their brown bosses watched over them. In a store, matters of official business were to be addressed solely to the brown owner, sitting at his desk. The task of the black Tanzanian worker was to remain standing, receive orders barked at him by the owner and run inside to fulfill the customer's order. So, when I asked this worker about the availability of a certain product, the shocked stares of both the owner and the worker made it clear to me that I had broken a hierarchical chain of communication. Later, I met a black Tanzanian government employee at another coffee shop in Kisutu, who confirmed the existence of this hierarchy. He said,

> Indians of course think they are better than us. That's why, when we interact with them, it's only because of business. Sometimes they treat us badly. They don't have African friends. But we have also started to believe that Indians are better than us. In fact, if there are black workers, the Indian boss will treat them badly, not give them lunch and pay them less compared to an African boss. I may even give them lunch. But they will want to work with the Indian because this has become our mindset.[5]

In the weeks that followed, I begrudgingly accepted the existence of my brown privilege. However, what was particularly curious was the extent of my craving for equality in subalternity. Being subaltern is hardly a privileged position. Yet, self-indulgently I wanted to claim equality with black Tanzanians, despite not having any memory or experience of the colonial presence. Here there may be parallels between my self-indulgence and the regularity with which figures like Mugabe and Malema feature in the global political landscape. We may consider their politics to be despicable, brash, and ultimately fruitless. But they nonetheless demonstrate the extent to which the call for liberation continues to resonate and have political purchase. I have earlier attributed the length and protracted nature of the liberation struggle to the material prowess of the colonial endeavor. But the never-ending nature of the liberation struggle could also be attributed to the extent to which the colonized are undone by the colonial endeavor and alienated from their sense of self in a way that they do not have any memory of an identity sans the legacies of the colonization. Evidence of this undoing is present in Fanon's characterization of the African intellectuals who, despite their enthusiastic search for a national identity untarnished by colonial rule, unwittingly speak in categories (like the so-called "Negro culture") that are entirely colonial (Fanon 1963, 178). Aijaz Ahmad argued that English, as the colonizer's language, cannot simply be erased from the (formerly) colonized's identity because history is not open to retroactive course correction (Ahmad 1992, 77). But here too, it would seem, the experience of colonization is such that it leaves the colonized without any memory of a point in history to which they can return or refer in order to rebuild their national identity.

Of course, this loss of memory of a precolonial past "fits" my conception of the forming of colonial power at the beginning of this book. The consolidation of colonial rule, I argued, requires the "unforming or re-forming" of a colonized community in such a way that it institutionalizes the domination of the colonizer. As this unforming takes place through "trade, plunder, negotiations, negotiations, warfare, genocide, enslavement and rebellions" (Loomba 1998, 2), it is not a surprise that this process also undoes the colonized's sense of self—resulting, not least, in their craving the "white mask" (Fanon 1952). The concern, however, is far more acute for those living under settler colonial rule. As I have discussed in chapter 2, the settler colonial endeavor purposefully erases the existence of the indigenous. In Israel-Palestine this includes, among other things, the biological elimination of Palestinians, the erasure of evidence of Palestinian existence in Israeli museum exhibits and the appropriation of Palestinian cultural artifacts as Israeli. Similarly, the curriculum of residential schools in North America and Australia that house indigenous children who were forcefully removed from their parents' home was structured to deindigenize. This was evident, for example, in a school that used William Swinton's *Introductory Geography* to teach racial hierarchies to indigenous students—hierarchies that clearly designated "white people" as superior and the indigenous community as "savages" (Jacobs 2009, 250).

The (formerly) colonized are therefore compelled to perpetually struggle for their liberated self. This is precisely because of the way colonial rule in general, and settler colonialism in particular, undoes the colonized's identity, leaving them with no past and, as a consequence, no basis for building a liberated future. It is therefore all the more telling to find Fanon arguing that the colonized's national identity resides in the national anticolonial struggle itself (Fanon 1963, 178). This is something with which I would concur. This is not to suggest that the national struggle leads to a decolonized identity and liberation, but rather that the act of the struggle is the closest the oppressed comes to anything remotely resembling a decolonized sense of self. In Tanzania, Nyerere hoped to build a self-reliant nation after independence, and cultural liberation from the prominence accorded to the colonizer's language was the platform of this struggle. Almost two decades ago Robert Mugabe began the struggle for black Zimbabweans' economic independence through a program of fast-track land occupations. In 2018, the likes of Julius Malema in South Africa seemed to be aiming at a similar process of securing economic independence for black South Africans. In India today, more than seventy years after the official end of the British Raj, we lack the kind of white settler presence that is seen in southern Africa, yet we still struggle to find that point in history, untarnished by the occupier, on the basis of which we can conjure up our *liberated* identity.

Having been born and raised under British colonial rule, my grandfather would have experienced difficulty stripping himself of his Englishness. I, by contrast, have no memory of the colonial presence, yet I struggle to conduct a conversation entirely in my native tongue and am unable to dream in any other language than English. Some may even quip that the symbolic struggle for liberation was present in the acquisition of the iconic British brands Jaguar and Land Rover by the Indian automotive manufacturing company Tata Motors. Hindu nationalists in India would argue that, in their saffron garb, they embody religious, cultural, and ideological indigeneity. But when in 1992 Hindu nationalist activists tore down a sixteenth-century mosque, the Babri Masjid built by the Mughal general Mir Baqi, because it was believed to have been built on the site of the birthplace of the Hindu deity Rama, they too were attempting to "correct" the past. And, by effacing the remnants of a perceived occupier, they were striving to liberate the nation from certain aspects of its history.

Palestine may eventually be liberated from settler colonial rule. But, here too it is unlikely that the struggle for liberation will end with the withdrawal of the settler. On the contrary, weighed under the legacy of a settler colonial rule insistent on Palestinian nonexistence, the struggle for liberation is likely to continue—albeit in different ways, under different pretexts and justified for different kinds of political gains. Such struggle persists because we feel adrift somewhere between oppression and liberation. But since we have no memory of a precolonial independent existence, we persist with the struggle for liberation, irrespective of the presence or absence of the oppressor. Perhaps it is only while fighting for liberation and against oppression that the unliberated are able to enjoy the feeling, and possibly the relative reality, of liberation.

Notes

CHAPTER 1. DECOLONIZING PALESTINE

1. As opposed to the Egyptian permit that allowed me to use the Rafah border cross-ing, this permit officially granted me entry *inside* Gaza. However, securing the Palestinian permission is largely a ritual affair. It is the Egyptian permit that determines whether or not one is able to enter (or leave) Gaza.

2. The Battle of Gaza refers to the armed conflict between Hamas and Fatah that took place between June 10 and 15, 2007. I discuss the circumstances that led to this conflict in chapter 3 in the context of the Oslo-mandated norms of Palestinian politics.

3. Izz ad-Din al-Qassam Brigade is Hamas's military wing.

4. Author Interview, Gaza City, June 2013.

5. In *Collateral Language* John Collins and Ross Glover insist that language is rarely *just* a means of communication. Instead, the use of expressions like "terrorism," "freedom," "fundamentalism," and "The War on Poverty/Drugs" in political rhetoric, especially in times of war, can "target civilians," "generate fear," and manufacture consent for unsavory forms of politics and their human and material consequences (Collins and Glover 2002, 2).

6. Field Notes, Tel Aviv, December 2015.

7. Here my acquaintance is referring to Israel's unilateral disengagement from the Gaza Strip in 2005. This dismantling of Israel's military and civilian presence within Gaza was based on a disengagement plan first introduced by Israeli prime minister Ariel Sharon at the 2003 Herzliya Conference, that also included plans to evacuate four West Bank settlements (Sharon 2003). The plan was first approved by the Israeli government in June 2004 and then by the Knesset in October 2004. In August 2005 the withdrawal plan was finalized and implemented. Israeli settlers, who were evacuated from the Gaza Strip and the West Bank, were compensated as per a law on compensation procedures approved by the Knesset in February 2005 (ECF 2005). Since, at the time, Israeli settlers were a small minority in the Gaza Strip, this disengagement was presented by Prime Minister Sharon as a way of "preserving a Jewish majority" in the Israeli state (Peleg and Waxman 2011, 122). However, despite this official unilateral disengagement from within the Gaza Strip, Israeli authorities have since maintained control over Gaza's borders by air, land, and sea, not least by means of the ongoing siege of the coastal enclave.

8. Field Notes, Jerusalem, December 2015.

9. In this book I have also consciously avoided the term *occupation*, which usually refers to the territories occupied by Israel following the Six-Day War of 1967. I am largely concerned with the entire period following the establishment of the State of Israel in 1948. That said, some of my Palestinian interlocutors do use the term *occupation* as a way of describing the Israeli military presence in the West Bank, Jerusalem, and the Gaza Strip.

10. This term was originally coined by Mohammed Harbi (1980).

11. Field Notes, Gaza Strip, May 2013.

CHAPTER 2. ON THE SETTLER COLONIAL ELIMINATION OF PALESTINE

1. CCTV footage of the attack was published by the right-wing Israeli news out-let Arutz Sheva. The video is available at www.youtube.com/watch?v=aw8eYodVrVs (accessed June 14, 2019).

2. Field notes, Jerusalem, November 2015.

3. While my concern here is the manner in which Palestinians experienced the establishment of the State of Israel, it is nonetheless important to recognize that the emergence of political Zionism is deeply rooted in the European history (and legacy) of the persecution of Jewish communities (Laqueur 2003; Avineri 1981). It is this history of persecution that led to the urgency of the establishment of a Jewish state. And, Theodor Herzl, in the closing lines of *Judenstaat*, declared: "The Jews who wish for a State will have it. We shall live at last as free men on our own soil and die peacefully in our own homes" (Herzl 1896, 72).

4. Edited footage of the encounter is available at www.youtube.com/watch?v=zl0IhCr8Ya4&t=129s (accessed June 15, 2019).

5. A spiced dish of poached eggs and tomatoes.

6. The unedited footage of the encounter is available at http://teamcoco.com/video/web-exclusive-conan-talks-with-palistinian-activists (June 15, 2019).

7. Field notes, Beit HaPalmach Tel Aviv, November 2013.

8. Field notes, Tel Aviv, November 2015.

9. The video and video of the interview is available at www.democracynow.org/2018/4/19/rashid_khalidi_the_israeli_security_establishment (accessed June 15, 2019).

10. Video available at www.facebook.com/idfonline/videos/1863897166966478/ (accessed June 15, 2019).

11. The press release is available at www.facebook.com/IsraelMFA/photos/a.4595111 11316/10155543830186317/?type=3&theater.

12. The full statement is available at: www.youtube.com/watch?v=ET1cU5_A2YM (accessed June 15, 2019).

13. CCTV footage of the attacks on Haftom Zarum was published by the Israeli newspaper *Haaretz* on YouTube. The video is available at www.youtube.com/watch?v=GWjP2_PRjPQ (accessed June 15, 2019).

CHAPTER 3. PALESTINIAN POSTCOLONIALITY

1. Figures 3.1, 3.2, and parts of this chapter have been published in Sen 2015b. Figures 3.3 and 3.4 were previously published in Sen 2013a.

2. Arafat, al-Wazir and Khalaf were among those who founded Fatah in 1959, while Habash established the Popular Front for the Liberation of Palestine in 1967.

3. UN Security Council Resolution 242 was adopted on November 22, 1967, following the Six-Day War. It declared the acquisition of territory through war to be inadmissible. The resolution further affirmed that lasting (and just) peace in the region could only be achieved through the withdrawal of Israeli troops from the Palestinian territories and the recognition of the sovereignty and territorial integrity of every state in the region, as well as their right to peaceful existence free from external threats. UN Security Council Resolution 338 was adopted on October 22, 1973, and called for the end of the Yom Kippur War (1973) (UNISPAL 1993).

4. See Elgot 2013 and Agence France-Presse 2013.

5. I have also discussed this visit in Sen 2013a.

6. Field Notes, Gaza Strip, June 2013.

7. Author Interview, Gaza Strip, June 2013.

8. Author Interview, Gaza Strip, June 2013.

9. Author Interview, Cairo, January 2013.

10. Shuja'iyya is known for being home to a strong contingent of Palestinian fighters. During Operation Protective Edge in 2014 the neighborhood was the site of the deadliest Israeli attack that lead to the death of approximately 120 Palestinians (Beaumont, Sherwood, and Weaver 2014).

11. Author Interview, Gaza Strip, May 2013.

12. Author Interview, Copenhagen, December 2012.

13. Author Interview, Gaza Strip, May 2013.

14. Author Interview, Gaza Strip, May 2013.

15. Author Interview, Gaza Strip, May 2013.

16. The text of Arafat's speech can be accessed at www.youtube.com/watch?v= nyTQPV3AgzA.

17. It is important to recognize that this transformation was not without opposition from within the ranks of Fatah and the PLO. But, despite "spirited resistance," Arafat was able to win the approval of the Fatah central committee. From the PLO executive committee Arafat received only nine of eighteen votes in favor of the Accords but the "resignations or self-imposed absences of five opponents" meant that he was able to proceed with the Interim Agreement (Sayigh 1997b, 658).

18. At the time of writing, the most recent reconciliation agreement was signed between Hamas and Fatah on October 12, 2017.

19. Hamas has been pressured by the disincentives (war, siege and sanctions) of violating the Oslo Accords.

20. Author Interview, Gaza Strip, May 2013.

21. Author Interview, Gaza Strip, June 2013.

22. Author Interview, Gaza Strip, June 2013.

23. Author Interview, Gaza Strip, June 2013.

24. Field Notes, Gaza Strip, June 2013.

25. Author Interview, Gaza Strip, May 2013.

CHAPTER 4. ANTICOLONIAL VIOLENCE AND THE PALESTINIAN STRUGGLE TO EXIST

1. A significantly abridged version of this chapter has been published as Sen 2017.

2. Author Interview, Gaza Strip, June 2013.

3. I have never been able to find any publicly available sources confirming the rescue.

4. Field Notes, Gaza Strip, June 2013.

5. Author Interview, Cairo, January 2013.

6. This interaction took place following one of my public presentation.

7. I of course recognize the practical challenges of documenting in pictures and videos Hamas's militant operations as they happen. However, as I discuss later in this chapter, a tunneling operation in 2014 conducted by Hamas nevertheless involved operatives carrying a camera to document the incident.

8. Author Interview, Gaza Strip, June 2013.

9. Author Interview, Gaza Strip, June 2013.

10. Since Fanon characterized the colonial subject as a man, I have chosen to use the male form while paraphrasing his writings.

11. Author Interview, Ramallah, January 2014.

12. Field Notes, Gaza Strip, June 2013.

13. Author Interview, Gaza Strip, June 2013.

14. Author Interview, Gaza Strip, June 2014.

15. Author Interview, Gaza Strip, June 2013.

16. Author Interview, Gaza Strip, May 2013.

17. Author Interview, Gaza Strip, May 2013.

18. Author Interview, Gaza Strip, May 2013.

19. Author Interview, Gaza Strip, June 2013.

20. Referring to Operation Cast Lead (2008–9) and Operation Pillar of Defense (2012).

21. At the end of his answer I asked Hamad to clarify what he meant by "we." He replied, "By 'we,' I mean Palestinians."

22. Author Interview, Gaza Strip, June 2013.

23. Nom de guerre of the leader of the Zapatista Army of National Liberation (EZLN).

24. On January 1, 1994, EZLN soldiers temporarily captured the major urban centers in the Chiapas.

25. The main plaza in Mexico City.

26. Field notes, Beit HaPalmach, Tel Aviv, November 2013.

27. Author Interview, Gaza Strip, May 2013.

28. Author Interview, Cairo, January 2013.

29. Author Interview, Cairo, January 2013.

30. Author Interview, Gaza Strip, May 2013.

31. Author Interview, Gaza Strip, June 2013.

32. Field Notes, Gaza Strip, May 2013.

33. Author Interview, Gaza Strip, June 2013.

34. While outside the scope of this book, undeniably the relationship between gender roles, masculinity, violence, and nationalism plays an important role in such discussions.

35. These statistics are difficult to verify. According to the Palestinian Centre for Human Rights, 175,000 Palestinians were arrested during the First Intifada. Additionally, between 1967 and 1988, 600,000 Palestinians were held in Israeli prisons (Palestinian Center for Human Rights 2002). As of May 2019, there were 5,350 Palestinian political prisoners in Israeli prisons (Addameer 2019).

36. Author Interview, Gaza Strip, June 2013.

37. See image in Rudoren 2014.

38. Author Interview, Gaza Strip, May 2013.

39. Bose also had a controversial legacy because of his overtures to Nazi Germany and Imperial Japan in the effort to defeat the British Raj. For more on this aspect, see, Hayes 2011.

CHAPTER 5. POSTCOLONIAL GOVERNANCE

1. My interlocutors in the Gaza Strip often joked that the length of a person's beard indicated his political allegiances. "No beard" would signify a Fatah or PFLP supporter, while a beard that was "too long" could indicate a Salafist or an Islamic Jihad supporter.

2. See Palestinian Central Bureau of Statistics 2012.

3. Phone Interview, February 2015.

4. Author Interview, Gaza Strip, June 2013.

5. Here it is important to note that the Palestinian Authority's fiscal operations—not least its tax revenues—are greatly contingent on its relations with Israel as codified by the Paris Protocol signed on April 29, 1994. Over the years this has left the Palestinian economy increasingly vulnerable to the political tides of Israeli-Palestinian relations since Israel collects value-added taxes and customs on behalf of the Palestinian Authority and is able to decide whether or not these funds will be transferred to it (Fjeldstad and Zagha 2004, 195; GISHA 2011).

6. Since 2010 the Hamas government has imposed tax regulations that are separate from those stipulated by the Palestinian Authority in the West Bank. Over the years it has imposed additional taxes on fuel, smuggled goods, construction materials, and tobacco (McCarthy 2010; Rubinstein 2012; al-Ghoul 2014; Balousha 2015).

7. Author Interview, Gaza Strip, June 2013.

8. Author Interview, Gaza Strip, June 2013.

9. Ahmed Yousef is the secretary general of HOW. For more on the organization's objectives, see HOW 2010.

10. Author Interview, Gaza Strip, May 2013.

11. Author Interview, Gaza Strip, May 2013.

12. This book is not concerned with providing a genealogy of Hamas and its operational priorities. It is nonetheless important to recognize that Hamas's socio-civilian identity draws on its predecessor's, the Palestinian Muslim Brotherhood's legacy of socio-civilian activism under Israeli rule and in exile (Mishal and Sela 2000; Roy 2011; Gunning 2007; Knudsen 2005).

13. Author Interview, Gaza Strip, May 2013.

14. Author Interview, Gaza Strip, June 2013.

15. Author Interview, Gaza Strip, May 2013.

16. Abu Heen himself has insisted that SAFA is an independent media institution (Abdelal 2016, 148).

17. Author Interview, Gaza Strip, May 2013.

18. Author Interview, Gaza Strip, June 2013.

19. Author Interview, Gaza Strip, June 2013.

20. Field Notes, Gaza Strip, June 2013.

21. I have adopted this expression from chapter 1 ("Gender Makes the World Go Round") of Enloe 1990.

22. Author Interview, Gaza Strip, May 2013.

23. Author Interview, Gaza Strip, May 2013.

24. Author Interview, Gaza Strip, June 2013.

25. Author Interview, Gaza Strip, May 2013.

26. Author Interview, Gaza Strip, June 2013.

27. Author Interview, Gaza Strip, May 2013.

28. Author Interview, Gaza Strip, June 2013.

29. Email Correspondence, June 2014.

30. Author Interview, Gaza Strip, June 2013.

31. Author Interview, Phone Interview, March 2015.

CHAPTER 6. THE PALESTINIAN MOMENT OF LIBERATION

1. The Gaza-based journalist introduced in chapter 5.

2. Author Interview, Gaza City, June 2013.

3. Phone Interview, March 2018.

4. In a discussion of the role of international donors and stakeholders who are political and financially responsible for the upkeep of the Palestinian Authority and its (violent) statelike conduct, Pace and Sen argue that external investments should be contingent on the extent to which the Palestinian Authority operates in service of securing Palestinian rights and not on the extent to which it is able mimic a "real" state (Pace and Sen 2019, 86–87).

CHAPTER 7. ON LIBERATION

1. That is to suggest that an individual cannot be happy if she/he identifies as anything *but* Turkish—say, for instance, as Kurdish.

2. Author Interview, Diyarbakir, January 2015.

3. See excerpt from Mugabe's speech at https://www.youtube.com/watch?v=Ape ZWRcJI0U (last accessed on May 28, 2018).

4. "Chimurenga" means "fight" or "struggle" in the Shona language.

5. Field Notes, Dar es Salaam, February 2018.

Bibliography

Abdelal, Wael. 2016. *Hamas and the Media: Politics and Strategy.* Oxon: Routledge.

Abufarha, Nasser. 2008. "Land of Symbols: Cactus, Poppies, Orange, and Olive Trees in Palestine." *Identities: Global Studies in Culture and Power* 15(3): 343–368.

Abunimah, Ali. 2006. "Hamas Election Victory: A Vote for Clarity." *Electronic Intifada,* January 26. http://electronicintifada.net/content/hamas-election-victory-vote-clarity/5847.

Abunimah, Ali. 2012. "Hummus and Falafel Are Already 'Israeli.' Now They're Coming for Palestine's Olive Oil Too." *Electronic Intifada*, January 16. https://electroni cintifada.net/blogs/ali-abunimah/hummus-and-falafel-are-already-israeli-now-theyre-coming-palestines-olive-oil-too.

Addameer. 2012. "Eyes on Israeli Military Court: A Collection of Impressions." December 31. http://www.addameer.org/publications/eyes-military-court-collection-impressions.

Addameer. 2019. "Statistics: May 2019." Accessed June 15. http://www.addameer.org/statistics/20190529.

Agence France-Presse (AFP). 2013. "Gaza Children Play War in Hamas Summer Camp." July 18. https://www.youtube.com/watch?v=9Pw8SO0GOJU.

Ahmad, Aijaz. 1994. *In Theory: Classes, Nations, Literature.* New York: Verso.

Akram, Fares, and Jodi Rudoren. 2014. "Executions in Gaza Are a Warning to Spies." *New York Times*, August 22. http://www.nytimes.com/2014/08/23/world/mid dleeast/israel-gaza.html.

Al Aqsa. 2014. "Hamas Spokesman Fawzi Barhoum in an Interview to Hamas's Al-Aqsa TV Channel." July 12. https://www.youtube.com/watch?v=wxZIASHyjLA.

Alexander, Jocelyn. 2006. *The Unsettled Land: State-making and the Politics of Land in Zimbabwe, 1893–2003.* Athens: Ohio University Press.

Al-Ghoul, Asmaa. 2014. "Source: Hamas Resorts to Tobacco Taxes to Pay State Employees." *Al Monitor*, January 20. http://www.al-monitor.com/pulse/originals/2014/01/gaza-government-hamas-cigarette-taxes-pay-state-employees.html#.

Al-Muqtafi. 2019. "Legal System and Legislative Process in Palestine." *Institute of Law, Birzeit University*, June 16. http://muqtafi.birzeit.edu/PDFPre.aspx?PDFPath=en/Uploads/supportive_research_and_studies/dd.pdf.

Amnesty International. 2017. "Gaza: Looming Humanitarian Catastrophe Highlights Need to Lift Israel's 10-Year Illegal Blockade." June 14. https://www.amnesty.org/en/latest/news/2017/06/gaza-looming-humanitarian-catastrophe-highlights-need-to-lift-israels-10-year-illegal-blockade.

Atkinson, David W. 1993. "Tagore's *The Home and the World*: A Call for a New World Order." *International Fiction Review* 20(2): 95–98.

Authority of the Secretary of the Interior. 1884. *Regulation of the Indian Department.* Washington, DC: Government Printing Office.

Avineri, Shlomo. 1981. *The Making of Modern Zionism: The Intellectual Origins of the Jewish State.* New York: Basic Books.

Ayyash, Mark Muhannad. 2010. "Hamas and the Israeli State: A 'Violent Dialogue.'" *European Journal of International Relations* 16(1): 103–123.

Bakr, Amena. 2014. "Hamas Leader Says Gaza Only a 'Milestone to Reaching Our Objective.'" *Reuters*, August 28. https://www.reuters.com/article/us-mideast-gaza-meshaal-rafah/hamas-leader-says-gaza-only-a-milestone-to-reaching-our-objective-idUSKBN0GS24Q20140828.

Balousha, Hazem. 2015. "Hamas Imposes New Taxes to Meet Payroll Dues." *Al Monitor*, April 29. https://www.al-monitor.com/pulse/originals/2015/04/palestine-hamas-employees-taxes-payroll-economy-gaza-strip.html.

Batchelor, John. 2014. "Hamas' Attack Tunnels Are Transforming War with Israel." *Al Jazeera America*, July 29. http://america.aljazeera.com/opinions/2014/7/gaza-tunnels-hamasisraelidf.html.

Beaudoux, Edith Kovats. 2003. *Les blancs créoles de la Martinique. Une minorité dominante*. Paris: Editions L'Harmattan.

Beaumont, Peter. 2017. "Hamas and Fatah Sign Deal over Control of Gaza Strip." *The Guardian*, October 12. https://www.theguardian.com/world/2017/oct/12/hamas-claims-deal-agreed-fatah-control-gaza-strip.

Beaumont, Peter, Harriet Sherwood, and Matthew Weaver. 2014. "Gaza Crisis: Palestinian Death Toll Climbs Past 500 as Hospital Is Hit." *The Guardian*, July 21. https://www.theguardian.com/world/2014/jul/21/gaza-crisis-obama-ceasefire-fighting-goes-on.

Bender, Dave. 2014. "Residents of Nahal Oz Respond to Video of Hamas Attack—'How Can Children Continue to Live Here?'" *Algemeiner,* July 30. http://www.algemeiner.com/2014/07/30/residents-of-nahal-oz-respond-to-video-of-hamas-attack-how-can-children-continue-to-live-here-video.

Benvenisti, Meron. 2002. *Sacred Landscape. The Buried History of the Holy Land since 1948*. Berkeley: University of California Press.

Bhasin, Tavishi, and Maia Carter Hallwark. 2013. "Hamas as a Political Party: Democratization in the Palestinian Territories." *Terrorism and Political Violence* 25(1): 75–93.

Blusse, Leonard. 1995. "Retribution and Remorse: The Interaction between the Administration and the Protestant Mission in Early Colonial Formosa." In *After Colonialism: Imperial Histories and Postcolonial Displacements*, edited by Gyan Prakash, 153–182. Princeton, NJ: Princeton University Press.

Boserup, Rasmus Alenius. 2009. "Collective Violence and Counter-State Building." In *Crisis of the State: War and Social Upheaval*, edited by Bruce Kapferer and Bjørn Enge Bertelsen, 241–264. New York: Berghan Books.

Bourdieu, Pierre. 1998. *Practical Reason: On the Theory of Action*. Stanford, CA: Stanford University Press.

Brown, Nathan J. 2012. *Gaza Five Years On: Hamas Settles In*. Beirut: Carnegie Endowment for International Peace.

Brynen, Rex. 2000. *A Very Political Economy: Peacebuilding and Foreign Aid in the West Bank and Gaza*. Washington, DC: United States Institute for Peace.

B'Tselem. 2010. "Kept in the Dark: Treatment of Palestinian Detainees in the Petah Tikva Interrogation Facility of the Israel Security Agency." October 26. https://www.btselem.org/download/201010_kept_in_the_dark_eng.pdf.

B'Tselem. 2015a. "Security Forces' Duty to Protect Civilians Must Not Become a License to Kill without Trial." November 23. https://www.btselem.org/press_releases/2015 1123_extrajudicial_killings.

B'Tselem. 2015b. "Your Responsibility for Permitting a De Facto Death Penalty." November 25. https://www.btselem.org/download/20151125_letter_to_pm_on_extrajudicial_killings_eng.pdf.

B'Tselem. 2017a. "Unprotected: Detention of Palestinian Teenagers in East Jerusalem." October 24. https://www.btselem.org/ota/152823.

B'Tselem. 2017b. "Torture and Abuse in Interrogations." November 11. http://www. btselem.org/torture.

Bunck, Julie M. 1994. *Fidel Castro and the Quest for a Revolutionary Culture in Cuba.* University Park: Penn State Press.

Caridi, Paola. 2012. *Hamas: From Resistance to Government.* New York: Seven Stories Press.

Chatterjee, Partha. 1993. *The Nation and Its Fragments: Colonial and Postcolonial Histories.* Princeton, NJ: Princeton University Press.

Clausewitz, Carl von. 1976. *On War.* Oxford: Oxford University Press.

Cleveland, Todd. 2005. "'We Still Want the Truth': The ANC's Angolan Detention Camps and Postapartheid Memory." *Comparative Studies of South Asia, Africa, and the Middle East* 25(1): 63–78.

Cliffe, Lionel. 2000. "Land Reform in South Africa." *Review of African Political Economy* 27(84): 273–286.

Cliffe, Lionel, Jocelyn Alexander, Ben Cousins, and Rudo Gaidzanwa. 2011. "An Overview of Fast Track Land Reform in Zimbabwe: Editorial Introduction." *Journal of Peasant Studies* 38(5): 907–938.

Cobham, David, and Nu'man Kanafani. 2004. "Introduction." In *The Economics of Palestine: Economic Policy and Institutional Reform for a Viable Palestinian State*, edited by David Cobham and Nu'man Kanafani, 1–11. New York: Routledge.

Collier, George A., and Elizabeth Lowery Quaratiello. 2005. *Basta! Land and the Zapatista Rebellion in Chiapas.* Oakland: Food First Books.

Collins, John, and Ross Glover. 2002. "Introduction." In *Collateral Language: A User's Guide to America's New War*, edited by John Collins and Ross Glover, 2–13. New York: New York University Press.

Collins, John. 2011. *Global Palestine.* New York: Columbia University Press.

Cousins, Ben. 2009. "Land Reform in South Africa." *Journal of Agrarian Change* 9(3): 421–431.

Dana, Tariq. 2014. *A Resistance Economy: What Is It and Can It Provide an Alternative?* Ramallah: Rosa Luxemburg Stiftung Regional Office Palestine.

Darwish, Mahmoud. 2000. *The Adam of Two Edens: Selected Poems.* Syracuse, NY: Syracuse University Press.

Darwish, Mahmoud. 2010. *State of Siege.* Syracuse, NY: Syracuse University Press.

Dawson, Suzanne. 2011. "The First Chimurenga, 1896–1897: Uprising in Matabeland and Mashonaland and the Continued Conflicts in Academia." *Constellations* 2(2): 144–153.

Dehnert, Elspeth. 2017. "A Tea Shop Founded by Indian Immigrants Is Bridging Cultural Divides in Tanzania." *Vice: Munchies*, March 16. https://munchies.vice. com/en_us/article/z4kwyy/a-tea-shop-run-by-indian-immigrants-is-bridging-cultural-divides-in-tanzania.

Dekker, Marleen, and Bill Kinsey. 2011. "Contextualizing Zimbabwe's Land Reform: Long-Term Observations from the First Generation." *Journal of Peasant Studies* 38(5): 995–1019.

Dunning, Tristan. 2016. *Hamas, Jihad, and Popular Legitimacy: Reinterpreting Resistance in Palestine.* Oxon: Routledge.

Economic Cooperation Foundation (ECF). 2005. "Disengagement Plan Implementation Law." February 17. http://ecf.org.il/issues/issue/97.

The Economist. 2017. "How Robert Mugabe Ruined Zimbabwe." February 26. https://www.economist.com/blogs/economist-explains/2017/02/economist-explains-20.

Efrat, Elisha. 2006. *The West Bank and Gaza Strip.* New York: Routledge.

Elgot, Jessica. 2013. "Gaza Children Play 'Kidnap The Soldier' at Military Summer Camp." *Huffington Post,* June 14. http://www.huffingtonpost.co.uk/2013/06/13/gaza-summer-camp_n_3433221.html.

Elkins, Caroline, and Susan Pederson. 2005. "Settler Colonialism: A Concept and Its Uses." In *Settler Colonialism in the Twentieth Century,* edited by Caroline Elkins and Susan Pederson, 1–20. New York: Routledge.

Enloe, Cynthia. 1990. *Bananas, Beaches, and Bases: Making Feminist Sense of International Politics.* Berkeley: University of California Press.

European Union Police and Rule of Law Mission for the Palestinian Territory (EUPOL COPPS). 2014. "Police and Rule of Law Mission for the Palestinian Territories." Last modified February 2015. http://eeas.europa.eu/csdp/missions-and-operations/eupol-copps-palestinian-territories/pdf/factsheet_eupol_copps_en.pdf.

Ezzedeen Al-Qassam Brigades. 2014. "Military Communique: Press Release of Abu Obeida, Al Qassam Spokesperson." August 20. http://www.qassam.ps/statement-1509-Press_Release_of_Abu_Obeida_Al_Qassam_spokesperson.html.

Ezzedeen Al-Qassam Brigades—Information Office. 2019. "About Us." Accessed June 16. http://www.qassam.ps/aboutus.html.

Fanon, Frantz. 1952. *Black Skin, White Masks.* London: Pluto Press.

Fanon, Frantz. 1963. *The Wretched of the Earth.* New York: Grove Press.

Fanon, Frantz. 1964. *Towards the African Revolution.* New York: Grove Press.

Fernandes, Sujatha. 2006. *Cuba Represent! Cuban Arts, State Power, and the Making of New Revolutionary Cultures.* Durham, NC: Duke University Press.

Finkelstein, Norman. 2018. *Gaza: An Inquest into Its Martyrdom.* Berkeley: University of California Press.

Fjeldstad, Odd-Helge, and Adel Zagha. 2004. "Taxation and State Formation in Palestine 1994–2000." In *State Formation in Palestine. Viability and Governance during Social Transformations,* edited by Mushtaq Husain Khan, George Giacaman, and Inge Amundsen, 192–214. New York: Routledge Curzon.

Frisch, Hillel. 1998. *Countdown to Statehood: Palestinian State Formation in the West Bank and Gaza.* Albany: State University of New York Press.

Gaess, Roger. 1997. "Interview with Mousa Abu Marzook." *Middle East Policy* 5(2): 113–128.

Gangahar, Manisha. 2013. "Decoding Violence in Kashmir." *Economic and Political Weekly* 48(4): 35–42.

Geismar, Peter, and Peter Worsley. 1969. "Frantz Fanon: Evolution of a Revolutionary: A Biographical Sketch; Revolutionary Theories." *Monthly Review* 21(1): 22–51.

Gilbert, Mads. 2014. "Brief Report to UNRWA: The Gaza Health Sector as of June 2014." United Nations Relief and Works Agency for Palestine Refugees in the Near East (UNRWA), July 3. http://www.unrwa.org/sites/default/files/final_report_-_gaza_health_sector_june-july_2014_-_mads_gilbert_2.pdf

Ginsburg, Mitch. 2014. "IDF Treats Hundreds of Soldiers for PTSD-like Symptoms Post-Gaza." *Times of Israel,* November 5. http://www.timesofisrael.com/idf-treats-hundreds-of-soldiers-for-ptsd-like-symptoms-post-gaza.

GISHA–Legal Center for Freedom of Movement. 2011. "The Tax System. Scale of Control." November 14. http://gisha.org/en-blog/2011/11/14/the-tax-system.

GISHA–Legal Center for Freedom of Movement. 2017. "Unemployment in Gaza in Early 2017: Over 40 Percent." July 4. http://gisha.org/updates/7962.

Gleis, Joshua L., and Bendetta Berti. 2012. *Hezbollah and Hamas: A Comparative Study.* Baltimore, MD: Johns Hopkins University Press.

Grohs, G. K. 1968. "Frantz Fanon and the African Revolution." *Journal of Modern African Studies* 6(4): 543–556.

Gunning, Jeroen. 2007. *Hamas in Politics: Democracy, Religion, Violence.* London: Hurst & Company.

Gupta, Akhil. 1995. "Blurred Boundaries: The Discourse of Corruption, the Culture of Politics, and the Imagined State." *American Ethnologist* 22(2): 375–402.

Hage, Ghassan. 2003. "'Comes a Time We Are All Enthusiasm': Understanding Palestinian Suicide Bombers in Time of Exighophobia." *Public Culture* 15(1): 65–89.

Halevi, Ilan. 1998. "Self-Government, Democracy, and Mismanagement under the Palestinian Authority." *Journal of Palestine Studies* 27(3): 35–48.

Hanafi, Sari. 2009. "Spacio-cide: Colonial Politics, Invisibility, and Rezoning in Palestinian Territory." *Contemporary Arab Affairs* 2(1): 106–121.

Hansen, Emmanuel. 1974. "Frantz Fanon: Portrait of a Revolutionary Intellectual." *Transition* 46: 25–36.

Hansen, Thomas Blom. 2001. "Governance and State Mythologies in Mumbai." In *States of Imagination: Ethnographic Explorations of the Postcolonial State*, edited by Thomas Blom Hansen and Finn Stepputat, 221–256. Durham, NC: Duke University Press.

Hansen, Thomas Blom, and Finn Stepputat. 2001. "Introduction: States of Imagination." In *States of Imagination: Ethnographic Explorations of the Postcolonial State*, edited by Thomas Blom Hansen and Finn Stepputat, 1–40. Durham, NC: Duke University Press.

Harbi, Mohammed. 1980. *Le FLN: Mirage et réalité, des origins à la prise du pouvoir.* Paris: Jeune Afrique.

Hari, Johann. 2010. "Not His Finest Hour: The Dark Side of Winston Churchill." *Independent,* October 27. http://www.independent.co.uk/news/uk/politics/not-his-finest-hour-the-dark-side-of-winston-churchill-2118317.html.

Harlow, Barbara. 1987. *Resistance Literature.* New York: Methuen.

Hass, Amira. 2005. "Broken Bones and Broken Homes." *Haaretz,* November 4. https://www.haaretz.com/1.4880391.

Hayes, Richard. 2011. *Subhas Chandra Bose in Nazi Germany: Politics, Intelligence, and Propaganda 1941–1943.* London: Hurst.

Herbst, Jeffrey. 1996–97. "Responding to State Failure in Africa." *International Security* 21(3): 120–144.

Herzl, Theodor. 1896. *The Jewish State.* New Orleans: Quid Pro Books.

Herzl, Theodor. 1902. *Old–New Land.* Translated by Lotta Levensohn. New York: M. Wiener.

Hobbes, Thomas. 1651. *Leviathan.* London: John Bohn.

Hodgkins, Allison. 1996. *The Judaization of Jerusalem—Israeli Policies since 1967.* Jerusalem: Palestinian Academic Society for the Study of International Affairs.

House of Wisdom for Conflict Resolution and Governance (HOW). 2010. "Objectives." Last modified May 17. http://www.howgaza.org/english/house-of-wisdom/about-us/objectives.html.

Hovdenak, Are. 2009. "Hamas in Transition: The Failure of Sanctions." *Democratization* 16(1): 59–80.

Hroub, Khaled. 2006. *Hamas: A Beginner's Guide.* London: Pluto Press.

Human Rights Watch. 2002. "Fast Track Land Reform in Zimbabwe." March 8. https://www.hrw.org/report/2002/03/08/fast-track-land-reform-zimbabwe.

Human Rights Watch. 2004. "Razing Rafah: Mass Home Demolitions in the Gaza Strip." October 17. https://www.hrw.org/report/2004/10/17/razing-rafah/mass-home-demolitions-gaza-strip.

Inglis, Ken. 1993. "Entombing Unknown Soldier: From London and Paris to Baghdad." *History and Memory* 5(2): 7–31.

International Crisis Report. 2007. "After Gaza." Access June 12, 2019. https://d2071and vip0wj.cloudfront.net/68-after-gaza.pdf.

Israel Ministry of Foreign Affairs (MFA). 2014. "Behind the Headlines: The Myth of an Israeli Siege on Gaza." August 17. https://mfa.gov.il/MFA/ForeignPolicy/Issues/Pages/The-myth-of-an-Israeli-siege-on-Gaza-17-Aug-2014.aspx.

Jacobs, Margaret D. 2009. *White Mother to a Dark Race. Settler Colonialism, Maternalism, and the Removal of Indigenous Children in the American West and Australia, 1880–1940*. Lincoln: University of Nebraska Press.

Jalal, Rasha Abou. 2013. "Unemployment Drives Gaza's Graduates to Drugs." *Al Monitor*, June 13. http://www.al-monitor.com/pulse/originals/2013/06/gaza-students-drugs-tramadol.html#

Jeganathan, Pradeep. 2004. "Checkpoint: Anthropology, Identity, and the State." In *Anthropology in the Margins of the State*, edited by Veena Das and Deborah Poole, 67–80. Santa Fe: School of American Research Press.

Jensen, Michael Irving. 2009. *The Political Ideology of Hamas: A Grassroots Perspective*. New York: I. B. Taurus.

Jerusalem Post Staff. 2018. "Read the Full Jewish Nation-State Law." *Jerusalem Post*, July 19. https://www.jpost.com/Israel-News/Read-the-full-Jewish-Nation-State-Law-562923.

Johnston, Josee. 2000. "Pedagogical Guerrillas, Armed Democrats, and Revolutionary Counterepublics: Examining Paradox in the Zapatista Uprisings in Chiapas Mexico." *Theory and Society* 29(4): 463–505.

Jones, George E. 1946. "Bose and His 'Army' Cause Stir in India; Trials of Those Who Fought for Japanese a Bitter Issue—Legend Being Created." *New York Times*. February 8.

Kane, Paul. 1859. *Wanderings of an Artist among the Indians of North America*. London: Longman, Brown, Green, Longmans, and Roberts.

Kazziha, Walid. 1979. *Palestine in the Arab Dilemma*. London: Croom Helm.

Khalidi, Rashid. 1997. *Palestinian Identity: The Construction of Modern National Consciousness*. New York: Columbia University Press.

Khalidi, Walid. 1992. *All That Remains: The Palestinian Village Occupied and Depopulated by Israel in 1948*. Washington, DC: Institute for Palestine Studies.

Khalili, Laleh. 2007. *Heroes and Martyrs of Palestine: The Politics of National Commemoration*. Cambridge: Cambridge University Press.

Khan, Mushtaq Husain, George Giacaman, and Inge Amundsen, eds. 2004. *Formation in Palestine: Viability and Governance during Social Transformations*. New York: Routledge Curzon.

Knudsen, Are. 2005. "Crescent and Sword: The Hamas Enigma." *Third World Quarterly* 26(8): 1373–1388.

Knudsen, Are. 2010. *The Public Services under Hamas in Gaza: Islamic Revolution or Crisis Management?* Oslo: Peace Research Institute of Oslo.

Korn, Alina. 2008. "The Ghettoization of the Palestinians." In *Thinking Palestine*, edited by Ronit Lentin. New York: Zed Books.

Kriger, Norma J. 1991. *Zimbabwe's Guerrilla War: Peasant Voices*. Cambridge: Cambridge University Press.

Krinninger, Theresa. 2015. "Zimbabwe's Fast-Track Land Reform Shows Little Benefit 15 Years On." *Deutsche Welle*, May 19. http://www.dw.com/en/zimbabwes-fast-track-land-reform-shows-little-benefit-15-years-on/a-18461592.

Kristianasen, Wendy. 1999. "Challenges and Counterchallenges: Hamas's Response to Oslo." *Journal of Palestine Studies* 28(3): 19–36.

Kubovich, Yaniv. 2018. "Israel to Top Court: Gaza Protests Are State of War, Human Rights Law Doesn't Apply." *Haaretz*, May 3. https://www.haaretz.com/israel-news/.premium-israel-gaza-protests-are-state-of-war-human-rights-law-doesnt-apply-1.6052794.

Kusno, Abidin. 1998. "Beyond the Postcolonial: Architecture and Political Cultures in Indonesia." *Public Culture* 10: 549–75.

Lancaster House Agreement. 1979. "Southern Rhodesia Constitutional Conference Held at Lancaster House, September—December 1979." December 21. http://sas-space.sas.ac.uk/5847/5/1979_Lancaster_House_Agreement.pdf.

Laqueur, Walter. 2003. *The History of Zionism*. New York: I. B. Taurus.

Leander, Anna. 2004. "Wars and the Un-making of States: Taking Tilly Seriously in the Contemporary World." In *Contemporary Security Analysis and Copenhagen Peace Research*, edited by Stefano Guzzini and Dietrich Jung, 69–80. New York: Routledge.

Lee, Gregory B., and Sunny S.K. Lam. 1998. "Wicked Cities: Cyberculture and the Reimagining of Identity in the 'Non-Western' Metropolis." *Futures* 30(10): 967–79.

Legere, Karsten. 2006. "JK Nyerere of Tanzania and the Empowerment of Swahili." In *"Along the Routes to Power": Explorations of Empowerment through Language*, edited by Martin Putz, Joshua A. Fishman, and JoAnne Neff-van Aertselaer, 373–404. Berlin: Walter de Gruyter.

Le More, Anne. 2004. "Foreign Aid Strategy." In *The Economics of Palestine: Economic Policy and Institutional Reform for a Viable Palestinian State*, edited by David Combham and Nu'man Kanafi, 205–226. New York: Routledge.

Loomba, Ania. 1998. *Colonialism/Postcolonialism*. London: Routledge.

Lund, Christian. 2006. "Twilight Institutions: Public Authority and Local Politics in Africa." *Development and Change* 37(4): 685–705.

Ma'an News Agency. 2014a. "Palestinian Teen Abducted, Killed in Suspected Revenge Attack." July 2. http://www.maannews.net/eng/ViewDetails.aspx?ID=709299.

Ma'an New Agency. 2014b. "Official: Autopsy Shows Palestinian Youth Burnt Alive." July 5. http://www.maannews.net/eng/ViewDetails.aspx?ID=710089.

Ma'an News Agency. 2014c. "Haniyeh Hails Palestinian Resistance 'Victory' in Massive Gaza Rally." August 27. http://www.maannews.com/eng/ViewDetails.aspx?id=723841.

Malesevic, Sinisa. 2012. "Wars that Make States and Wars that Make Nations: Organised Violence, Nationalism, and State Formation in the Balkans." *European Journal of Sociology* 53(1): 31–63.

Mamdani, Mahmood. 1996. *Citizen and Subject: Contemporary Africa and the Legacy of Late Colonialism*. Princeton, NJ: Princeton University Press.

Mamdani, Mahmood. 1998. "When Does a Settler Become a Native? Reflections of the Colonial Roots of Citizen in Equatorial and South Africa." *Citizenship Rights in Africa Initiative*, May 13. https://citizenshiprightsafrica.org/wp-content/uploads/1998/05/mamdani-1998-inaugural-lecture.pdf.

Mamdani, Mahmood. 2008. "Lessons of Zimbabwe." *London Review of Books* 30(23): 17–21.

Martin, David, and Phyllis Johnson. 1981. *The Struggle for Zimbabwe—The Chimurenga War*. Johannesburg: Ravan Press.

Masalha, Nur. 2012. *The Palestine Nakba: Decolonising History, Narrating the Subaltern, Reclaiming Memory*. London: Zed Books.

Masalha, Nur, and Lisa Isherwood. 2014. "Introduction." In *Theologies of Liberation in Palestine-Israel: Indigenous, Contextual and Postcolonial Perspectives*, edited by Nur Masalha and Lisa Isherwood, xi–xviii. Eugene, OR: Pickwick Publications.

Masiiwa, Medicine, and Lovemore Chipungu. 2004. "Land Reform Programme in Zimbabwe: Disparity between Policy Design and Implementation." In *Post-Independence Land Reform in Zimbabwe: Controversies and Impact on the Economy*, edited by Medicine Masiiwa, 1–24. Harare: Friederich Ebert Stiftung/Institute of Development Studies, University of Zimbabwe.

Massad, Joseph A. 2001. *Colonial Effects: The Making of National Identity in Jordan*. New York: Columbia University Press.

Matar, Dina. 2011. *What It Means to be Palestinian: Stories of Palestinian Peoplehood*. London: I. B. Taurus.

Matondi, Prosper B. 2012. *Zimbabwe's Fast Track Land Reform*. London: Zed Books.

Mbembe, Achille. 2003. "Necropolitics." *Public Culture* 15(1): 11–40.

McCarthy, Rory. 2010. "Hamas Imposes New Gaza Taxes to Pay for Burgeoning Bureaucracy." *The Guardian*, April 8. http://www.theguardian.com/world/2010/apr/08/hamas-taxes-gaza.

McDonald, David. 2006. "Performing Palestine. Resisting the Occupation and Reviving Jerusalem's Social and Cultural Identity through Music and the Arts." *Jerusalem Quarterly* 25(1): 5–18.

Melber, Henning. 2003. "'Namibia, Land of the Brave': Selective Memories on War and Violence within Nation Building." In *Rethinking Resistance: Revolt and Violence in African History*, edited by Jon Abbink, Mirjam de Bruijn, and Klaas van Walraven, 305–327. Boston: Brill.

Meredith, Martin. 2002. *Mugabe: Power and Plunder in Zimbabwe*. Oxford: Public Affairs Press.

Middle East Monitor. 2014. "Torture in Israeli Prisons: 200 Methods Used against Palestinian Prisoners." October 29. https://www.middleeastmonitor.com/news/middle-east/14957-torture-in-israeli-prisons-200-methods-used-against-palestinian-prisoners.

Migdal, Joel. 1988. *Strong Societies and Weak States: State-Society Relations and State Capabilities in the Third World*. Princeton, NJ: Princeton University Press.

Milton-Edwards, Beverly. 2008. "The Ascendance of Political Islam: Hamas and Consolidation in Gaza Strip." *Third World Quarterly* 49(8): 1585–1599.

Milton-Edwards, Beverly, and Alastair Crooke. 2004. "Elusive Ingredient: Hamas and the Peace Process." *Journal of Palestine Studies* 33(4): 442–459.

Mishal, Shaul, and Avraham Sela. 2000. *The Palestinian Hamas: Vision, Violence, and Coexistence*. New York: Columbia University Press.

Mitchell, Timothy. 1991. "The Limits of the State: Beyond Statist Approaches and Their Critics." *American Political Science Review* 85(1): 77–96.

Mukerjee, Madhusri. 2011. *Churchill's Secret War: The British Empire and the Ravaging of India during World War II*. New York: Basic Books.

Murray, J.A.H., ed. 1971. *The Compact Edition of the Oxford Dictionary*. Vol 2. Oxford: Oxford University Press.

Najjar, Orayb Aref. 2007. "Cartoons as a Site for the Construction of Palestinian Refugee Identity: An Exploratory Study of Cartoonist Naji al-Ali." *Journal of Communication Inquiry* 31(3): 255–285.

Nasser, Wisam. 2015. "Pregnant Palestinian Woman Killed in Air Strike Buried." *Al Jazeera*, October 13. https://www.aljazeera.com/indepth/inpictures/2015/10/pregnant-palestinian-woman-killed-air-strike-buried-151011190120562.html.

Negotiations Affairs Department—Palestinian Liberation Organization (NAD-PLO). 1994. "The Palestinian-Israeli Interim Agreement on The West Bank & The Gaza Strip." April 9. http://www.nad-plo.org/userfiles/file/Document/ParisPro.pdf.

Neumann, Michael. 2002. "Israelis and Indians." *Counterpunch*, April 9. http://www.counterpunch.org/2002/04/09/israelis-and-indians.

Nevel, Donna. 2014. "But Hamas." *Tikkun Daily*, August 14. http://www.tikkun.org/tikkundaily/2014/08/14/but-hamas.

Nkrumah, Kwame. 1968. *Handbook of Revolutionary Warfare: A Guide to the Armed Phase of the African Revolution*. New York: International Publishers.

O'Brien, Jean. 2010. *Firsting and Lasting: Writing Indians out of Existence in New England*. Minneapolis: University of Minnesota Press.

Oonk, Gijsbert. 2013. *Settled Strangers: Asian Business Elites in East Africa (1800–2000)*. London: Sage Publications.

Osborne, Samuel. 2018. "South Africa Votes through Motion to Seize Land from White Farmers without Compensation." *Independent*, March 1. https://www.independent.co.uk/news/world/africa/south-africa-white-farms-land-seizure-anc-race-relations-a8234461.html.

Oxford Dictionary of English. 2010. Edited by Angus Stevensen. Oxford: Oxford University Press.

Pace, Michelle, and Somdeep Sen. 2019. *The Palestinian Authority in the West Bank: The Theatrics of Woeful Statecraft*. Oxon: Routledge.

Palestinian Basic Law. 2007. "2003 Amended Basic Law." December 13. http://www.palestinianbasiclaw.org/basic-law/2003-amended-basic-law.

Palestinian Center for Human Rights. 2002. "Arrests, Imprisonment and Torture." Last modified October 4. http://www.pchrgaza.org/arrests_torture_stat.html.

Palestinian Center for Policy and Survey. 2013. "Palestinian Public Opinion Poll No. 48." June 13–15. http://www.pcpsr.org/en/node/163.

Palestinian Center for Policy and Survey. 2019. "Public Opinion Poll No. 71." April 9. https://www.pcpsr.org/sites/default/files/Poll%2071%20English%20full%20text%20March%202019.pdf.

Palestinian Central Bureau of Statistics. 2012. "Almar'aa wa alrajul fii Filastiin" [Women and Men in Palestine]." Accessed June 15. http://www.pcbs.gov.ps/Portals/_PCBS/Downloads/book1936.pdf.

Pappe, Ilan. 2006. *The Ethnic Cleansing of Palestine*. Oxford: One World.

Parsons, Nigel. 2005. *The Politics of the Palestinian Authority: From Oslo to al-Aqsa*. New York: Routledge.

Parsons, Nigel. 2010. "Israeli Biopolitics, Palestinian Policing: Order and Resistance in the Occupied Palestinian Territories." In *Policing and Prisons in the Middle East: Formations of Coercion*, edited by Laleh Khalili and Jillian Schwedler, 57–76. London: Hurst & Company.

Pascovich, Eyal. 2012. "Social-Civilian Apparatuses of Hamas, Hizballah, and Other Activist Islamic Organizations." *Digest of Middle East Studies* 21(1): 126–148.

Paterson, Thomas G. 1994. *Contesting Castro: The United States and the Triumph of the Cuban Revolution*. New York: Oxford University Press.

PEGASE. 2017. "Action Document for PEGASE: Direct Financial Support to Recurrent Expenditures of the Palestinian Authority." https://ec.europa.eu/neighbourhood-enlargement/sites/near/files/b_c_2017_1096_palestine_sm_2017_annex_1_pegase.pdf.

Peleg, Ilan, and Dov Waxman. 2011. *Israel's Palestinians: The Conflict Within*. New York: Cambridge University Press.

Perez-Stable, Marifeli. 2012. *The Cuban Revolution: Origins, Course, and Legacy*. New York: Oxford University Press.

Quraishy, Samira. 2009. *The Judaization of Jerusalem: A Review of Israel's Escalating Campaign of Land Seizures, House Demolitions, and Eviction of Palestinians*. London: Middle East Monitor.

Radcliffe, Sarah. 2001. "Imagining the State as a Space: Territoriality and the Formation of the State in Ecuador." In *States of Imagination. Ethnographic Explorations of the Postcolonial State*, edited by Thomas Blom Hansen and Finn Steppatat, 123–145. Durham, NC: Duke University Press.

RAND Corporation. 2005. *Helping a Palestinian State Succeed: Key Findings*. Arlington, VA: Rand Corporation.

Reuters. 2017. "Hamas Chief in Gaza says Palestinian Unity Deal Is Collapsing." *Reuters*, December 21. https://www.reuters.com/article/us-palestinians-hamas-reconciliation/hamas-chief-in-gaza-says-palestinian-unity-deal-is-collapsing-idUSKBN1EF2C5.

Riches, David. 1986. "The Phenomenon of Violence." In *The Anthropology of Violence*, edited by David Riches. Oxford: Basil Blackwell.

Robinson, Glenn E. 1997. *Building a Palestinian State: The Incomplete Revolution*. Bloomington: Indiana University Press.

Rose, David. 2008. "The Gaza Bombshell." *Vanity Fair*, March 3. http://www.vanityfair.com/news/2008/04/gaza200804.

Rose, Deborah Bird. 1991. *Hidden Histories: Black Stories from Victoria River Downs, Humbert River and Wave Hills Stations*. Canberra: Aboriginal Studies Press.

Roy, Sara. 1987. "The Gaza Strip: A Case of Economic De-development." *Journal of Palestine Studies* 17(1): 56–88.

Roy, Sara. 1995. *The Gaza Strip. The Political Economy of De-development*. Washington, DC: Institute of Palestine Studies.

Roy, Sara. 2000. "The Crisis Within: The Struggle for Palestinian Society." *Critique* 17: 5–30.

Roy, Sara. 2011. *Hamas and Civil Society in Gaza: Engaging the Islamist Social Sector*. Princeton, NJ: Princeton University Press.

Rubinstein, Danny. 2012. "Rafah Tunnels Smugglers Fed Up with Hamas' Heavy Taxes." *Al Monitor*, February 15. http://www.al-monitor.com/pulse/tr/business/2012/02/smugglers-fed-up-with-hamas-taxe.html.

Rudoren, Jodi. 2014. "Tensions High in Jerusalem as Palestinian Teenager Is Given a Martyr's Burial." *New York Times*, July 4. http://www.nytimes.com/2014/07/05/world/middleeast/israel.html?_r=0.

Sa'di, Ahmad, and Lila Abu-Lughod, eds. 2007. *Nakba: Palestine, 1948, and the Claims of Memory*. New York: Columbia University Press.

Said, Edward. 1979. *The Question of Palestine*. New York: Vintage Books.

Said, Edward. 1993. "The Morning After." *London Review of Books* 15(2): 3–5.

Said, Edward. 1995. *Peace and Its Discontents: Essays on Palestine in the Middle East Peace Process*. New York: Vintage Books.

Saleh, Yasmine. 2014. "Court Bans Activists of Islamist Hamas in Egypt." *Reuters*, March 4. http://www.reuters.com/article/2014/03/04/us-egypt-hamas-idUSBREA230F5 20140304.

Sayigh, Rosemary. 1979. *The Palestinians: From Peasants to Revolutionaries*. London: Zed Books.

Sayigh, Yezid. 1997a. "Armed Struggle and State Formation." *Journal of Palestine Studies* 26(4): 17–32.

Sayigh, Yezid. 1997b. *Armed Struggle and the Search for State: The Palestinian National Movement: 1949–1993*. New York: Oxford University Press.

Sayigh, Yezid. 2007. "Inducing a Failed State in Palestine." *Survival* 49(3): 7–39.

Sayigh, Yezid. 2009. *Fixing Broken Windows: Security Sector Reform in Palestine, Lebanon, and Yemen*. Beirut: Carnegie Endowment for International Peace.

Sayigh, Yezid. 2011. *We Serve the People: Hamas Policing in Gaza*. Waltham, UK: Crown Center for Middle East Studies.

Scheper-Hughes, Nancy. 1995. "The Primacy of the Ethical: Propositions for a Militant Anthropology." *Current Anthropology* 36(3): 409–440.

Scoones, Ian, Nelson Marongwe, Blasio Mavedzenge, Jacob Mahenehen, Felix Murimbarimba, and Chrispen Sukume. 2010. *Zimbabwe's Land Reform: Myths and Realities*. Suffolk, UK: James Currey.

Scott, James. 1998. *Seeing like a State*. New Haven: Yale University Press.

Sen, Amartya. 1983. *Poverty and Famines: An Essay on Entitlement and Deprivation*. Oxford: Oxford University Press.

Sen, Somdeep. 2013a. "Summer Fun, Hamas-Style." *Open Democracy*, July 12. http://www.opendemocracy.net/somdeep-sen/summer-fun-hamas-style-0.

Sen, Somdeep. 2013b. "Little Pride, Little Joy: The Tragedy Behind Assaf-Mania." *Huffington Post*, July 17. http://www.huffingtonpost.com/somdeep-sen/little-pride-little-joy-t_b_3603356.html.

Sen, Somdeep. 2013c. "Reporting Gaza: Trials and Tribulations of 'Getting the Story Out.'" *Huffington Post*, November 1. http://www.huffingtonpost.com/somdeep-sen/gaza-reporters_b_4191567.html.

Sen, Somdeep. 2015a. "Bringing Back the Palestinian State: Hamas between Government and Resistance." *Middle East Critique* 24(2): 211–225.

Sen, Somdeep. 2015b. "It's Nakba, Not a Party: Re-Stating the (Continued) Legacy of the Oslo Accords." *Arab Studies Quarterly* 37(2): 161–176.

Sen, Somdeep. 2017. "To Fight Is to Exist: Hamas, Armed Resistance, and the Making of Palestine." *Interventions: International Journal of Postcolonial Studies* 19(2): 201–217.

Shain, Yossi, and Gary Sussman. 1998. "From Occupation to State-building: Palestinian Political Society Meets Palestinian Civil Society." *Government and Opposition* 33(3): 275–306.

Shalhoub-Kevorkian, Nadera. 2015. *Security Theology, Surveillance, and the Politics of Fear*. Cambridge: Cambridge University Press.

Sharon, Ariel. 2003. "Address by PM Ariel Sharon at the Fourth Herzliya Conference." December 18. https://jcpa-lecape.org/wp-content/uploads/2017/10/Discours-de-Sharon-à-Herzliya.pdf.

Strickland, Patrick. 2014. "Amnesty: Pattern of Israeli 'War Crimes' in West Bank." *Electronic Intifada*, February 28. https://electronicintifada.net/blogs/patrick-strickland/amnesty-pattern-israeli-war-crimes-west-bank.

Strickland, Patrick. 2015. "Israel Continues to Criminalise Marking Nakba Day." *Al Jazeera*, May 14. https://www.aljazeera.com/news/2015/05/israel-nakba-palestine-150514080431980.html.

Suliman, Mohammed. 2013. "Gaza Students Stranded by Rafah Border Closure." *Al Monitor*, September 26. http://www.al-monitor.com/pulse/originals/2013/09/gaza-students-rafah-erez-crossing.html.

Swedenburg, Ted. 1990. "The Palestinian Peasant as National Signifier." *Anthropological Quarterly* 63(1): 18–30.

Swedenburg, Ted. 1995. *Memories of Revolt: The 1936–1939 Rebellion and the Palestinian National Past*. Minneapolis: University of Minnesota Press.

Tagore, Rabindranath. 1919. *The Home and the World*. London: Macmillan.

Tamimi, Azzam. 2007. *Hamas: A History from Within*. Northampton, MA: Olive Branch Press.

Tartir, Alaa, Sam Bahour, and Samer Abdelnour. 2012. "Defeating Dependency, Creating a Resistance Economy." *al-Shabaka,* February 13. https://al-shabaka.org/briefs/defeating-dependency-creating-resistance-economy.

Tharoor, Shashi. 2017. *Inglorious Empire: What the British Did to India*. London: Hurst.

Tilly, Charles. 1992. *Coercion, Capital, and European States: AD 990–1992*. Oxford: Blackwell.

Times of Israel Staff. 2018. "Netanyahu Hails Troops on Gaza Border, Says Israel Acts Firmly to Defend Itself." *Times of Israel*, March 31. https://www.timesofisrael.com/netanyahu-hails-troops-on-gaza-border-says-israel-acts-firmly-to-defend-itself/.

Topan, Farouk. 2008. "Tanzania: The Development of Swahili as a National and Official Language." In *Language and National Identity in Africa*, edited by Andrew Simpson, 252–266. Oxford: Oxford University Press.

Turki, Fawaz. 1972. *The Disinherited: Journal of a Palestinian Exile*. London: Monthly Review Press.

Turki, Fawaz. 1996. "Palestinian Self-Criticism and Liberation of Palestinian Society." *Journal of Palestine Studies* 25(2): 71–76.

Turner, E. Randolph. 1985. "Socio-Political Organization within the Powhatan Chiefdom and the Effects of European Contact, A.D. 1607–1646." In *Cultures in Contact: The Impact of European Contacts on Native American Cultural Institutions A.D. 1000–1800*, edited by William W. Fitzhugh, 193–224. Washington, DC: Smithsonian Institution Press.

United Nations (UN). 2017. "Gaza Ten Years Later." July 12. https://unsco.unmissions.org/sites/default/files/gaza_10_years_later_-_11_july_2017.pdf.

United Nations Children's Fund (UNICEF). 2019. "In Gaza, a Crisis for Children." Accessed June 16. https://www.unicef.org/infobycountry/oPt_74620.html.

United Nations General Assembly/Security Council. 1993. "Declaration of Principles on Interim Self-Government Arrangements (Oslo Accords)." September 13. https://peacemaker.un.org/israelopt-osloaccord93.

United Nations High Commissioner for Refugees (UNHCR). 1995. "Israeli-Palestinian Interim Agreement on the West Bank and the Gaza Strip." September 28. http://www.refworld.org/pdfid/3de5ebbc0.pdf.

United Nations Information System on the Question of Palestine (UNISPAL). 1993. "Israel-PLO Recognition: Exchange of Letters between Rabin and Arafat." September 9. http://unispal.un.org/UNISPAL.NSF/0/36917473237100E285257028006C0BC5.

Vale, Lawrence J. 1992. *Architecture, Power, and National Identity*. New Haven, CT: Yale University Press.

Veracini, Lorenzo. 2010. *Settler Colonialism: A Theoretical Overview*. New York: Palgrave Macmillan.

Veracini, Lorenzo. 2011. "Introducing Settler Colonial Studies." *Settler Colonial Studies* 1(1): 1–12.

Vishwanathan, Gauri. 1995. "Coping with (Civil) Death: The Christian Convert's Rights of Passage in Colonial India." In *After Colonialism: Imperial Histories and Postcolonial Displacements*, edited by Gyan Prakash, 183–210. Princeton, NJ: Princeton University Press.

Wacquant, Loic J. D. 1995. "The Pugilistic Point of View: How Boxers Think and Feel about Their Trade." *Theory and Society* 24(4): 489–535.

Watson, Geoffrey R. 2000. *The Oslo Accords: International Law and the Israeli-Palestinian Peace Agreements*. Oxford: Oxford University Press.

Wiegand, Krista E. 2010. *Bombs and Ballots: Governance by Islamist Terrorist and Guerrilla Groups*. Burlington, VT: Ashgate Publishing Group.

Wolfe, Patrick. 1999. *Settler Colonialism and The Transformation of Anthropology: The Politics and Poetics of an Ethnographic Event*. New York: Cassell.

Wolfe, Patrick. 2006. "Settler Colonialism and the Elimination of the Native." *Journal of Genocide Studies* 8(4): 387–409.

Wolfenstein, Victor. 1971. *The Revolutionary Personality*. Princeton, NJ: Princeton University Press.

World Bank. 2019. "Palestinian Partnership for Infrastructure Trust Fund." Last modified March 13. http://www.worldbank.org/en/programs/palestinian-partnership-for-infrastructure-trust-fund.

Yeoh, Brenda. 2001. "Postcolonial City." *Progress in Human Geography* 25(3): 456–468.

Zanotti, Jim. 2018. "U.S. Foreign Aid to the Palestinians." *Congressional Research Service*, December 12. https://fas.org/sgp/crs/mideast/RS22967.pdf.

Zink, Valerie. 2009. "A Quiet Transfer: The Judaization of Jerusalem." *Contemporary Arab Affairs* 2(1): 122–133.

Index

Italicized page numbers indicate photographs. Page numbers followed by n or nn indicate notes.

CPSIA information can be obtained
at www.ICGtesting.com
Printed in the USA
LVHW090045240820
663915LV00023B/56